SOCIAL CONDITIONS IN SUB-SAHARAN AFRICA

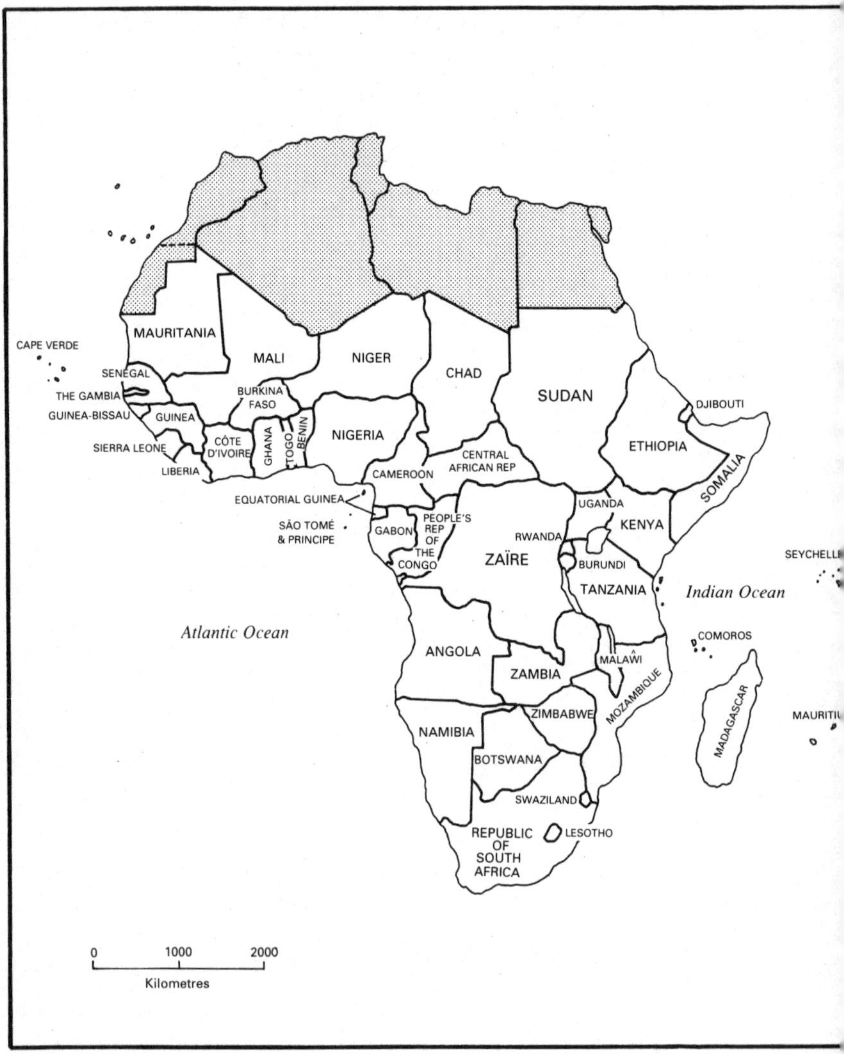
CAPE VERDE
MAURITANIA
MALI
NIGER
CHAD
SUDAN
DJIBOUTI
SENEGAL
THE GAMBIA
GUINEA-BISSAU
GUINEA
BURKINA FASO
SIERRA LEONE
LIBERIA
CÔTE D'IVOIRE
GHANA
TOGO
BENIN
NIGERIA
ETHIOPIA
CENTRAL AFRICAN REP
CAMEROON
SOMALIA
EQUATORIAL GUINEA
SÃO TOMÉ & PRINCIPE
GABON
PEOPLE'S REP OF THE CONGO
UGANDA
KENYA
RWANDA
ZAÏRE
BURUNDI
SEYCHELLES
TANZANIA
Indian Ocean
Atlantic Ocean
COMOROS
ANGOLA
MALAŴI
ZAMBIA
MOZAMBIQUE
MADAGASCAR
ZIMBABWE
MAURITIUS
NAMIBIA
BOTSWANA
SWAZILAND
REPUBLIC OF SOUTH AFRICA
LESOTHO
0 1000 2000
Kilometres

Sub-Saharan Africa

Social Conditions in Sub-Saharan Africa

Roy A. Carr-Hill

Senior Research Fellow at the
Centre for Health Economics, University of York

M
MACMILLAN

First published 1990

Published by
MACMILLAN ACADEMIC AND PROFESSIONAL LTD
Houndmills, Basingstoke, Hampshire RG21 2XS
and London
Companies and representatives
throughout the world

Printed in Great Britain by WBC Ltd., Bridgend

ISBN 0–333–52589–2

British Library Cataloguing in Publication Data
Carr-Hill, Roy A.
Social conditions in Sub-Saharan Africa.
1. Africa south of the Sahara. Social conditions
I. Title
967

ISBN 0–333–52589–2

Contents

Preface

The purpose of this book is to present a picture of trends in social conditions in Africa on the basis of a critical assessment of the available statistical data. It is clear that the main problems faced by most rural populations in Africa are disease, shortage and maldistribution of food, low incomes and skewed income distribution and illiteracy, but it is less clear that the data available are adequate to assess the extent to which these and other 'basic needs' are being met.

It should be emphasised that this is not a review of economic and social statistics in Africa. For that, the reader should turn to the excellent book of the same name by G.M.K. Kpedekpo and P.L. Arya published by George Allen and Unwin in 1981. Instead the intention is to bring together data bearing on a 'core set' of basic needs indicators and to caution against over interpretation of what is often very flimsy data.

Critical reflection about statistics obviously cannot substitute for positive action about poverty and many argue that we know enough to act even though the data are dubious. But this is an assumption and there is often a further presumption that everyone agrees what should be measured. Yet without a clear view of what should count as development and how it should be monitored, social planning of any kind is almost impossible.

The book grew out of a report to the Swedish International Development Agency (SIDA) as a background to a three day meeting on appropriate aid policies to sub-Saharan Africa for the 1990s. Obviously, if starting from scratch, it would be more sensible to organise a multi-authored compilation but that would then have posed a major problem of coordination. Instead, the emphasis here is on a consistent approach to the monitoring of social conditions and trends in respect of each major group of basic needs indicators.

Clearly this is a very ambitious exercise and I crave the reader's indulgence for my arrogance in attempting to write about each of the very disparate areas. But, whilst specialists fully appreciate the problems of data in their own sector, there is a tendency to presume that data from another sector are reliable and valid. The hope is that the critique of this book spanning several fields of economic and social statistics will add to the concern over the nature and quality of the data available for monitoring social conditions and trends and, eventually, lead to their improvement.

Foreword

Information gives power—at least potentially. Power to control, power to get things done, power to move minds, power to understand. It is crucial for everyone concerned with development. Yet as Roy Carr-Hill so eloquently argues in this book, information isn't just 'out there', to be picked up and used. Information, he tells us, is 'produced, not collected'; *what* is produced depends on the use for which it is intended. What is *not* produced, or not analysed, is often more important than what is.

And there is a great deal in this book that puts more 'official' statistics to shame—the excellent discussion on the status of women, for example, or the repeated and well-documented insistence that (civil) war has done more to worsen social conditions in Sub-Saharan Africa than virtually anything else. Both these subjects, and especially the latter, are usually absent from more conventional discussions or routinely published statistical series. Carr-Hill, fine statistician that he is, also gives many examples of how figures take on a life of their own: while the original source often discusses the (perhaps dubious) assumptions and weaknesses of the data, these soon are transformed into statistics of unquestioned authority, the basis for further elaborations or comparisons. Population figures provide a particularly striking instance. Again and again Carr-Hill tells us that we just don't know. And when we pretend to know, we're frequently wrong, and even more often, biased. Particularly striking is the repeated evidence that, not only governments, but also international agencies—even some of the most respected ones!—use statistics of dubious quality in order to make points, to prove the relevance or success of their policy, or to underpin their advocacy.

Roy Carr-Hill and I have for many years shared many concerns, and both of us, in different ways, have been deeply influenced by Dudley Seers—an influence much in evidence in this book. We have also disagreed, perhaps particularly on the interpretation of data which are not essentially statistical and where 'judgement' plays a greater role—in that spirit the following pages are also likely to lead to some interesting dialogue between us. But to harp on that would be ungenerous to a book which contributes so much to our better understanding of realities in Africa, and also to forget that such disagreements are healthy and necessary, and that they help keep the discussion lively on issues of fundamental human concern. With this book Roy Carr-Hill has done a service to students of development as well as to those involved in the making and implementation of policy: I hope all will fully use not only his many empirical insights, but also his explicit and implicit guidelines on how to interpret official and unofficial data.

Emanuel de Kadt
Institute of Development Studies
University of Sussex

List of tables

List of figures

Acronyms

CIMMYT	International Maize and Wheat Improvement Centre
ERS	Economic Research Service
GNP	Gross National Product
LDC	Least Developed Countries
NIC	Newly Industrialising Countries
OECD	Organisation for Economic Cooperation and Development
SADCC	Southern Africa Development Coordinating Committee
SWC	State of the World's Children
UNCHBP	United Nations Centre for Housing and Buildings Programmes
UNDP	United Nations Development Programme
UNESCO	United Nations Educational, Scientific and Cultural Organisation
UNICEF	United Nations International Children's Fund
UNRISD	United Nations Research Institute for Social Development
USAIO	United States Agency for International Development
USDA	United States Development Administration
WHO	World Health Organisation

Acknowledgements

This book has grown out of a paper prepared for a seminar organised by the Swedish International Developmental Agency (SIDA) held at Saltsjobaden in September 1988. David Pearce, who was at that seminar, encouraged me to publish the material and suggested the manuscript to Macmillan. It has been substantially revised on the basis of comments received at that seminar and subsequently, and the author is especially grateful to Gunilla Rosengart of SIDA for her detailed comments on the original manuscript.

I have received substantial assistance from several people: in particluar Jacky Kulkarni helped me draft Chapter 12 on the status of women and Alex Murray compiled the basic data for Chapter 11 on the impact of state violence and warmongering.

The typescript has been prepared, several times, by Jenny Hardy at high speed; the diagrams and figures have been prepared by Ian Taylor of Computype Manuscript Services, who has also re-set the text more than once without complaint; and the proof-readers at Macmillan have been especially patient. To all those I owe a debt of thanks.

Finally, despite many late nights, I want to express my gratitude to my household who have been wonderfully supportive throughout.

Introduction

We are living through the disturbing end of several international 'Decades'. There has been a Decade for Solving Environmental Problems (1972–1982), a Decade for World Hunger (1974–1984), a Decade for Women (1975–1985); and we are nearly at the end of the International Water Supply and Sanitation Decade (1980–1990). Yet Third World 'development' has gone astray in the 1980s: the well-publicised UNICEF study *Adjustment with a Human Face* (referred to as AwHF in this book) was only the latest in a long line of reports from international agencies to pronounce a dismal pattern of 'failure' of growth world-wide.

In particular, many see sub-Saharan Africa as in 'decline'. Whilst this is highlighted by spectacular media coverage of famines 'caused' by drought and other 'natural' disasters, the basis for many of these claims of doom and gloom is statistical data of dubious quality and erratic interpretation. But it is inadequate to simply acknowledge that 'our ideas about aggregative change in rural Africa are therefore quantitatively very rough' (Rimmer, 1988, p.12), and then either speculate or treat existing data as gospel. The correct conclusion is that data must be treated carefully as providing partial evidence from an unsavoury witness (Fetter, 1985).

The emphasis on statistical data might seem curious but case study material cannot convey an understanding of scale. This is, in no way, meant to deny the value of more qualitative studies. Without the realism of case studies it is easy for glib elitist stereotypes of the stupid, ignorant and lazy poor to persist and be reinforced by statistical data. Moreover, whilst Seers exaggerated in saying that

> there are virtually no statistics anywhere on most of the aspects of life that really matter—the average distance people have to carry water and food; the number without shoes; the extent of overcrowding; the prevalence of violence; how many are unable

> to multiply one number by another, or summarize their own country's history...
>
> (Seers, 1983, pp.5–6)

he was, of course, right to argue that

> many of the more important social factors are inherently unquantifiable: how safe it is to criticize the government publicly, or the chance of an objective trial or how corruption affects policy decisions.
>
> (Seers, 1983, p.6)

The limitations of quantification do indeed need to be borne in mind. But they can provide a useful corrective to the casual impressions and information obtained from media coverage or from the most vocal. For example, we are much less likely to hear about the long term consequences of food insecurity than about an imminent drought-induced famine. Similarly, whilst it is undoubtedly true that, with 'structural adjustment' (international financier's code; it usually boils down to price liberalisation), civil servants and others on fixed salaries have lost out, it is not so easy to ascertain the effects on the poor who are the focus of this book.

At the same time, the way in which decision makers and the elite conceive their information needs depends on the existing framework of data collection and presentation.

> The series a statistical office chooses to prepare and publish exercise a subtle and pervasive influence on political, social and economic development. This is why *the apparently dull and minor subject of statistical policy is of crucial importance.*
>
> (Seers, 1975, p.3, my emphasis)

It is equally, perhaps even more, important to be careful in commenting upon existing data. Hence the purpose of this book: to present a more nuanced picture of trends in social conditions in Africa on the basis of a critical assessment of the available statistical data.

The book is organised into three sections. The first section discusses the basic methodological background; the second section presents the evidence; and the third section considers ways in which data collection could be improved.

The first step is to decide what should be measured.

Traditionally—over the last 40 years, that is—'progress' has been measured in terms of average rate of growth of gross national product (GNP). But much useful output is not accounted for within the GNP framework and much of the output included does not contribute to well-being. Indeed,

> really fast growth (e.g. in the NICs) is not merely accompanied by the increased 'output' of military services ... and growing social inequalities and increasing debt: it requires them.
>
> (Seers, 1983, p.21)

The irrelevance of GNP to the assessment of trends in social conditions is explained in Chapter 1.

There is nothing new here, but recently over 800 parliamentarians from five countries found it necessary to request the President of the World Bank to make increased use of social indicators, arguing that

> the conditions of the poor can best be measured by social indicators such as the mortality rates of children under 5; life expectancy; access to safe water; the adult literacy rate, particularly among women; and the proportion of children suffering from malnutrition.
>
> (UNICEF, 1989, p.85)

Their emphasis on what is essentially the basic needs framework promoted by the International Labour Office in the early 1970s is to be welcomed. But we need to guard against any attempt to substitute an Index of Basic Needs for the GNP measure (see Carr-Hill, 1978). The approach adopted in this book is explained in Chapter 2.

Describing social conditions in terms of people's basic needs rather than in terms of levels of production focuses attention on the accuracy of the basic population data. These are often inadequate, both in themselves and as a basis for other analyses (see Appendix 1). Given their significance to the book as a whole, the sources of population data and the estimation techniques used are discussed in detail in Chapter 3.

Section 2 presents the evidence. Due to the data constraints, the approach adopted is very pragmatic. Chapters 4 and 5 examine the availability of food, fuel and water, as these are the basic requirements for survival. The next four chapters consider the health and educational status of, separately, children and adults. Access and equity are important issues for both health and education, and are considered in Appendices 2 and 3.

The last three chapters of Section 2 are rather different in that they are thematic rather than being concerned with a 'basic need'. Chapter 10 examines the overlapping issues of industrialisation, modernisation and urbanisation; Chapter 11 presents data on refugees, destabilisation and war; and Chapter 12 data on the status of women.

The concluding section of the book is concerned with how to improve the collection and deployment of data. In Chapter 13, the difficulties of constructing a functional system of social statistics are discussed; it is clearly a very long term project even if desirable. Instead, in Chapter 14, we consider the possibilities of bottom up, local based monitoring; whilst inevitably small-scale, such efforts are more likely to reflect population needs.

The final chapter comes clean: this book has been written by one European—albeit with considerable bibliographical help—concerned by the ideological hegemony of GNP-speak. Could not real scholars help local populations to monitor what is happening to them?

Section 1: Monitoring Social Conditions

We first have to decide what to measure. Many accounts of the African 'crisis' start with poor rates of growth in the Gross National Product (GNP). In Chapter 1, we demonstrate the inadequacy of the basic data in many African countries and the universal difficulty of interpreting movements in the index; we conclude that this index is of little relevance to understanding how living conditions are changing, especially in the African context. In Chapter 2, the approach adopted in this book—a variant of the Basic Needs Approach—is explained; the discussion highlights the importance of accurate population data as the basis for all assessments of social conditions. The section concludes, in Chapter 3, therefore, with a review of the reliability of population data for African countries and, in particular, of the evidence for the postulated growth rates.

1 Growth—the African disease

Economic development in sub-Saharan Africa—as measured by growth rates in GNP—has stagnated during the 1980s: 'More than two decades of growth have been lost ... for the majority of poor African countries' (AwHF, p.20). What impact have these recessionary trends had on social conditions for their populations? How can, or should, these trends be monitored?

1.1 AFRICA A VICTIM

The picture from the North is of Africa—and especially of sub-Saharan Africa—as being a victim of global market forces. In AwHF, Cornia describes how the 'crisis' of the Northern industrial market economies is 'transmitted to' ('imposed upon'?) the South. Because world trade has stagnated, the demand for primary commodities—one of the LDCs' major exports—stagnated. With its (financial) power the North has profited from the technological possibilities of substituting synthetics for raw materials and the declines in the volume of manufactured production (in the North) to push down commodity prices. The flow of development aid, although only a small fraction of the donor countries' GNP, has also stagnated. Combined with the 'necessity' to service the large accumulated debt of the 1970s, many countries of the South were *exporting* resources to the North by the middle of the decade.

Consequently, growth rates in *per capita* gross domestic product (GDP) for Africa have changed from +2.4% during 1976–80 to –3.1% during 1981–85 (AwHF, p.16). Of 32 African countries analysed by Cornia, cumulative growth rates had declined by more than 20% in six, and by more than 10% in another ten.

More recently, of course, the World Bank suggests there has been a 'turnaround' with estimated overall GDP growing at more than 2.3% per year on average during 1985/1986/1987. But the die had been cast: people were 'worse off' (*per capita* GNP had dropped in many countries). Thus, many commentators painted a picture of the African victim, with media attention focused on drought and famines, but little attention focused on the extent to which day to day conditions are different or not. International agencies joined in the chorus: for example, the UNICEF publication analysing the impact of adjustment policies upon the conditions of children and on other vulnerable groups claimed that 'serious problems have emerged during the last few years and action is needed urgently' (AwHF, pp.21–2).

Neither this author, nor any of those he has read, would dispute the persistence of serious problems of health or of nutrition (the ones singled out by AwHF) in sub-Saharan Africa. But the claim in UNICEF's conclusions, that the serious problems have *emerged*—rather than always being there—is contentious. They freely admit that the 'information remains fragmentary and scattered' (p.21) but argue that it would be unjustified to wait to take action. Correct—but what action?

It is crucial to know how and to what extent the situation is changing, before endorsing the focus in AwHF on macro-economic solutions to problems which, in large part, have been brought about by the application of previous macro-economic solutions.

The exclusive focus on the economic dimension is excused in AwHF (p.7); the authors claim that their concern is to influence (international) policy makers without which 'broader approaches to adjustment' cannot be considered. Many African writers take a different view. Gakou (1987), for example, argues that the recent emphasis upon food production, irrigation and the lot of the peasantry in the rural areas does not derive solely from a humanitarian, moral concern. The particular form of implementation of these humanitarian projects was often to safeguard a workforce for the (further) penetration of agro-processing companies: and the extension of credit and the international or state provision of relatively expensive irrigation promotes the incorporation of the peasantry into the market economy, thereby hastening the break-up of communal solidarity. Instead, Gakou argues for democracy, for the free organisation of the peasantry, for popular alliances which will enable African peoples to delink their own development from the demands of transnationalisation.

That's all very well, replies the economist—but you still need economic growth.

1.2 DOES AFRICA NEED 'ECONOMIC (GNP) GROWTH'?

The fundamental issue is the measure of development: this is not a new concern. Nordhaus and Tobin wrote in 1973, at the beginning of many 'Decades' of development:

> A long decade ago, economic growth was the reigning fashion of political economy. It was simultaneously the hottest subject of economic theory and research, a slogan eagerly claimed by politicians of all stripes, and a serious objective of the policies of governments. The climate has changed dramatically.
>
> (Nordhaus and Tobin, 1973, p.509)

Even James Grant (later Executive Director of UNICEF) admitted:

> Contrary to expectations, increased output of goods and services has failed to 'trickle down' to the poorer half of the populations ... [A] rising GNP growth rate alone is no guarantee against worsening poverty ... Development planners need to be equally concerned, if not more so, with *how* the GNP increases than with the *rate* by which it increases.
>
> (Grant, 1973, p.43)

But we have not moved very far since then. The most recent UNICEF report repeats that average *per capita* GNP says very little about the standard of living of the poor. Development effort should be refocused on the poorest groups, the GNP *per capita* of the poorest 40% of a country's population. Unfortunately, these data do not exist for the majority of countries. Table 1.1 presents data for the few African countries where estimates have been made, and for the Netherlands and the USA for comparison.

Table 1.1 GNP per capita and estimated share of poorest 40% of households

Country	*GNP per capita in US$, 1985* Total	Poorest	*% total GNP accruing to poorest 40% of households*
Netherlands	9,180	5,141	22.4
USA	16,400	7,052	17.2
Egypt	680	281	16.5
Mauritius	1,070	308	11.5
Zambia	400	108	10.8
Kenya	290	65	8.9
Cote d'Ivoire	620	132	8.6

Source: UNICEF, *State of the World's Children*, 1989, p.76.

The countries are ranked differently according to which measure is used.

- The overall GNP per capita of Mauritius is more than 50% higher than for Egypt, whilst the GNPs *per capita* for the poorest 40% are nearly the same.
- The GNP *per capita* in Egypt and in Cote d'Ivoire is approximately the same but the GNP of the poorest 40% is twice as high in Egypt as in Cote d'Ivoire.

Moreover, our concern here is with describing (improvements in) the actual living conditions of the poor, not in their changing share of GNP.

1.2.1 Can GNP be measured accurately?

A special assumption of the System of National Accounts is that *reliable* statistics do, in fact, exist for a large fraction of the economic activities of these countries (Seers, 1983). Yet all these figures are highly suspect. Because of the structure of developing countries' economies, the basic building blocks for the GNP measure—the accounts of inputs and outputs—are rarely available.

There is the problem of identifying the type of income or the industrial origin of income. Caldwell (1977) agrees '...we have not been able to show satisfactory relationships of provable accuracy between stated income and other characteristics of respondents'. Also, although 'the failure to disclose all earnings, investment and expenditure to interviewers is conventionally explained as fear of taxation authorities; ... [probably] a much more potent fear is that the responses will be overheard by relatives'. Bondestam (1973) says: 'income data for a majority of the population—farmers, livestock breeders and other own account workers, and those under- and quasi-employed—are extremely unreliable' (p.30). The calculation of gross national output is further complicated by unmarketed products where there is no estimate of quantity and there is no unit price. In particular, the estimate of agricultural output from farmers, made by combining estimates of acreage, average yield and unit price, is arbitrary and extremely unreliable; it is almost impossible to assess the value of the products used for own consumption.

> Statistical conventions are bedevilled by the coexistence of organised economic activity, activity that is unorganised but remunerated, and household activity carried on without payment, often all producing the same product.
>
> (Kpedekpo and Arya, 1981, p. 232)

Blades (1980) concludes that the margin of error in African GDP estimates averages 20% and that some sectoral components of these estimates (including agricultural output) could be out by up to 50%. Similarly, balance of payments figures have been described as 'part fantasy' (Berg, 1975, p.4). Rimmer (1988, p.12) concludes:

> there appears to be no ground for expecting any trend of improvement in the quality of such estimates. Their inadequacy is itself a datum of economic and social research in tropical Africa.

Even the World Bank (1989) now agrees that 'the statistics commonly reported mask a more complex, less dismal picture ...' They admit that 'statistical anomalies have contributed to the pessimistic picture', pointing to the difference in interpretations according to the prices and exchange rates used (World Bank and the UNDP, 1989, pp.2–3). If 1987 exchange rates rather than 1980 exchange rates had been used, aggregate statistics, rather than showing stagnation, would have shown a cumulative growth rate of 13%. Such variations are comic more than correctable.

1.2.2 Does GNP measure welfare?

Kpedekpo and Arya (1981, p.231), reviewing the value of GNP statistics, argue that:

> subsistence agriculture ... is the starting point of a socially oriented development plan. The whole treatment of non-monetary output in the ... accounts reflects an assumption that this type of activity is an excrescence of the body economic, something for which an allowance can be added on (very approximately) after economic activity proper of various kinds has been estimated ...

Even if accurate national accounts could be constructed for more countries (see, for example, Kravis 1981; Kravis, Heston and Sommers, 1982) it is debateable whether we would be much the wiser. For as 'national income adds together different types of output ... the incomes of people from different ethnic groups, classes, regions, etc., one does not know how to interpret changes in it' (Seers, 1983, p.19).

Even ignoring the problem of interpreting changes, the GNP cannot be interpreted as a measure of economic—let alone social—welfare. Again, Seers provides a succinct summary of the problems:

> the use of prices which reflect highly concentrated distributions of income and severe market imperfections, especially in developing countries; or the reliance on actual expenditures on government services ... as an indication of their value, or the failure to make deductions either for social costs, such as pollution, or for the destruction of assets by war or disaster or even for the depletion of forests, soil and non renewable resources.
>
> (Seers, 1983, p.19)

AwHF itself focuses upon changes in (child) welfare and argues that there is 'no excuse for inaction'. But this is no more (and no less) valid than it has been ever since Europe colonised Africa: the problem is what kind of action—must it necessarily be 'economic growth'? The presumption is widespread: thus, even Amin says 'the reason for seeking greater output per farmer is precisely in order to make possible a higher degree of urbanisation' (Gakou, 1987, p.x). Surely it should also be to create the possibility to manufacture *selected* goods and services, nearly all on (the rural) site, e.g. water, sanitation, housing, and not to increase output *per se*.

The Ecologist is more aggressive: development, as currently understood, means more deforestation, more soil erosion, more floods, more droughts, more poverty, more malnutrition and more misery.

> Third World countries are being asked to exchange the indispensable—their forests, their soil, their water, their culture, and, in the long term, their physical survival, for the gadgetry, the tawdry mass produced goods, the junk foods, and the rest of the paraphernalia of the modern way of life.
>
> (Goldsmith, 1985, p.211)

The issue, therefore, is the composition of the national product—*which* goods are produced and with what resources—and who gets it in terms of access, availability and price. The next question, which sets the agenda for this book, is how to assess social conditions and trends. For example, whilst no-one would dispute the importance of agricultural 'development', the crucial issue is whether land reform or the provision of technical inputs actually improves the lot of the poor over a specified time period and in specified ways. A generalised faith that 'growth' will yield unspecified benefits sometime in the future will not do.

It is much more difficult to agree on the dimensions of 'improvement'. Continuing with the same example, an assessment of the overall impact upon individual households of peasant families probably should include the impact upon their health, their learning, their prospects for joyful participation in the community, etc. as well as food availability and consumption.

The range of criteria which perhaps ought to be taken into account appears vast. A 'short list' provided by Bondestam (1973) illustrates the problem.

> Some of the alternative measures of development, which could be used instead of the overall GNP per capita, are: division of economic wealth among the various economic groups, measured in, for example, purchasing power and related to a minimum standard of living: the proportion of the population which is under constant threat of famine: the economic possibilities of the various economic groups to fulfil the most immediate daily needs, like housing, sufficient calorie and protein intake, and clothing; the proportion of the population within the monetary sector of the economy; distribution of economic growth among the various groups; economic dependency between the various economic groups, between rural and urban areas, between the actual country and industrialised countries etc; trends in concentration or deconcentration of capital, land and wealth; type of industry (light or heavy), rate of investments and rate of industrialisation, measured in production as well as employment, security against confiscation of land, eviction from land, loss of job, etc.; access to medical and health services, education, community development services, technical assistance in agriculture, etc.
>
> (Bondestam, 1973, p.42)

The problem, therefore, is to *specify* exactly which factors should be included in an overall assessment and the importance or weight we attach to each of them. Without these prior decisions—and evidence as to the relation between GNP growth and these factors—the question as to whether Africa needs GNP growth cannot easily be answered.

1.3 THE PQLI

One alternative which has frequently been canvassed is the Physical Quality of Life Index (the PQLI). The US Overseas Development Council were looking for a measure to assess nutritional success in very poor countries. As they said, 'the ultimate test, obviously, was the physical quality of life achieved …' (Morris, 1979). Morris argued that a useful measure should meet the following criteria:

(i) the measure should not depend too heavily (if at all) on market performance (or on GNP data);
(ii) the index should avoid measures that assume that LDCs will inevitably develop along lines followed by developing countries;
(iii) the index should avoid measures that are excessively ethnocentric;
(iv) measures of performance probably should not be based on absolute minima;
(v) the index or indicators must be sensitive to distribution results;
(vi) the measure must be simple.

Morris proposed the PQLI, defined as the average weighted rank of each country in respect of life expectancy, infant mortality, and literacy. The measure satisfies the first and fourth criteria and, with a *sufficiently broad definition of literacy,* might well pass the second and third tests. But it is clearly not very sensitive to the extremes (because the data are ranked), and its operating characteristics—the way it reflects any specific situation—are not simple to understand.

This last point—the way in which one overall index tends to obscure rather than clarify issues—is, of course, one of the original objections to the GNP measure being used as an index of (economic) progress. Proposing the PQLI was rather like jumping out of the frying pan into the fire.

1.4 ALTERNATIVE SCHEMATA

Many other weird and wonderful schemes have been proposed. For example, during the late 1970s and early 1980s, the World Bank supported the construction of social accounting matrices. These were an extension of the input–output methods, obtained by sub-dividing production of commodities into, say, modern and traditional methods, and households or consumers into urban and rural, rich and poor, and so on. There have been suggestions that these could be extended to include educational and eventually cultural activities.

But this and many other system-based schemes are too sophisticated for the data available. Often, in their enthusiasm to illustrate the advantages of a particular framework or scheme for analysis, authors are cavalier about the precise factors which should be included and rely on inappropriate proxies; nearly always they underestimate the fragility of the data base. These are the concerns addressed here: exactly which factors should be included in an assessment of social conditions; and how adequate are the data to reflect current conditions and trends?

2 Which social conditions to report?

Ideally—from the point of view of a desk-bound commentator—we would define a basic set of minimum standards, search for corresponding data, and present standard tables. The world is not like that. In Chapter 14 we go further to argue that such an approach is inappropriate. In any case, the approach in this chapter is more modest: to identify a number of basic themes which most people agree *should* be incorporated into an assessment of social conditions in sub-Saharan Africa.

From this perspective, the basic needs approach promulgated in the 1970s by the International Labour Office (ILO) seems to offer an appropriate framework. This chapter explains how the approach adopted in this book is both close to and distanced from that approach.

2.1 THE BASIC NEEDS APPROACH

The 'basic needs approach' aimed to take into account both what goods and services were available and who were the beneficiaries in terms of consumption. Thus the 'definition of a set of basic needs, together constituting a minimum standard of living, would *at one and the same time* assist in the identification of these (poorest) groups and provide concrete (production) targets against which to measure progress' (ILO, 1976, p.31; this author's insertions and emphasis).

The Programme of Action of the 1976 Employment Conference defines needs and a basic needs approach as follows:

(1) Strategies and national development plans and policies should include explicitly as a priority objective the promotion of employment and the satisfaction of basic needs of each country's population.

(2) Basic needs, as understood in this Programme of Action, include two elements. First, they include certain minimum requirements of a family for private consumption: adequate food, shelter and clothing, as well as certain household equipment and furniture. Second, they include essential services provided by and for the community at large, such as safe drinking water, sanitation, public transport and health, educational and cultural facilities.
(3) A basic-needs-oriented policy implies the participation of the people in making the decisions which affect them through organizations of their own choice.
(4) In all countries freely chosen employment enters into a basic-needs-policy both as a means and as an end. Employment yields an output. It provides an income to the employed, and gives the individual a feeling of self-respect, dignity and of being a worthy member of society.

(ILO, 1976, p.182)

The basic needs approach (BNA) to development gives priority to meeting the basic needs of *all* the people. The approach aims to define both what goods and services should be made available and who should be the beneficiaries (ILO, 1976, p.31). It was not a new or sophisticated idea (Carr-Hill, 1978, p.6) but a restatement of 'the simple view that development should be concerned with removing absolute deprivation, as a first priority' (Stewart, 1985, p.1). It *seemed* to be different because, in contrast to the (prior) emphases upon growth-maximisation and industrialisation, the objectives were defined, however vaguely, *in physical terms;* and that is also the essence of poverty or wealth. For, neither a certain money income per head (obtained by effectively dividing the GNP among all registered members of the population), nor (however it is defined) full employment (the means to such an income) can ensure that essential goods and services are produced in the right quantities at the right time and actually reach the right people.

2.2 THE PERVERSION OF THE BASIC NEEDS APPROACH

On the one hand, a working definition of needs and a core list of needs is proposed. On the other hand, during the late 1970s, the ILO laid heavy emphasis upon participation: 'the main thrust of a basic-needs strategy must be to ensure that there is effective mass participation of the rural population in the political process in order to safeguard their interests' (Sheehan and Hopkins, 1979, p.59).

The BNA has since fallen into disrepute: critics argue that it is (variously) utopian, romantic, populist, anarchic, inefficient, slow, and that it obscures the fundamental international problems that frequently underlie poverty. Instead, they point to the need for freer trade or for fairer prices (take your pick) in order to resurrect growth-oriented development (see Wisner, 1988a).

But the special feature of the basic needs approach was a very belated recognition of the fact that welfare must be measured in concrete terms for each individual prior to homogenisation in terms of a monetary, or any other, unit, and prior to any aggregation across people in terms of a 'growth' index. However, just as the policy implications of the approach were soon perverted (see Wisner, 1988a), so were the statistical implications.

2.2.1 The BNI trap

For, despite this initial affirmation of the importance of identifying basic needs in physical quantities, the applications in the latter half of the 1970s were eager to find a one dimensional yardstick (Hicks and Streeten, 1979) and sometimes a monetary equivalent. Indeed the empirical papers in *Employment Growth and Basic Needs* (ILO, 1976) are expressly designed to show what *growth rates* would be required to satisfy a given collection of basic needs. Similarly, a 'basic needs income' (BNI) should be calculated by identifying 'the marginal household which *absorbs* the stipulated quantities ... [the] *total* expenditure of this household ... yields ... [the] BNI' (my emphasis).

This was taken to ridiculous extremes. Thus, Streeten (1977), using Kahn's (1976) estimates of shortfalls in basic needs in Bangladesh, produced the figures shown in Table 2.1. The BNI is presumably then calculated by dividing $1,940 million by the number of poor?

Even without the sums, the last column is pure fiction in terms of satisfying the requirements of the poor for food, clothing, water and shelter:

Table 2.1 Estimates of basic needs income

Item	*Shortfall quantity*	*Unit cost to consumer*	*Additional income required*
Food	2.5m. tons of cereal	$440 per ton	$1,100m
Clothing	100m. sq. metres	$1 per sq. metre	$100m
Water	Hydrants for 44% of pop.	Free	–
Shelter	6.7m. dwellings	$125 per family per yr	$840m
Total additional income required by the poor =			$2,040m

- How does 2.5 million tons of cereal get *distributed* to the needy population and using what resources? (It will depend entirely on where and when it is produced.)
- Some of the clothing is required by tradition (see, for example, Kahn 1976) and so the estimates given assume that these traditions will not change significantly (most historical experience suggests that rising income influences clothing habits).
- How on earth are water hydrants *free?* (In fact in this particular economy—Bangladesh—water hydrants are supplied by the public authorities and it is presumably being assumed that the necessary finance is being supplied from external aid or, God forbid, by taxing the bourgeoisie.)
- Why is there a *continuous* need for housing? (Because Kahn, or Streeten, are assuming that the need will be met by commercial constructions built to fall down rather than self-help-built, long-lasting structures flexible to the needs of many kinds of households.)

2.2.2 The GOBI desert

This perversion of the BNA can be seen most clearly in the health programmes proposed by international agencies. For example, GOBI (*G*rowth monitoring, *O*ral rehydration therapies (for diarrhoea), *B*reast-feeding and expanded *I*mmunisation programmes) was promoted at a UNICEF meeting in New York in September 1982,

> to recapture the past modest momentum of health and nutrition and nutrition progress especially with respect to protecting and accelerating progress for the world's poorest billion from the risks of malnutrition, infections, disease and lack of sanitation.
> (Cash, Kuesch and Lamstein, 1987, p.2)

This set of strategies was rapidly perceived to be a technical (GOBI) desert and so they added the three Fs—*F*amily planning, *F*emale education and *F*ood supplementation—reiterating that they should not detract from other UNICEF programmes.

Does GOBI-FFF work? A conference held in 1985 by involved participants is illustrative of the problems. All the substantive papers are competent reports on programmes or reviews of research but they do tend to stop just where the argument gets interesting.

One of the best examples is the discussion on oral rehydration therapy (ORT). Hirschorn (1987) acknowledges that there is a 'terrific polemic with ideological colour ... over whether ORT should be delivered as WHO "full" formula packets ... or by teaching mothers to make salt and sucrose solutions at home' (p.35) but he makes only a few technical observations on a debate about hierarchy, participations and power in a couple of paragraphs! Yet the author also concludes that 'the principal obstacles to the widescale acceptance and use of ORT are lack of organisation, will, resources, understanding of the social and cultural milieu and lack of innovation ...' and 'No strategy stands a chance ... as long as the world's resources are directed to war, weapons and oppression instead of human welfare.' But these are seen as peripheral not central issues. Scrimshaw's (1987) summary records happily that 'few [countries] would dare to reject the goals of "GOBI"' (p.249); but few seem prepared to match their rhetoric with implementation because that would imply a massive redistribution.

The opportunists try hard to escape the technological fix. Thus Scrimshaw proposes that: the *G* should be interpreted as *G*rowth monitoring, as a *G*uide to improved nutrition and health care; the *O* as *O*ral rehydration plus *H*ygiene; the *B* as *B*reast-feeding plus *C*omplimentary feeding; and *P* for *P*overty should be brought in somewhere (totally unexplained, perhaps as part of a monetarist strategy?). Unsurprisingly, after concluding that the entire expression, *for clarity* would have to be GG-OH-BC-I-FFF (P?), he then collapses into an espousal of Integrated Child Survival and Development strategies *whether or not* restricted to the specific technical package. But who would ever dispute such a worthy cause? Who has ever disagreed that any of these is a 'good thing'? So what?

2.3 BASIC NEEDS AND EQUITY

The problem is that many aid agencies are not only concerned with attaining basic needs. For example, Chenery (1977), in discussing agrarian reform as part of the *Redistribution with Growth* package promoted by the World Bank, explains:

> more importantly, there is a general thesis that once the peasantry's immediate demands for land are met, it becomes a conservative force, a *bulwark of the [new] status quo*. Provided the process is *controlled,* therefore, a land reform in a setting where land ownership is initially highly concentrated can do much to alleviate the lot of the poor without tearing apart the fabric of society.
>
> (Chenery, 1977; my emphasis)

The preservation of the system is a major concern: as the President of the World Bank said:

> the real issue is not whether land reform is politically easy. The real issue is whether indefinite procrastination is politically prudent. An increasingly inequitable situation will pose a growing threat to political stability.
>
> (World Bank, 1973)

Another excuse for retreating from a 'full-blown' BNA has been the argument that the satisfaction of basic needs contradicts the attainment of a fast rate of economic (GNP) growth. There are several possible variants of the relationship between GNP per capita and inequality of income distribution: either

(a) income distribution first becomes less equal, and only then more equal (Kuznets, 1972; Adelman and Morris, 1973); or

(b) economic growth is retarded by emphasising income redistribution; or
(c) the distribution of income is determined by external factors.

Papanek (1978) believes there is no one correct conclusion:

> at all levels of per capita income, some countries are quite egalitarian and some have quite unequal distributions ... there is nothing inevitable about changes in its distribution as average [national] income rises.

Instead of sterile debates about redistribution and/or growth (in order to meet basic needs), the issue here is whether we can assess progress or recession in respect of basic needs directly with the data available and, if not, how it should be assessed.

2.4 MONITORING MINIMUM SOCIAL CONDITIONS

The question is the choice of measure. Elsewhere, this author has argued that the specification of what to measure is highly political (Carr-Hill, 1984a). At the same time, there are 'areas of concern' which can be incorporated in a wide variety of world views: health, learning, human activities, physical and social environment, and personal security.

The focus should be on the 'end results' of the development process rather than on inputs to it. Ideally, these would be judged by the people involved rather than by an outside 'expert'. In the absence of effective mass participation of populations in deciding what should be development priorities (see Chapter 14), it is important that the presumptions behind each choice are made clear.

Furthermore, given the choice of measures, the specification of indicators is not simply arbitrary, or worse, merely a technical matter; thus, whilst most commentators would go along with the major headings chosen in Section 2 (food, fuel and water; education and health; urbanisation; war; and women), the way in which the discussion is presented will appear as idiosyncratic to some and as objectionable to others. In order to counter at least the charge of arbitrariness, the choice of indicators in each chapter has been set, very briefly, against the background of current literature where appropriate. This is not to say that the indicators are being fully justified by the theoretical literature. The claim is much more modest: that data for these indicators would form part of anyone's 'minimum data set' for monitoring social conditions in sub-Saharan Africa.

The main problem is that the nature and quality of the statistical series for the monitoring of economic and social conditions which are available in Africa leave much to be desired. Where possible, comparisons are made between country trends over time rather than between countries at a certain date. This is because, whilst there may well have been changes in classification or coverage within countries over time, often undocumented, such changes are likely to be less than the differences in classification and coverage between countries. At the same time, in a comparative trend analysis, the differences between countries may be less important, as a trend in data with incomplete coverage may reflect a similar trend in the overall picture.

These difficulties are discussed where appropriate in each chapter. Here, we simply emphasise that we must be clear what is meant in any context by a 'basic needs approach'; whether it is restricted to the delivery of services *to* the poor or includes the choice of and control over services *by* the poor; and that any proposal to monitor the attainment of basic needs must be very carefully designed.

In particular, in order to monitor the attainment of basic needs, the data—whether on education, food, fuel, health or war—have to be related to individuals. This characteristic distinguishes indicators for monitoring the social conditions of populations from other economic and social statistics. It imposes the requirement for accurate population data: this is so important that the next chapter is devoted entirely to a detailed examination of population data.

3 The real population problem

For some, the basic problem of development is population control. Bigger populations obviously pose different sets of problems than smaller ones do, but unless there is an acute shortage of fertile land—as, for example, in Hong Kong—the size of the population is only a problem when it consumes excessive natural resources per capita (as does the North). There are, of course, pressures on the most fertile land and on the resource base of sub-Saharan Africa, but these do not in the main arise from the indigenous populations.

In any case, the real problem for this book is that the estimates of population and of population growth are awful.

3.1 STRAIGHTFORWARD APPROACHES

The obvious way to count the population, to know its shape and size, is to carry out a census of the entire population. But these are not trouble free. Kpedekpo and Arya (1981) give examples of some common types of error:

(1) *Geographical coverage and distribution of the population*
Kpedekpo (1967) discusses the nature and extent of errors in the 1960 Ghanaian census: even the well prepared Tanzanian census of 1967 encountered 'almost unsurmountable difficulties in the field work' and organisational problems. Egero (1973) cites a study by the Bureau of Statistics putting a possible maximum figure of 2% on the loss.

(2) *Absolute population*
In a census, individuals are recorded at their residence sometimes *de facto* (where they spent the night prior to the enumeration) or *de*

jure (according to usual place of residence). In a highly mobile population, this poses difficulties.

(3) *Conceptual problems*
Western concepts are untranslatable. For example, the economic classification of women: their double role as home maker and agricultural worker is unclassifiable according to instructions modelled on an industrially developed society.

(4) *Age data*
The Western concept of birthday is alien. Firstly, people do not remember their age by celebrating their birthdays. Secondly, people just do not know their birthdays.

(5) *Fertility and mortality*
Kpedekpo and Arya (1981) comment:

> statistics on fertility and mortality that are based on questions about births and deaths in the household are not only unreliable but even useless in any form of planning unless adjusted.

Egero (1973) sums up as follows:

> The question on current fertility appears to have resulted in over-reporting of children born due to misconception about the reference period. Retrospective fertility, on the other hand, would seem to be under-reported, a common error due to memory lapses and exclusion of children deceased soon after birth.

Indeed, there is a widespread reluctance to tell enumerators about deceased children.

As Gunnar (1968) remarked when comparing Ghana's population growth, 'observed growth rates are 1.8% for 1948–57 and 3.1% for 1958–67, a difference which would imply an unrealistically high decline in the death rates'. One is tempted to conclude that the reliability of census data has changed little over the century and that the caustic reflections by Fetter (1985) on population statistics based on data from colonial censuses still apply—they should be treated as an unsavoury witness whose testimony must be verified from other sources and cross-checked for internal consistency. In any case, they are too infrequent for assessing short-term change.

There are basically four other methods of counting births and deaths: civil registration, sample surveys of the population, routine health service records, and recording by paramedical workers.

(1) *Civil registration* of births, deaths, marriages and divorces. *If* they can be organised, they are accurate and timely. Very few developing countries have such a system (Habicht and Chamie, 1982). Moreover, although compulsory registration of the restricted set of vital events (births and deaths) is almost universal, the data actually available in Africa are subject to similar kinds of errors as census data.

There is very substantial under-registration of events as well as various inaccuracies in the recording of events. Kpedekpo and Arya (1981) give several examples of impossibly low rates of registration. Also, registration of births—and sometimes deaths—is often late (Kpedekpo, 1970). It is therefore difficult to be confident about these data, except in small well organised countries like Botswana and Mauritius.

(2) *Sample surveys* of the population are the most practical way of collecting detailed data. They provide good estimates *so long as* the sampling frame is reliable. Without a reference population from a previous reliable census, or a system of civil registration, household registration or national identity cards, this is problematic. Moreover, whilst a sample design might look simple on paper, they are not always easy to carry out. Official reports of surveys frequently include references to failures to carry out the sample design fully or to gain cooperation in all sampled areas. The general problem of surveys is considered further in Chapter 14: here we simply record that they too are probably not appropriate for regular and routine monitoring of population change.

(3) *Routine health service records.* Hospital and health care statistics may well be kept accurately for administrative purposes but they are difficult to interpret because people attending health care institutions are usually unrepresentative of the population as a whole. Several studies have shown how the use of hospital facilities for births and

deaths is affected by attitudes to Western medicine in general and to the hospital concerned in particular, and by geographical, financial and social access to hospital care, amongst other factors.

(4) *Recording by paramedical workers.* In some countries, primary health care (PHC) workers have been asked to collect basic information about the households they visit. The approach appears to motivate workers and to provide useful information (Nabarro and Graham-Jones, 1987); the validity of the data is, of course, impossible to assess.

The importance of reliable statistical series on (infant and child mortality) for planning purposes is widely recognised. But few developing countries have been able to establish satisfactory data collection programmes for compiling them on a regular basis. A recent review of the data situation showed that despite the almost universal existence of legislation requiring the compulsory registration of vital events, hardly any developing countries have satisfactory civil registration systems.

> Several countries seem . . . to have been mis-classified as to the reliability of their vital statistics.
>
> (WFS, 1983, p.16)

3.2 INDIRECT ESTIMATES

The alternative is to rely on indirect methods of estimation. There are four indirect techniques of mortality estimations.

(1) *Intercensal survival technique:* where the numbers of persons by age and sex at two different points in time (e.g. 30–35 year olds in 1971 with 40–45 year olds in 1981) are compared to derive an estimate of mortality during the 1970s. This technique assumes knowledge of the in- and out-migration of this group and that there has been no change in the pattern of age reporting.

(2) *Retrospective mortality questions:* a survey or census which asks about the number of individuals who died in a household over the last 12 months. Whilst in theory this should give good results, in practice,

according to the UN themselves 'it does not prove to be very satisfactory' (UN, 1984, p. 36). In fact, given the reluctance to talk about those recently deceased, the results are almost useless.

(3) *Multi-round survey:* visiting a household more than once in a given period. The problems of forgetting and misreporting of events, that plague retrospective questionnaires, can be eliminated. Events occurring between rounds can be well documented, as the reporting period is fixed by the first survey. However, it is expensive.

(4) *Survivorship questions:* a respondent is asked about the number surviving of a particular category of relative. Usually women are asked about the number of children ever born and the number surviving. This percentage can be converted, using various assumptions, into an estimate of child survivorship. This estimate of child survivorship is then converted, via a 'model life table'—which is basically a set of fixed relationships between the different age-specific mortality rates—into an estimate of mortality in all age groups (and therefore life expectancy).

This latter is the most common procedure (UN, 1983). The basic estimate of child survivorship depends on assumptions about fertility and infant survival but also on correct age reporting and on the willingness of the respondent to answer truthfully. Yet in many cultures, there are taboos about revealing exact family size. The plausibility of the final estimate of life expectancy further depends on the plausibility of the 'Model Life Table'. As the original Coale and Demeny (1966) tables were based on empirical examples from developed countries with 'complete' vital registration systems, the UN Population Division prepared another set for developing countries (UN, 1982).

On the basis of high quality data from 22 less developed countries, 72 life tables (36 male, 36 female) were constructed. Statistical comparison, *via* a form of principal components, suggested they fell into four clusters, labelled the Latin American pattern, the Chilean pattern, the South Asian pattern and the Far Eastern pattern. There was no 'African' pattern. Other life tables, e.g. from Israel and Kuwait, as well as those for the female populations of Hong Kong and the Republic of Korea, did not fit, so were omitted! For each of the eight groups (two genders, four patterns) life tables were constructed for 41 different levels of mortality. Within each table, calculations have been made allowing for a rate of natural increase (the crude birth rate minus the crude death rate) between –1% and +5% per year.

In principle, these tables can be used to identify the rate of natural increase which best describes any given population. Demographers search for the Coale and Demeny age column which best matches the pyramid under study. The matching procedure requires precise population estimates broken down by gender into 5–year intervals. Even then, the procedure is highly problematic as columns for low rates of natural increase from tables of high mortality can closely resemble columns for higher rates of natural increase at a lower mortality.

If only one age-specific mortality is used to estimate life expectancy, the choice of a model has a significant impact. With an infant mortality rate of 100, estimated life expectancy varies from 50 to 59, depending on the choice of model (see Murray, 1987, Fig. 1, p.775).

In devising life tables for developing countries in Africa, the United Nations team, after a brief examination, is categorical:

> The results of these comparisons are disappointing. . . . If the seven countries analysed are representative, African data show a wide variety of mortality patterns. . . . given the unreliability of the data at hand, statements about the age pattern of mortality in this region must remain tentative.
>
> (quoted in *Levels and Trends in Mortality Since 1950,* p.15)

This discussion has assumed that there actually are some empirical data—probably on child survivorship—even if only from a (small) sample of women in the population. Unfortunately this is rare in Africa and most sources make estimates based on a variety of assumptions. The choice of sources is obviously crucial.

3.3 THE CHOICE OF SOURCES

Murray's (1987) excellent review of sources has been used as the basis for this sub-section.

The Division of Health Studies Assessment of the WHO produces a *World Health Statistics Annual* based on reports from countries. However, their comparative table on life expectancies in 1970–75 and 1980–85, published in the 1984 *Annual,* was based on the UN Population Division *World Population Prospects: Estimates and Projections as Assessed in 1982*.

The UN Secretariat produces three sets of life expectancy estimates.

(1) The *Demographic Yearbook* is based on country responses to a questionnaire; if there is no response, the Population Division estimates are used. Consequently there is no consistency from year to year for one country. Where country estimates are used (about 40% of the time according to Murray, 1987, p.776), they are of unknown reliability, given the possibility of political distortion as well as the lack of detail on data quality and estimation techniques.

(2) The *World Population Prospects* is produced by the Estimates and Projections Sub-Division. Their mandate from the Population Commission is to produce population estimates up to the year 2025. To produce population projections they need a fertility estimate and a mortality estimate (or life expectancy at birth) for each country for each 5–year period. They first derive a base year measurement in a particular country: and then *assume* that each country's life expectancy will increase by 2½ years—or 2 years (low variant) or 3 years (high variant)—every five years until 62.5, thereafter gains are less. The original estimate of 2½ years was based on life tables reported by 27 developed nations and nine developing countries (seven in Latin America, two in Asia, none in Africa). This 'model' has hardly changed in 30 years, and there is certainly no reason to suppose it applies in sub-Saharan Africa.

For many countries the base year is from the early or mid 1960s. In these cases, including many from Africa, the estimate for life expectancy in 1980–85 is just the empirical measurement for 1960–65 with eight years (using the low variant) tacked on. For some other sub-Saharan states, an average of neighbouring countries' life expectancy provides a base year measurement. Even when new data appear, Murray (1987) reports that the Estimates and Projection

Sub-Division are reluctant to make large changes in their 'assessments', as they have to preserve historical continuity. Murray (1987, p.777) shows how, in the case of the Congo, new data from the 1974 census implying much higher life expectancies were mostly ignored.

(3) The *World Population Trends and Policies Monitoring Report* is produced by the UN Trends and Structures Sub-Division, whose mandate (also from the Population Commission) is 'to monitor and measure population, fertility and mortality levels and trends'. They are therefore concerned with empirical data and measurements only, not with hypothetical rates of gain. They produce estimates for some 70 developing countries only, since if there is no reliable data available, they will not publish an estimate. This includes only *two* countries in sub-Saharan Africa.

The most recent data of the *1983 Monitoring Report* was published in 1985. The results from the 1980 round of censuses were not included, so it is potentially out-of-date. In fact, much of this report is based on the life expectancy estimates produced by the US Bureau of the Census.

The Center for International Research of the US Bureau of the Census publishes, every two years, *World Population—Recent Demographic Estimates for the Countries and Regions of the World.* Only data 'based on reliable population censuses, vital registration systems, and/or sample surveys' are presented. The most recent report (for 1983) gave life expectancy for only 104 out of its target of 158 developing countries.

However, the most widely used source is that of the World Bank. Life expectancy for about 126 developing countries is published annually by the Population and Nutrition Department. The World Bank has its own technique for updating old empirically based mortality estimates. Their model was based on the relationship between change in life expectancy and educational level. They claimed to find a different relationship depending on the level of female primary school enrolment, but since their data were drawn from the UN Estimates and Projections Sub-Division, their actual 'model' closely follows the UN model.

The Bank use their model to project backward to 1950 and forward to 2025 from the more recent base year. Murray (1987, p.779) comments that the life expectancy estimates for Africa:

> are consistently higher than the corresponding Estimates and Projections Sub-Division figures . . . because they are based on the childhood mortality rates derived from child survivorship figures being produced by the Estimates and Projects Sub-Division [who do not themselves, as yet, use them].

The differences can be large.

> The estimate for the Congo in 1980–85 of 60.5, which is 15 years higher than the UN estimate, was based on an estimate of child survival from the 1974 Census. The estimate for South Africa of 63.5 in 1980–85 for the total population is ten years higher than the UN.... As a consequence of this estimate for South Africa, Namibia, whose estimate is based on an average of neighbouring countries, has a life expectancy of 60.4 in 1980–85 according to the Bank and a life expectancy of 48.2 in 1980–85 according to the UN.
>
> (Murray, 1987, p.779)

The Bank is also willing to incorporate data from new surveys—if it implies higher life expectancy—and to alter the whole historical sequence from 1980.

3.4 THE REAL POPULATION PROBLEM: USING POPULATION DATA

It cannot be too strongly emphasised that most current population estimates rely on these techniques, and especially on these model life tables for the derivation of the final estimates. To the extent that these models do not accurately represent reality, the estimates obtained will be biased. Moreover, because of these assumptions, one must be very careful in analysing the relation between estimated populations or rates of population growth and other socio-economic variables. The pitfalls are illustrated in Appendix 1.

There is no easy 'fix'. Blacker (1987, p.197) concluded:

> there is still no method of estimating either fertility or mortality in developing countries lacking reliable vital registration which can be guaranteed to give accurate results.

These various assumptions (about fertility and mortality), whilst usually specified quite clearly in the source documents, tend to be forgotten as the statistical series—reproduced in one international publication after another—take on a life of their own. It is startling to realise how out-of-date empirically-based estimates for fertility are for many African countries. Murray (1987) explains:

> In Africa alone, Djibouti, Equatorial Guinea and Somalia's life expectancy estimates are based on averages of neighbouring countries, while nine other countries have had no survey data since the fifties or early sixties.

For 23 African countries, even though both use the same data, their estimates of life expectancy produced by the UN and the World Bank differ by more than three years.

> The review of 52 selected developing countries concluded that, given the limited potential of measuring infant mortality trends on an annual basis, worldwide progress in reducing infant mortality could meaningfully be reported only once every 3 or 4 years.
>
> (Carlson, 1985, p.56)

There is little to add to Murray's general conclusion: 'that reliable empirical information on change in life expectancy exists for only a handful of countries' (p.781). For sub-Saharan Africa, the present estimates of changes in the rates of fertility and of mortality and, therefore, of population growth, are so bad that it is difficult to draw any inferences at all.

No-one would want to deny that population has increased in Africa (as elsewhere). But the precise growth rate matters. If, for example, the growth rate of population were estimated to be 3% when it is really 2½% (2%), then that difference—which is very small relative to the variations discussed above—would make a difference of 23% (57%) in estimated projections of additional population after 10 years. These very large uncertainties must be borne in mind whenever we discuss *per capita* trends.

Section 2: A Critical Examination of the Statistical Data

The purpose of this section is to examine critically the statistical data available about levels and trends in social conditions. The organisation of the material into chapters is based loosely upon the list of basic human needs suggested by the International Labour Office in the mid–1970s. Chapters 4 and 5 present data on the availability of food, fuel and water; Chapters 6 and 7 on child development and on adult health; and Chapters 8 and 9 on the availability of basic primary education and on literacy. For each of these concerns there is a particular concern with the distribution between geographical regions and between social groups, and data on disparities and inequalities in health and education have been collected together in Appendix 2 and 3 respectively.

In the remaining chapters of this section, data are presented on three 'cross-cutting' concerns, and on the groups which are rendered especially vulnerable in the maelstrom of development. In Chapter 10 data are presented on urbanisation and the relative status of the rural and urban poor; in Chapter 11, material is brought together on refugees, destabilisation and war; and, finally, in Chapter 12, evidence about the status of women is examined.

4 Food production and food security

The issue for this chapter is whether or not people have an adequate diet. Whilst the 'end result' is nutritional adequacy, the chapter is more broadly concerned with food (in)security. Hence, we consider data on domestic food production, food availability both geographically and over the season, and finally the impact upon households' food security.

4.1 (THE MEASUREMENT OF) DOMESTIC FOOD PRODUCTION

The Food and Agriculture Organisation (FAO) claims that between 1970 and 1980, *per capita* food production fell by 11%. Their indices show an increase of 20%, which is equivalent to a 1.8% compound annual growth rate over the period.

Indices of agricultural production for sub-Saharan Africa

1950	*1955*	*1960*	*1965*	*1970*	*1975*	*1980*	*1985*
56	61	68	76	85	91	102	105

On the basis of an estimated 2.7% population growth rate, this represents an annual decline of 0.9% per capita. The picture for food production for specific countries in Figure 4.1. looks convincing.

But these indices of agricultural production are calculated by combining together into one index the marketed outputs of different products according to the prevailing prices on 'the market'. This is exactly the GNP trap: and besides telling us nothing about what is happening to actual food availability, it tells us very little about domestic crop production. (For completeness, however, FAO statistics, comparing growth pre- and post-1980, have been included as an Annex to this chapter.)

Figure 4.1 Indices of agricultural production, 1980 (1969–71 = 100)

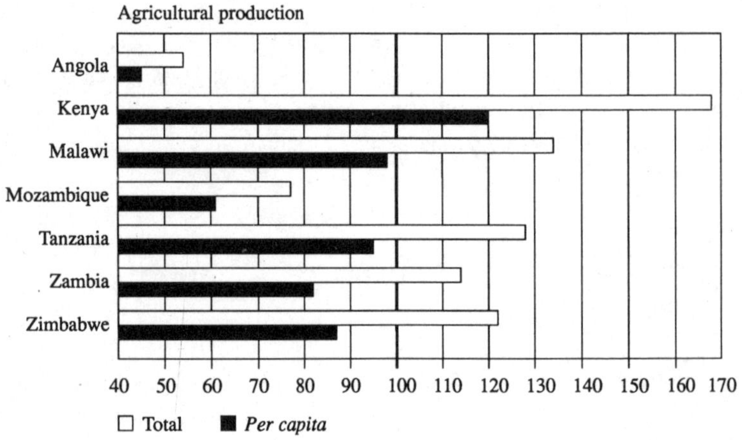

Source: World Indices of Agricultural and Food Production (1981), USDA-ERS, *Statistical Bulletin.*

The methods used by the FAO to estimate crop production are not documented. Uncertainties abound. Thus, Bondestam (1973) cites an early study claiming that 'less than 15% of the total farm product is marketed and the small surpluses yielded by subsistence cultivation are usually traded in markets within the traditional economy' (US Dept. of Commerce, 1967). Many subsequently have challenged FAO statistics for particular countries (see for example Fresco, 1987; Guyer, 1984; Jamal and Weeks, 1988; Koley, 1973) for the same kind of reason. Cheater (1988) remarks 'It is all too easy ... to forget that African statistics on food *production* are *at best* 'guesstimates' extrapolated off what little is known of *recorded* marketing.' Food production and food supply on official markets are *not* the same.

The relevant statistics are, therefore, very weak but apparently there was a dramatic fall in African food production in 1980–82 and a dramatic rise in 1985–86 in that average food production in 1986 *per capita* was more than 90% of the 1980 level in most SSA countries. Agricultural production is either highly volatile or poorly measured. Rimmer (1988) suggests that

> Statistics may have been politicised in the bad years ... to trigger international relief: emergency food aid could be used to supplement government resources as well as to feed people.

Indeed, it has been suggested that estimates of national agricultural production for some of the larger countries (e.g. Zaire, Nigeria, Ethiopia, Sudan) are little better than random numbers (Fieldhouse, 1986, p.98, quoting Michael Lipton).

The Ethiopian famine

According to both FAO and USDA indices of *per capita* food production remained above the base year in the mid 1970s until 1984, when they both fell substantially (to 90 and 98 respectively). The estimates included areas outside government control and relied on very out-of-date population estimates (contrast the FAO 1983 estimate of 33.7 million with the 1984 census figures of 42 million). Meanwhile, donors presumed the Relief and Rehabilitation Commission (RRC) had exaggerated its food requirements, which led to a growing scepticism and eventually to the well-known donations by the Western public.

Some authors suggest 'that official statistics for output have diverged further and further from actual output in recent years and that neither the magnitude of the divergence nor, in many cases, the direction of the divergence is known' (Berry, 1983). It is presumed that the low level of prices prevailing on official markets (whether for export or home consumption), is a major cause for stagnation in the production and delivery of food to the official market: the same logic suggests that producers will shift into the production of food for themselves or for unofficial markets. Raikes (1986, p.162) concludes:

> it is simply not clear what has happened to food production in much of tropical Africa ... there can be no doubt that [food supply on the official markets] has deteriorated, but it is not at all clear what the trends in food production have been.

In the absence of good data on agricultural production, there is a tendency to make inferences based upon other data about the economy (e.g. Green and Kirkpatrick, 1982) and in particular upon aggregate import volumes. As imports have increased sharply over the last quarter of a century, it is then deduced that there have been substantial declines in domestic food production *per capita*.

In fact, Shatz (1986) argues 'the import data do not tell us anything of the kind'. At the start of the 1980s, African food production amounted to roughly 85% of food consumption whilst imports were 15%. Aggregate food imports of sub-Saharan Africa almost exactly quadrupled between 1961–63 and 1980–82—equivalent to a 7.6% increase per annum. This increased *total* food supplies by approximately 1.1% per annum.

Given the presumed annual population growth of 2.7% per annum, if total African food production had remained constant, then in 20 years consumption *per capita* would have dropped to 72% of the already inadequate level of, say, 1960. If consumption has remained constant, then domestic aggregate food production has risen substantially—by 1.6% per annum. In fact, the World Bank claims calorie supply *per capita* rose from 2056 calories per day in 1977 to 2156 calories per day in 1982, an increase of 0.9% per annum. This would have absorbed virtually all the additional food made available through rising food imports. Hence, Schatz (1986) argues that domestic food production *per capita* has remained about level.

Cheater's final comment is:

> because most food production goes unrecorded ... and because demographic data are unreliable, the spurious accuracy of those statistics which make Africa the world's worst basket case must be questioned.
>
> (Cheater, 1988)

4.2 FOOD AVAILABILITY AND DISTRIBUTION

The publicity attached to famines has made it difficult to assess the actual levels of and trends in food availability in Africa. The data in the latest *State of the World's Children* are presented in Figure 4.2.

Figure 4.2 Daily *per capita* calorie supply as percentage of requirements, 1985

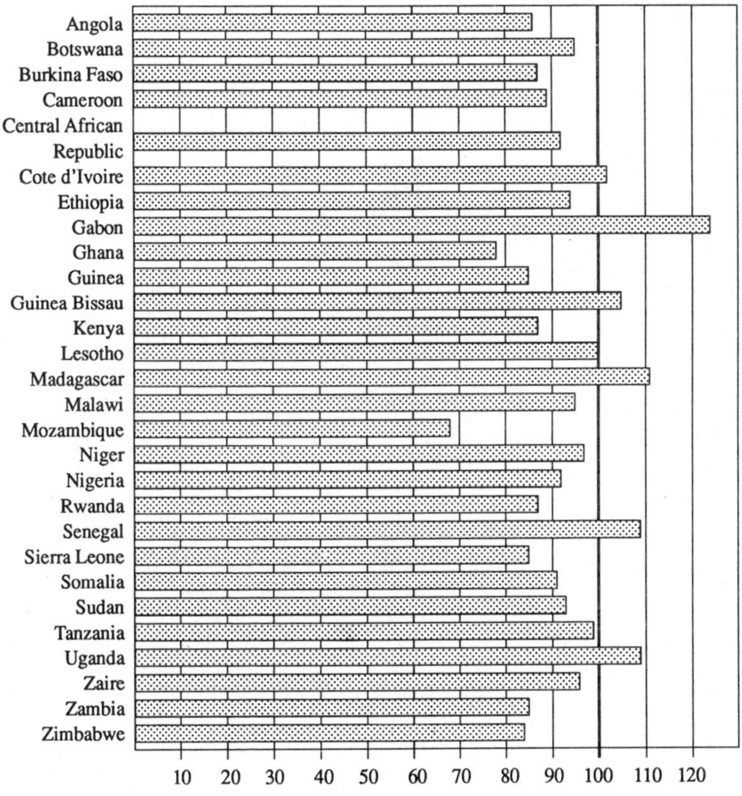

Source: UNICEF (1989), Table 2, p.96.

For 11 of the 28 countries, daily *per capita* supply was estimated in 1985 to be less than 90% of requirements. Trend data, based on these countries with Food Balance Sheets calculated for both 1969–71 and 1971–81, are given in Table 4.1. These show that there were increases in *per capita* dietary energy supplies for about half of the countries and decreases in the other half.

Table 4.1 Per capita dietary energy supplies (DES) 1969–71 and 1979–81, estimated population growth rate 1970–80 and calculated growth rate in DES 1969–71 to 1979–81

	DES	*DES*	*Growth rates*	
Country	*1969–71*	*1979–81*	*Pop.*	*DES*
Benin	2,105	2,174	2.9	0.3
Botswana	2,176	2,398	2.6	1.0
Burkina Faso	1,987	1,694	2.4	–0.1
Cameroon	2,151	2,217	2.2	0.3
Central African Republic	2,186	2,117	2.1	–0.3
Cote d'Ivoire	2,484	2,641	4.1	0.6
Gambia	2,348	2,151	3.0	–0.4
Ghana	2,230	1,766	3.0	–2.3
Guinea	2,040	1,880	2.5	–0.8
Kenya	2,260	2,012	3.8	–1.2
Lesotho	2,032	2,424	2.3	1.8
Madagascar	2,469	2,491	2.5	0.1
Malawi	2,282	2,207	3.1	–0.3
Mali	2,065	1,790	2.6	–1.4
Mozambique	2,088	1,881	2.5	–1.0
Niger	2,074	2,441	2.8	1.6
Nigeria	2,255	2,446	3.1	0.8
Rwanda	2,049	2,274	3.0	1.0
Senegal	2,299	3,346	2.8	0.2
Sierra Leone	2,071	1,955	2.6	–0.6
Somalia	2,163	2,004	5.1	–0.8
Sudan	2,102	2,312	2.7	1.0
Swaziland	2,204	2,494	2.6	1.2
Tanzania	1,980	2,371	3.0	1.8
Togo	2,191	2,138	2.6	–0.2
Uganda	2,260	1,797	3.0	–2.3
Zambia	2,167	2,145	3.1	–0.1
Zimbabwe	2,056	2,094	3.3	0.2

Source: FAO (1985) *The Fifth World Food Survey*, Table 2.4.

Given the quality of the basic data, it is difficult to draw any overall conclusion other than that many in Africa have been living on the breadline for some time.

The initial availability of food is only the first step. The next step is getting it to those who need to eat it! There are problems of geographical distribution within countries and the seasonality of food supply and of wastage.

4.2.1 Geographical distribution

The importance of geographical distribution obviously varies according to the possibility of geographical redistribution. There is no systematic data on the potential for re-distribution within a country, but Hey and Rukuni (1988) have examined the potential for mutual aid between the SADCC countries. They show that output has fluctuated wildly but that, even though there is a high degree of correlation between variations in national outputs, the inter-annual variations within individual SADCC countries are greater than variations within the SADCC Region as a whole. In principle therefore, within the SADCC group, countries in surplus one year could assist their neighbours; and the same argument almost certainly applies to districts within a country. But the transport difficulties are legion.

The point here is that aggregate assessments at a national level tell us very little about food availability *in practice* at *local* level. Chambers (1974, 1983) argues for seasonal analysis of food availability by local level staff. Schuftan (1981), reviewing the experience of 24 African countries, also argues that we need data on quantities of locally grown food per season; and on quantities of food exported from and imported to a given community or region.

Assuming local availability, the major constraint on adequate calorie intake is price. On a national level, Scandizzo (cited in Horton, Kerr and Diakosavvas, 1988) claims to have established a relationship between calorie intake per capita and cereal prices, but there must be suspicions that each series might be partly estimated from the other. On a local level, Kumar (1988), investigating the relation between food availability and the area planted among households in Chipata,

Zambia, suggests that his results are best interpreted by presuming food is treated as a wage good.

4.2.2 Seasonal variation

There are substantial seasonal variations in food supply. Energy requirements increase substantially during harvesting season and usually coincide with low food availability. Kumar (1988) investigated the relation between labour inputs, malnutrition and production. As agricultural work loads rise, food consumption rises, but so does malnutrition (see Table 4.2). Kumar (1988) finds that low levels of food stocks in the post harvest period and their availability during the heavy work period in the rainy season, as well as the use of non-household agricultural labour, can reduce the area planted.

Table 4.2 Seasonal distribution of malnutrition for adults, Chipata, Zambia (below 29 weight-for-height ratio)

	Males		*Females*		
Season 1981/82	*Labour input*	*% Mal-nutrition*	*Labour input*	*% Mal-nutrition*	*Activity*
Sept./Oct.	15	57	20	41	Clearing
Jan./Feb.	41	67	43	49	Planting/Weedin[g]
May/June	13	67	19	48	Harvesting

Source: Kumar, 1988, Tables 1 and 2.

The impact, of course, varies according to the pattern of activity nomadic herders can significantly reduce energy outlay by restin[g] during the rainy period; peasants embroiled in cash-cropping have t[o] work harder. But seasonal hunger has been documented for over 2[0] years (Hunter, 1967): whilst the loss is usually less than 10% of bod[y] weight and hence may have no functional significance for adult males for pregnant women, lactating mothers and children, such a loss ma[y] be injurious (Hussain, 1985).

4.3 FOOD SECURITY

Seasonal variation in food availability obviously affects those already at the margin. For example, Matomara reports on surveys conducted in villages selected as part of a PHC programme. One of the annual surveys compared 202 households with severely malnourished children to 3,757 other households during 1983. The 202 households had more children being fed only with pap (uji), had only 50kg or less grain reserve, cultivated only two or less acres of land, and their fields were two or more miles away. Any seasonal 'variation' would be dramatic.

Following Bryceson (1989) one can distinguish three types of food inadequacy:

Malnutrition—a chronic state of under-nutrition or malnourishment—reflecting a deficient intake of calories and/or proteins relative to body requirements. This may be caused by infection generating high nutritional requirements, as well as inadequate amounts of food;

Seasonal hunger—a cyclical dip in dietary intake causing a temporary state of under-nutrition, usually most acute in the pre-harvest rainy season;

Famine—severe calorie deprivation arising from natural or human events.

The FAO—and many other agencies—presume the increases in food production should be the main focus of policy to alleviate food inadequacy. But 'malnutrition is almost universally a consequence of people's inability to afford food which is available' (Tarrant, 1980, p.4).

This is well illustrated by understanding how families attempt to cope with famine or the possibility of famine. On the basis of studies on Ethiopia and the Sudan, Corbett (1988) suggests that families follow a three-stage sequence.

Stage One—Insurance Mechanisms

- changes in cropping and planting practices
- sale of small stock
- reduction of current consumption levels
- collection of wild foods

- use of interhousehold transfers and loans
- increased petty commodity production
- migration in search of employment
- sale of possessions

Stage Two—Disposal of Productive Assets

- sale of livestock
- sale of agricultural tools
- sale or mortgaging of land
- credit from merchants and moneylenders
- reduction of current consumption levels

Stage Three—Destitution

- distress migration

Their 'strategies' are focused primarily on raising income, not on their own food production and intake. Reardon, Matlon and Delgado (1988) also show how households spread income risk not only across occupations but also across locations although the success of such strategies varies between regions.

Many authors would argue that cash cropping increases vulnerability to famine, because the poorer groups will not grow staples in sufficient quantities. However, there is some contrary data. Kennedy and Cogill (1988) report on the impact of increased cash cropping upon household food security in South western-Kenya, the area with the highest infant mortality rate of the country. The newest sugar factory was established in 1977 and data were collected from the households of new and established sugar farmers (N=181) and a matched group of non-sugar farmers (N=231) during 1984. They observed no significant differences in the allocation of land, food stocks or mean energy intake between the three groups of farmers, and energy consumption did not seem to be related to farm size. They further show how the incomes of sugar farmers are higher, but that this extra income tends to be spent on non-food items—e.g. housing and school fees.

The authors acknowledge that the baseline consumption and nutritional status of sugar and non-sugar farmers may have been different. They do show, however, that differences in wealth between the groups are unlikely to account for the finding: in their follow-up study two years later, new entrants whose baseline income was initially the same as that of non-sugar farmers, had significantly higher incomes. They concluded that the

> conventional wisdom that an increased emphasis on commercial agricultural production necessarily results in a deterioration of household food security is not borne out by [their] data.
>
> (Kennedy and Cogill, 1988, p.1080)

Von Braun (1988) traced the impact of technological change in agriculture to production and income effects, and to consumption and nutritional effects among 200 households/compounds in central Gambia. A large-scale rice irrigation project covering 1500 hectares was implemented in 1983, giving priority to women during the registration of the plots. But focusing investment on a 'woman's' crop in this way did not necessarily help women farmers:

(1) The more a new technology increased labour productivity in rice, the more there was a takeover of the rice production by male producers and the more the crop became a 'communal' crop for household food security.
(2) Household income increased and much of the increased income was spent on increased calorie consumption.

Calorie consumption levels differed substantially by income level with the widest gap in the 'hungry' wet season. Differences in malnutrition (measured by weight for age with NCHS/WHO standard) were also widest in the wet season (see Table 4.3).

Table 4.3 Calories *per capita* per day

Household per capita income	*Calories per capita per day*		*Weight for age less than 80% of standard children 60-120 months Per cent of childen*	
	Wet season	*Dry season*	*Wet season*	*Dry season*
Lowest quartile	1,893	2,176	33	17
Top quartile	2,917	2,972	15	11
Total average	2,380	2,522	26	17

Source: Von Braun 1988, p.1085.

4.4 ENDPOINTS: THE FOOD CRISIS AND ELIGIBILITY

> Clearly over the last decade Africa did experience a food crisis. The incidence of famine is proof of the most awful kind that there was a severe food crisis in several countries. But the unreliability of the data implies that researchers should re-examine with care prevailing notions of the extent and sources of the crisis at a country and regional level.
>
> (Borton and Clay, 1988, p.144)

In particular, there is general agreement that the countries worst hit by famine and widespread starvation were Chad, Ethiopia, Mali, Mozambique and Sudan (FAO, 1985a; ODI, 1985; USAID, 1986). None of these is thickly populated, even by African standards, and whilst drought and economic and environmental problems were all crucial contributory factors, the fact that all of these countries, except Mali, were involved in a civil conflict at the time should not be forgotten.

There is a problem of domestic food production in sub-Saharan Africa. But given the apparently sharp rise in 1985–86, it can be questioned whether domestic food production in Africa has got substantially worse. If one is really concerned about the availability of food to those in real need and their security of access to it, then one must also take into account forms of 'entitlement to food' (Sen, 1981a). The famines in Sahelian countries during 1973 occurred without any decline in the overall availability of food (Sen, 1981a)—in fact Mali and Senegal continued to export cash crops. A drought affects individuals' (classes') abilities to 'command commodities in general and food in particular' differentially.

This does not imply that food production should be ignored. But different ways of increasing food production have different effects upon the pattern of entitlement. The impact of both cash cropping and technological change upon food availability varies: more generally poorer income groups are more adversely affected. Moreover, in using the term 'entitlement', Sen was referring not only to purchasing power but also to non-market distribution and redistribution within the household. What affects households is the food available to them, and individuals are also affected by the intra-household distribution of food.

ANNEX

Table 4A.1 presents data on growth rates in food production pre- and post-1980. In about half the countries the rate is higher before 1980 and in the other half the rate is higher after 1980. One is tempted to query data which are distributed so evenly.

Table 4A.1 Growth rates in food production during the 1970s and the first half of the 1980s

	Net food productivity growth rate	
Country	*1971–80*	*1980–84*
Angola	0.36	0.38
Benin	2.85	2.88
Botswana	–3.55	0.97
Burkina Faso	2.25	0.34
Burundi	2.30	2.68
Cameroon	1.97	0.60
Central African Republic	1.82	1.02
Congo	2.11	0.58
Cote d'Ivoire	6.16	1.68
Ethiopia	2.03	–0.98
Gabon	0.16	2.17
Gambia	–3.58	1.83
Ghana	–1.75	1.47
Guinea	0.66	2.76
Guinea Bissau	1.79	8.55
Kenya	2.09	3.51
Lesotho	0.85	–0.27
Madagascar	1.38	2.48
Malawi	1.51	2.49
Mali	3.66	0.81
Mozambique	–0.48	–1.30
Niger	5.11	–2.40
Nigeria	2.88	0.95
Rwanda	4.78	2.96
Senegal	0.13	1.74
Sierra Leone	1.19	0.33
Somalia	0.93	0.19
Swaziland	3.48	3.33
Tanzania	5.79	–0.33
Togo	1.52	–0.85
Uganda	0.69	10.01
Zaire	1.64	3.30
Zambia	2.83	1.40
Zimbabwe	1.44	–6.98

Source: FAO, *The State of Food and Agriculture*, 1985, Table 2.16, pp.92–3.

5 Fire and water

The purpose of this chapter is to describe what we know about access to essential energy and water.

Fuel is one of the very few areas where the trend appears incontrovertible although the data are weak. The majority of the energy consumed in Africa is wood based, and the first half of the chapter focuses only on this with a short discussion of the time costs of collection. There is more dispute over exactly what should count as an adequate supply of water; after presenting the basic data (also very weak) the difficulty of assessing the health benefits and time savings of improved water availability are discussed in the second half of the chapter.

5.1 ENERGY CONSUMPTION

Everyone agrees that wood is the main source of fuel, especially in rural areas. Moreover, whilst no-one would dispute that electricity is a very desirable amenity, it can only be used for lighting or the radio (because few have a cooker, a fridge or other household appliances).

> The benefits of rural electrification, including the social benefits, tend to be overestimated and the costs understated. Multi-million dollar schemes, it appears, are repeatedly based on conventional wisdom fueled by extraneous motives rather than arithmetic. The role of subsidies is therefore debateable, particularly in countries yet unable to satisfy needs more basic than access to electricity.
>
> (Fluitman, 1983, p.53)

In any case, electricity use is low, even in a relatively well-off country like Zimbabwe (see Table 5.1).

Table 5.1 Per capita income and electricity use in selected African countries, 1982

Country	*Per capita income use (US dollars)*	*Electricity (million kilowatt hours)*	*Per capita electricity use (kilowatt hours)*
Zimbabwe	849	7,614	1,015
Zaire	203	4,392	143
Kenya	420	1,998	110
Senegal	541	633	105
Niger	338	350	60

Source: World Bank, '1982 Power/Energy Data Sheets for 104 Developing Countries' (Washington DC, July 1985).

It is, however, virtually impossible to make sensible estimates of household consumption of woodfuel. For example, Enabor (1976) comments:

> There are no published data on production and consumption of wood and wood based products ... The major source ... is FAO's Country Table ... FAO's data are compiled from information supplied by individual reporting countries ... Nevertheless, the published statistics of wood products in Nigeria are entirely inadequate and unsatisfactory.

Table 5.2 presents data from Agarwal (1986), themselves derived from FAO figures which 'are generally considered the best available at the macro level'. However,

> no precise macro estimates exist of the use of woodfuel in different countries ... The figures relate to annual production of firewood plus charcoal ... which is typically assumed to equal annual woodfuel consumption. For some countries, the figures given are either based on FAO's own estimates or obtained from unofficial sources. For others, they are official figures supplied by the countries and would usually cover only recorded removals from forests [and therefore] would tend to underestimate actual consumption ... Further, although FAO gives country-specific figures for imports and exports of fuelwood plus charcoal, the world aggregates do not balance: the 1982 world export figure was only 74% of the world import figures (FAO, 1984). (Agarwal, 1986, p.6)

Table 5.2 Commercial and woodfuel energy consumption in Africa, 1982

Country	*Commercial energy per capita kg. CE*	*Woodfuel consumption per capita*		*Woodfuel as a percentage of total energy*	*Similar estimates from Hall et al*
		Cu.m	*kg. CE*		
Angola	126	0.96	319	72	>70
Benin	40	1.05	348	90	>80
Central African Republic	42	1.06	353	89	>90
Chad	22	1.62	541	96	>90
Cote d'Ivoire	287	0.78	260	48	46
Ethiopia	31	0.83	276	90	>90
Ghana	122	0.60	199	62	>70
Kenya	103	1.48	492	83	>70
Madagascar	67	0.59	197	75	>80
Malawi	50	0.90	301	86	nc
Mali	30	0.58	194	87	>90
Niger	47	0.58	192	80	>80
Nigeria	186	0.84	279	60	>80
Rwanda	21	1.11	371	95	>90
Senegal	200	0.55	183	48	nc
Sudan	84	1.75	584	87	>80
Uganda	25	1.77	590	96	nc
Upper Volta	31	1.04	347	92	nc
Zaire	69	0.91	304	82	nc
Zambia	389	0.87	290	43	35
Zimbabwe	636	0.96	321	34	28

Notes:
nc = not cited
CE = coal equivalent
Woodfuel consumption relates to fuelwood and charcoal.
The total energy estimates do not include other traditional sources of energy such as cattle dung, crop residues, etc. (lack of data).
Conversion factor used for woodfuel: 1 cubic metre = 0.33 metric tons CE.

Sources:
Data on total commercial energy taken from United Nations (1984), *Energy Statistics Yearbook*, 1982, Dept. of International Economic and Social Affairs, Statistical Office.
Data on total woodfuel consumption taken from FAO (1984),1982 *Yearbook on Forestry Products*, FAO Forestry Statistics, Sires, Rome. (Note: production is assumed as equal to consumption in this data source).
Data on population taken from World Bank (1984), *World Development Report*, 1984.

In a masterpiece of understatement, Agarwal concludes 'the FAO woodfuel-related statistics need to be treated with caution' (p.6).

Elkan (1988a) also cites an estimate from Hall et al (1982) and those figures—presumably relating to the late 1970s—are included to provide some indication of trend. In five cases the later estimate is lower and in four it is higher; a cynic might conclude that both estimates are equally unreliable.

Until relatively recently this level of consumption was not a concern: but the rise in oil prices focused attention on all aspects of energy and it was recognised that woodlands—especially around towns—are being rapidly depleted. It is unclear whether this is due to an increasing demand for woodfuel or due to the intensification and extension of agriculture.

Rural populations are, of course, even more dependent on woodfuel than urban populations who are more likely to use electricity, gas or kerosene. Despite this, the rate of depletion in rural areas *by households* is likely to be small because fuel gatherers (mainly women) prefer to collect or cut off branches rather than fell whole trees. The main reason for depletion in rural areas is, therefore, cash-cropping (*pace* Rimmer, 1988).

Attempts at reafforestation, despite World Bank backing, have not been particularly successful in current commercial conditions where remaining indigenous wood is still virtually free. Elkan (1988b) supports French (1985) in suggesting that farmers might be persuaded to plant enough trees and the right species to protect the soil and to ensure that the land does not dissolve into sand. The incorporation of environmental costs and of externalities can, probably, be encouraged by differential pricing; but this depends, fundamentally, upon a different view of development.

5.2 TIME COSTS OF COLLECTING WOODFUEL

Whilst the rate at which depletion is taking place is disputed, no-one questions that women now have to walk further to collect the same amount of wood. It should therefore be emphasised that the studies presented in Table 5.3 reflect the situation in the mid-1970s, not currently.

Table 5.3 Time taken and distance travelled for firewood collection

		Firewood collection		
Country	*Year of data*	*Time taken*	*Distance travelled*	*Data source*
Burkina Faso	na	4.5 hrs/day	na	Ernst (1977)
Ghana	na	4-5 hrs/day	2½-7 m	DEVRES (1980)
Kenya	na	3-3.5 hrs/day	na	Earthscan (1983)
Niger	c1977	4 hrs/day	na	Ernst (1977)
Sahel	c1977	3 hrs/day	10 km	Floor (1977)
	c1981	3-4 hrs/day	na	Ki-Zerbo (1981)
Sudan/Bara	1966-67	0.33 hrs/day	na	Digernus (1977)
	1976-77	1-2 hrs/day	na	
Tanzania	1975-76	1.6 hrs/day	na	Fleuret and Fleuret (1978)

na = information not available.

5.3 COVERAGE OF WATER SUPPLY AND SANITATION SERVICES

According to Saunders and Warford (1976, p.10), annual investment on rural water supply in Africa in 1970 was little more than £8 million. At then current costs, this was enough to build water supplies for one million people a year out of an estimated rural population of 170 million. Meanwhile, three times this sum was being spent on water supplies for the much smaller urban population.

Whilst there have been substantial increases in the coverage of water supply and sanitation services since then, these have been overtaken by increases in population—although it is hard to tell by how much as aggregate data is very poor. The information on community water supply is generally better than on excreta disposal facilities and countries tend to have better data on the urban than on the rural situation. Also the numbers of people served with water through house connections are undoubtedly better estimated than the numbers supplied from standpipes or public outlets. The definition of what constitutes 'reasonable access to safe water' (see box) is not clear-cut, particularly for rural areas and may well vary from country to country or from one survey to the next in the same country.

Reasonable access. In an urban area, a public fountain or standpipe located not more than 200m from a house may be considered as being within reasonable access of that house. In rural areas, reasonable access would imply that the housewife or members of the household do not have to spend a disproportionate part of the day in fetching water for the family's needs.

Moreover, estimates usually ignore semi-permanent breakdowns of supply, dispersal of populations from source, and rely on very crude estimates of coverage. With all these caveats, the current estimates of the availability of water and of sewerage are given in Tables 5.4 and 5.5.

Awareness has slowly spread, that simply to build water supplies is not enough, and that without adequate maintenance they break down (Cairncross and Feachem, 1977). Indeed, in some countries, they have been breaking down as fast as new ones are built. Donor aid, which is increasingly important in this sector, has not always been helpful in, for example, pressing governments to buy the donor's own national brand of equipment, so that a country ends up with several different models and requirements for spares.

Table 5.4 Coverage of water supply and sanitation services

	Water supply				*Sanitation*		
	1970	*1980*	*1983*		*1970*	*1980*	*1983*
	Percentage of population				*Percentage of population*		
Proportion covered by Report							
Urban	67	52	64		60	28	23
Rural	55	63	70		50	32	38
Of these, proportion covered by services							
Urban	70	62	61		40	59	68
Of which							
House connections	39	30	33	Sewer	8	16	18
Standposts	30	32	27	Other	32	44	50
Rural	10	24	26		19	21	25

Source: Deck, 1986, Tables 1, 2 and 3.

Table 5.5 Changes in coverage of water supply (19 countries) and sanitation (12 countries), 1970-83

	Water supply		*Sanitation*	
	Increased population 000s	*Increases in population served*	*Increased population 000s*	*Increases in population served*
Urban	+21,844 (+139%)	+12,406 (+125%)	+7,303 (+115%)	+5,126 (+126%)
House	+21,844 (+139%)	+8,019 (+151%)	+7,303 (+115%)	+2,452 (433%)
Rural	+22,889 (+30%)	+15,311 (+183%)	+18,007 (+30%)	–1,311 (–8%)

Source: Deck, 1986, Tables 6 and 8.

Note, however, that data inadequacies are not just a problem for developing countries (in Africa). Day (1988) reports how a programme to monitor Australia's diverse water resource base 'collapsed under the weight of data inadequacies along with administrative and political problems that only states, territories and federal governments can together generate' (p.230).

5.4 HEALTH BENEFITS OF WATER SUPPLIES

There are three kinds of possible benefits of water supplies:

- improvements in health
- direct economic benefits from water use
- indirect benefit through saving labour.

White, Bradley and White (1972) themselves found no measurable reduction in water-related disease. They considered possible economic spin-offs such as livestock, brewing, communal gardens, but found no effect; and pump-priming by Government appears to encourage villagers to demand more pump-priming rather than to be galvanised into a process of sustained and enthusiastic self-help. The time saving was evident. The first category of benefit is considered in the remainder of this section and the third category in the next.

Bradley (1972) defined four ways in which disease can be transmitted by water:

Water-Borne	pathogens are present in water supplies	*Water-Washed* *Water-Scarce*	spread of the pathogen is affected by amounts of water available for hygiene
example:	diarrhoeal infections, cholera, typhoid	example:	scabies, trachomas, pinworm infection
control:	water quality	control:	water quantity, soap hygiene education
Water-Based	the pathogen must spend part of its life cycle in aquatic intermediate host or hosts	*Water-Related* *Insect Vector*	the pathogen is spread by insects that feed or breed in water (flies and mosquitoes)
example:	1 guinea worm infection 2 schistosomiasis 3 lung fluke infection	example:	malaria, yellow fever, Bancroftian filariasis Onchocerciasis
control:	excreta disposal (2,3) water quality (1) water access (1,2)	control:	surplus water drainage and management, insecticides
Soil-Based	the excreted organism is spread through the soil		
example:	bookworm infection		
control:	excreta disposal		

Source: *Waterlines,* 7, (1), 16.

Measuring the presumed health benefits of water supplies is extremely difficult. For example, in Egypt, despite a massive expansion of water services in the 1950s, infant mortality remained obstinately above 100 per 1000 (White and White, 1986). They suggest that local practices of excreta disposal, food handling and water use may be the cause. A study evaluating a combined water and sanitation project in Imo State, Nigeria showed a substantial decline in wasting (80% weight-for-height of the NCHS reference values) over a three year period in the intervention village and no change in the control village (The Imo State Evaluation Team, 1989). However, they also acknowledge that health impact studies are difficult to conduct.

Cairncross (1988) illustrates the complexity from a study in Tanzania comparing two villages where different proportions of the population have piped water. Whilst those who drink piped water in the better provided village have lower rates of diarrhoea and of antibodies to typhoid than those drinking from dug holes in the lesser provided village, the highest rate for diarrhoea is among those with piped water in the village with the lowest overall proportion of piped water and the lowest rate for typhoid is among those drinking from wells in the better provided village (Figure 5.1).

Figure 5.1 Source of water and susceptibility to disease

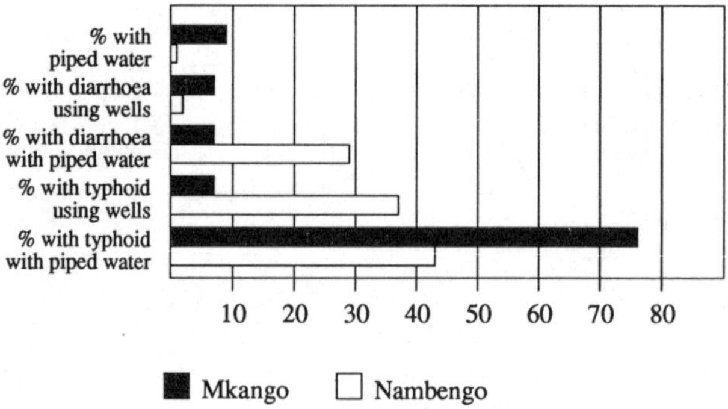

Source: Adapted from Cairncross (1988).

Changes in water supply will have differential effects on the incidence of the four kinds of disease. For example, at a given level of pathogens, more water will *increase* the incidence of water-borne diseases but *decrease* the incidence of water-washed diseases.

In the African context, the major concern is with faeco-oral diseases. Whilst planners have tended to assume these are water-borne, increasing evidence suggests that the endemic paediatric diarrhoeas of poorer communities are water-washed, as they are not substantially affected by improvement in water quality when hygiene and access to water are changed.

If this is the case, then it is important to take into account the *quantity* of water used as well as the level of access and quality of the supply (cf DeWolfe Miller 1986). WHO suggest that typical pattern of use is as shown in Table 5.6

Table 5.6 Average water use from different kinds of source

	Distance	*Water used (litres per capita per day)*
Well	>2,500 m	5
Post	<2,500 m	15
Standpost	<250 m	15 – 35
Piped yard tap		75

On the basis of the handful of studies available, Cairncross suggests that the relationship between domestic water consumption and level of access is non-linear (Figure 5.2).

Figure 5.2 Schematic representation of the relationship between time taken to collect a bucket of water and the quantity used in litres *per capita* per day (lcd)

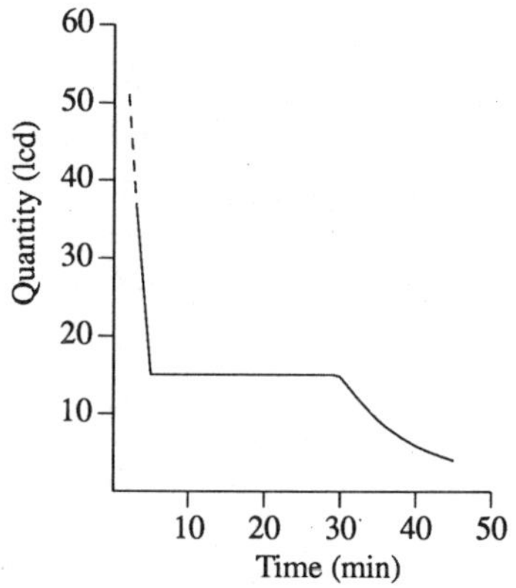

Source: Adapted from Cairncross, 1988, p.54.

> As the time required to collect a bucket of water is reduced, water use increases progressively until it reaches a plateau at around 30 minutes equivalent to a walking distance of 1 km. each way. *Within this range, bringing the water source closer to the home does not lead to increased consumption*
>
> (Cairncross, 1988, p.53, my emphasis)

To increase direct health benefits, water supplies with house connections are required.

Cairncross suggests that house connections might be encouraged. This requires delicate differential pricing: for example, an analysis of the quantity of water consumed in Khartoum showed that the consumption per capita is positively related to lot size and negatively related to price and number of household members and that the price elasticities were high (Khadam, 1988). Proposals to introduce user charges must ensure that quantity consumed does not, as a result, fall below a minimum safe level.

5.5 TIME SAVING

Until recently, few writers have referred to the benefit of time saving, probably because they are (Western educated) men and the water carriers are (African) women. For example, World Bank policy from the mid 1970s closely followed Saunders and Warford (1976), who only gave it passing consideration.

Esoteric methods of measuring the 'benefit' have been proposed. For example, Bradley and White (1972, pp.93–8) measured the length of the water collection journey and attempted to value it by estimating the calories of energy consumed and thence the cost of food to provide or replace those calories; others have attempted to ask hypothetical questions of women about how they would spend their time and put a value on the percentage spent on 'productive' work.

Neither is satisfactory: the former, if applied to a high status civil servant, would put an improbably low value on his work; the latter, apart from the inherent difficulty of interpreting the responses, makes the usual sexist assumptions about what is productive or unproductive. Time budget observation suggests that where women are relieved of some excess labour, either by being able to share their work (Feachem et al, 1978) or because water collection time is reduced, they tend to reallocate their time to other household work and to rest (see Table 5.7).

Table 5.7 Average time budgets of adult women

	Before installing water supply	*After installing water supply*	*Difference*
Fetching water	131	25	–106
Grinding	84	98	+14
Housework	126	161	+35
Agriculture	154	160	+6
Rest	385	433	+48
Total	880	877	–3

Source: Cairncross (1988) based on time budgets of 110 and 118 women days.

If the relief of drudgery is taken as a basic human right then water installation is very cost effective: Cairncross (1988) reports an earlier estimate of about 7p per woman-hour saved, which is much less than the prevailing unskilled wage rate.

Despite the rhetoric, one still finds bizarre cost-benefit solutions being adopted. Sule and Oni (1988) propose a simulation model to determine the optimal location of standpipes for a given level of service availability and a given maximum round trip distance. Their assessment of benefit depends on calculations of the lost revenue to petty traders, which presumes an infinitely elastic market for their goods. After perpetrating this and other horrors, they choose a solution with a maximum round trip distance of 650m, thus ignoring nearly all the other evidence about patterns of water use.

Water, both of a certain level of purity and in sufficient quantity, is essential to reaching certain health standards. 'However, *if instead of asking how to provide more water the initial question is how water may best serve the well-being of the community,* a different kind of analysis results' (White, Bradley and White, 1972, p.251).

Possible improvements involve either choosing cheaper interventions so as to spread subsidies over a larger population or introducing user charges. The former could include simple protection of springs and wells so as to reduce or eliminate guinea worm (Cairncross, 1988) or the wet season well, providing water during the most difficult time of year for rural Africans (Chambers, 1983).

> Stressing the delivery of minimum quantities of potable water to every household would alter the design of major distribution lines.
>
> (Chambers, 1983, p.273).

6 Child mortality and nutrition

Many have argued that the most important general indicator of a nation's health is the pattern of child mortality (e.g. Kielmann, 1978), especially in the poorer developing countries where the rates are more than *ten times* higher than in the North.

Indeed, in presenting data on social and economic conditions, UNICEF ranks countries by the under-five mortality rate. However, given the relatively rapid decline in infant mortality rates, it is more appropriate to present a wider range of data (see also King, 1987). This chapter, therefore, presents data on childhood nutrition, morbidity, prophylaxis and birthweights as well as on mortality.

This and the next chapter comment on national data, but any proper analysis of malnutrition, morbidity and mortality has to take account not only of geographical inequities (considered in Appendix 2) but also of seasonal variation. Thus Chambers (1983) shows how, in tropical environments, the wet season is the most critical time of the year, especially for poorer people, women and children. At that time, malnutrition, morbidity and mortality peak: weight variations of up to 5% have been recorded for adults; the costs of sickness—to society in lost agricultural production, and to families in food and income forgone—are at their highest; sickness is most liable to make poor people permanently poorer; and health services are likely to be at their least effective. The impact, of course, varies according to the pattern of activity: nomadic herders can significantly reduce energy outlay by resting during the rainy period; peasants embroiled in cash-cropping have to work harder. These variations have to be remembered when interpreting the data.

6.1 INFANT AND CHILD MORTALITY

Published infant mortality rates (IMRs) (see Annex to this chapter) show a continuous fall since 1960 (*pace* AwHF, p.30) but they remain very high and they do not necessarily reflect the very high mortality rates in poor communities (see, for example, Heligman, 1978). For in most countries, data on the IMR is collected by health care institutions and *not* from civil registration data nor from a population survey. Mauritius is one of the rare exceptions in Africa with a comprehensive registration system, and its data also show a clear positive trend (Figure 6.1).

Figure 6.1 Mauritius

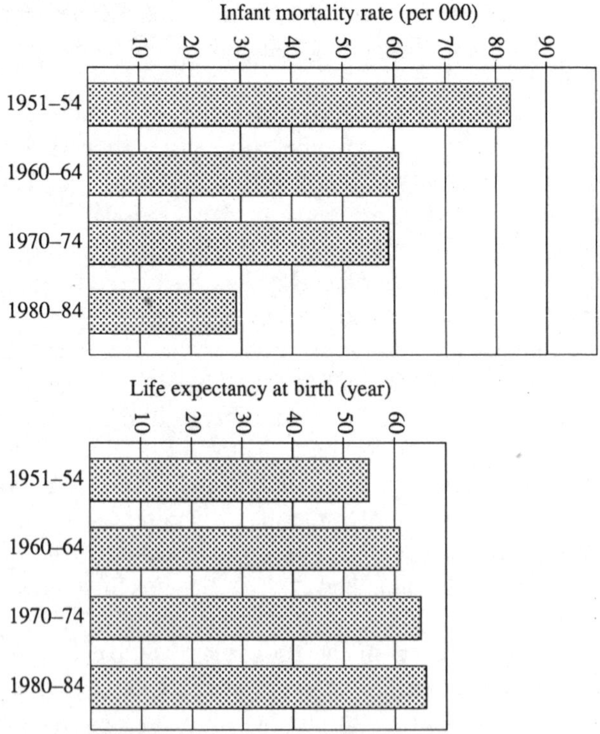

Source: R. Choolun, 'The Mauritius Health Service: The Population Changing Needs and Demands', *International Journal of Health Planning and Management*, 4.1, 1989, pp.63-72.

Otherwise, published rates are based on extrapolations from out-of-date and unreliable census material (see Habicht and Chamie, 1982 and Chapter 3). The only alternative is to use the results of the World Fertility Survey (WFS), carried out by the International Statistical Institute in some thirty developing countries during the 1970s. Their results are reported in Rutstein (1983); those for nine African countries are presented in Table 6.1.

When these results from Table 6.1 are compared to the most reliable indirect estimates (those from the US Bureau of the Census), the WFS estimates are substantially lower (at least 25 deaths per thousand) for Cameroon, Ghana, Mauritania and the Sudan. The most likely source of discrepancy is the misreporting of the age of the mother at census. Older mothers tend to underestimate their age: this would raise the proportions dead in the crucial 20–29 age group and therefore upwardly bias estimated mortality rates.

Table 6.1 Current levels of male and female infant and child (2–3) mortality 0–9 years before the survey

	Date of survey	*Infant mortality (under 1) 0-9 years before survey*		*Child mortality (aged 2-3) 0-9 years before survey*	
Country		*Male*	*Female*	*Male*	*Female*
Benin	1981-82	129.7	110.1	83.4	77.8
Cameroon	1978	107.7	101.1	61.5	62.0
Cote d'Ivoire	1980-82	142.2	114.3	49.8	44.8
Ghana	1979	81.1	66.4	35.9	37.6
Kenya	1977-88	96.5	87.2	36.4	35.7
Mauritania	1981-82	95.2	78.1	69.3	75.9
Lesotho	1977	132.6	125.4	29.3	26.6
Senegal	1978	124.9	108.0	107.0	106.8
Sudan (North)	1979-80	87.9	71.6	36.3	47.7

Source: World Fertility Survey, *Comparative Studies,* August 1988, Table 27, p.72.

According to the WFS findings presented in Table 6.2, in most cases there was a drop in both infant and child mortality during the 1960s and 1970s (see Table 6.2).

Table 6.2 Under 5 and infant mortality for five-year periods before the survey (children with mothers aged 20-29 at birth)

	Infant mortality (deaths under 1) Years prior to the survey				*Child mortality (deaths between 1 and 5) Years prior to the survey*			
Country	*0-4*	*5-9*	*10-14*	*15-19*	*0-4*	*5-9*	*10-14*	*15-19*
Benin	101.8	126.2	139.4	156.0	94.3	114.1	114.7	(121.1)
Cameroon	95.0	96.2	137.2	149.5	86.3	95.7	100.8	108.6
Cote d'Ivoire	101.3	133.3	154.2	169.8	57.7	89.2	91.4	119.6
Ghana	64.8	67.7	85.9	78.3	51.9	56.4	71.9	69.0
Kenya	83.2	88.2	96.1	121.0	51.6	59.9	60.4	72.0
Mauritania	82.0	68.8	68.4	111.9	106.5	97.5	94.9	(115.7)
Lesotho	121.9	123.1	138.9	115.3	43.9	53.8	49.1	54.0
Senegal	102.0	115.7	115.2	105 7	148.6	154.0	178.5	162.2
Sudan	66.6	72.2	71.3	49.1	62.8	50.8	68.7	(73.1)

Source: World Fertility Survey, *Comparative Studies,* August 1985, Table 30, p.75.

This does not, of course, directly provide any reliable evidence about trends in infant and child mortality rates during the *1980s*. The problem is, no other source does either. Despite the absence of concrete evidence, these estimated trends over the 1960s and 1970s make it seem rather unlikely that there has been a substantial increase in the 1980s.

Whilst it is difficult to mount censuses or national surveys, local community (small-scale) studies are being conducted all the time. They should be collated and compared on a regular basis.

6.2 ASSESSING MALNUTRITION

The concept of nutritional deficiency is clear:

> Nutritional anaemia is a condition in which the haemoglobin content of the blood is lower than normal as a result of a deficiency of one or more essential nutrients, regardless of the cause of such deficiency.
>
> (WHO, 1968)

Anaemia may lead to aggravation of many other disorders. It contributes to the overall mortality associated with malnutrition, both of mothers and of babies.

The emphasis on *essential* nutrients means that trends in food availability cannot be translated easily into nutritional availability, e.g. via daily calorie supply figures. For during infancy growth, when the infant requires much higher nutrients than older children, she may be given meals of bulky high-cellulose food, which pose not only problems of stomach capacity and processing the protein intake, but also of ensuring energy needs. The dietary pattern is as critical as the non-availability of food: witness the low proportion of endocrine diseases in contrast to the high proportion of digestive diseases.

Morley (1987) argues that the problem for the majority is not an inadequate intake of protein but an inadequate intake of food due to the bulkiness of the diet. In Africa, 'By the age of 2, in bulky traditional diets, the child requires a kilo of food per day' (p.10). He suggests increasing the amount of fats and oils in the diet, given that the average consumption in developing countries in 1980 figures is about one-third of that eaten in industrialised countries. Not always easy to do when poor.

The classification of undernutrition on the basis of growth-retardation was introduced by Gomez and associates (1955) as a heuristic device pointing towards appropriate immediate clinical management. Weight-for-age expressed as a percentage of the median of the National Center for Health Statistics of the US Department of Health, Education and Welfare is often used as the indicator of nutritional status. However, weight-for-age, obviously, reflects both weight-for-height and height-for-age, which appear to vary independently (Keller and Fillmore, 1983). Weight-for-age is considered an indicator of nutritional *wasting* or emaciation, reflecting current acute malnutrition, and height-for-age an indicator of nutritional *stunting* or dwarfing, reflecting long-term undernutrition.

These authors claimed no physiological or pathological basis for the cut-off points they proposed. There is no clear point of onset, no easily discernible dividing line between normality and disease. Similarly, the process by which a particular state is reached is multidimensional: the children may be deficient in a wide variety of nutrients (not only calories) and there are a range of other factors (such as infections) which also intervene. None of the gradations or classifications (the Harvard standard, the NCHS standard, etc.) have been *proved* to be valid indicators of the severity of undernutrition;

but, like many other similar criteria, they have since been set in tablets of stone.

The appropriateness of Caucasian/Western growth standards to assess the growth of other children is also questionable, although Habicht and colleagues have argued that genetic or ethnic variation in growth patterns across populations among well nourished young children is small compared to differences between well-nourished and malnourished children of the same ethnicity living in the same country (see, Habicht, Martorell and Yarborough et al, 1974; Martorell and Habicht, 1986). However, at given levels of average income, with access to safe water supply, and food consumption, children in South Asia (Haaga et al, 1985) appear to be lighter than children in Latin America, Africa or Eastern South Asia. Ethnic differences therefore cannot be ruled out.

The FAO reports for Africa that 26% of children have a low weight-for-age and 7% low weight-for-height. Haaga, Kenrick, Test and Mason (1985) provide data on the prevalence of child malnutrition (low weight-for-age on the NCHS standard) in 22 developing countries where there had been national random sample surveys since the world food crisis of 1972–74. Their article included data from seven African countries (Cameroon, Kenya, Lesotho, Liberia, Malawi, Sierra Leone and Togo).

It is noteworthy that the data from the African countries (Table 6.3) tend to be '*outliers*'. For whilst six of the seven African countries have very low GNP *per capita*, below US$400, they also have fairly low levels of malnutrition (below 35%) as measured by weight-for-age. The authors dismiss the possibility that GNP *per capita* is under-reported (on the basis of Kravis's (1981) analysis of 'real' GDP); instead they suggest that the distribution of income might be more egalitarian or that child health problems in Africa are just as severe but not manifested in low weight-for-age. Similarly, less than a third of the populations of the six African countries with data have access to safe water, yet they still have low proportions of underweight children. Whilst their own analysis shows that food availability is the major determinant of malnutrition (see Annex), Haaga et al (1985) conclude that these differences really do show different responses of child growth to deprivation.

Table 6.3 Child malnutrition and other developmental indicators in seven African countries around 1980

Country	*Year*	*% Children below 80% weight-for-age*	*GNP, 1980 $US (survey year)*	*Kcal per capita (2-year average around survey year)*	*% Access to safe water (1975)*	*% Adult women illiterate (most recent survey rate*	*Infant mortality rate (1975–80)*	*Child mortality rate (around 1980)*
Cameroon	1978	21.8	459	2,451	26	76	114	25
Kenya	1982	24.3	312	2,055	17	65	91	15
Lesotho	1976	22.0	255	2,152	17	32	120	20
Liberia	1976	24.7	335	2,347	20	91	160	16
Malawi	1981	31.0	201	2,219	33	88	179	25
Sierra Leone	1978	31.9	–	2,518	–	96	215	25
Togo	1977	24.2	303	2,015	16	93	115	25

Source: Haaga, Kenrick, Test and Mason (1985).

At the same time, the suggestion that a child might 'adapt' to under-nourishment is dangerous. There is a wealth of historical and worldwide evidence that poor growth is linked to early mortality (see Eveleth and Tanner, 1976; Floud, 1984). Data from national samples in the late 1970s presented in Table 6.4 suggested that many are at risk. Rosetta (1988), in a longitudinal, although small-scale, study in Senegal during 1981 and 1982 showed seasonal variations in height and weight velocities illustrating the vulnerability of children's growth. There should be no complacency whilst anyone, anywhere, suffers from lack of food.

Table 6.4 Percentages of children below 2 standard deviations height-for-age (NCHS reference)

<table>
<tr><th>Country</th><th>Date</th><th>N</th><th>Under 1 year</th><th>1 year</th><th>2 years</th><th>3 years</th><th>4 years</th></tr>
<tr><td>Botswana II</td><td>1979</td><td>679</td><td>25</td><td>56</td><td>37</td><td>46</td><td>40</td></tr>
<tr><td>Kenya urban</td><td>1979</td><td>866</td><td>18</td><td>26</td><td colspan="2">35</td><td>14</td></tr>
<tr><td>rural</td><td>1979</td><td>2,659</td><td>27</td><td>39</td><td colspan="2">39</td><td>35</td></tr>
<tr><td>Sierra Leone</td><td>1975</td><td>1,960</td><td>33</td><td>36</td><td>35</td><td>36</td><td>31</td></tr>
<tr><td>Togo</td><td>1977</td><td>5,407</td><td>18</td><td>34</td><td>31</td><td>40</td><td>38</td></tr>
</table>

Source: Keller and Fillmore (1983).

6.3 TRENDS IN MALNUTRITION

Given the complexities of measurement, the assessment of trends is tricky. Data collected via the health care system is likely to reflect diagnostic and referral capacities rather than incidence. Hence the increases in hospitalised cases of malnutrition observed, for example, in Zambia (see Table 6.5) have to be interpreted with caution.

Indeed, for the four African countries for which over-time prevalence data is available (see Table 6.6) it seems that there has been an overall decline in malnutrition (Gorstein and Akré, 1988). In Cape Verde, Lesotho and Malawi, as in other developing countries, this has occurred across all age groups, but in the Sierra Leone data, no decline was observed among the younger age groups. This latter probably accounts for the marked contrast between the 84% decline in wasting (low weight-for-height) and the 2% increase in stunting (low height-for-age).

Table 6.5 Zambia: malnutrition admissions in hospitals and health centres

	Total malnutrition admissions	*Malnutrition admission mortality*	*Estimated under 5 population (000s)*	*Estimated number of under 5 admissions as a percentage of under 5 population*
1974	10,609	12.1	902	1.1
1977	13,586	13.1	1,026	1.3
1980	15,970	15.5	1,205	1.5
1983	20,142	17.2	1,454	1.4

Source: Ministry of Health Statistics, Zambia.

Table 6.6 Trends in child malnutrition

		Year of survey % below cut off point		*Cut off point*
Cape Verde		*1977*	*1986*	
Ages	0-11	7.9	7.5	less than –2
in	12-23	26.8	19.1	standard
months	24-71	23.0	18.7	deviations
Lesotho		*1976*	*1981*	
Ages	0-11	14.8	8.2	less than
in	12-23	25.1	17.8	80% median
months	24-35	26.2	13.6	
	36-47	22.2	14.8	
	48-59	23.2	12.9	
Malawi		*1969-70*	*1981-82*	
Ages	0-11	23.5	17.1	less than
in	12-23	47.2	29.7	–2 standard
months	24-35	46.4	29.4	deviations
	36-47	35.6	19.2	
	48-59	32.6	17.0	
Sierra Leone		*1974-75*	*1978*	
Ages	0-11	21.2	23.1	less than
in	12-23	38.0	40.1	80% median
months	24-35	34.5	26.8	
	36-47	37.7	23.8	
	48-59	44.8	28.2	

Source: Gorstein and Akré, 1988, pp.48-58.

6.4 MORBIDITY AND PROPHYLAXIS

Few child deaths (under 5s) are 'caused' by a single episode of one disease:

> in the majority of cases, an infant or child death is the ultimate outcome of a combined process of multiple recurrent infections and nutritional deficiencies which cumulatively retard growth, lead to excessive loss of weight, and progressively wear down the individual's resistance.
>
> (van Norren, Boerma and Sempebura, 1989, p.1091)

6.4.1 Levels of morbidity

Maternal reporting of childhood morbidity varies between social groups (Tsui, DeClerque and Mangani, 1988) as in the North (see, for example, Blaxter, 1981, p.100), which makes it difficult to be precise about overall levels. But the incidence of serious conditions is high. For example, Sircar and Dagnow (1988) surveyed a population of 6236 under 5s for diarrhoeal mortality and morbidity in North Western Ethiopia in 1986, and found a prevalence of 14%, with 42% of deaths related to diarrhoea.

Other debilitating conditions can be very common indeed. Thus, Goyea (1988) reports on a study of common health problems among 43 proprietors of the low income pre-schools in Benin City and 353 mothers of children attending such groups (see Table 6.7); 415 of the children were also examined. Whilst malaria and catarrh were the commonest conditions according to the parents and proprietors, the physical examination established catarrh and ringworm as very common.

Table 6.7 Benin City: levels of morbidity among children

	Percent of victims acccording to		
	Proprietors (N = 43)	*Parents (N = 353)*	*Results of physical examination (N = 415)*
Catarrh	86	70	47
Ringworm	37	20	25
Malaria	93	55	Not assessed

Source: Goyea, 1988, Tables 2 and 3.

6.4.2 Prophylaxis

One of the four elements of UNICEF's child survival and development revolution was the Expanded Programme of Immunisation (EPI). An evaluation in the mid 1980s by Walsh (1987) of the EPIs was rather pessimistic, 'immunisation coverage remains discouragingly low: less than one third of infants in the *world* have received the EPI recommended doses of measles, BCG, polio and DPT' (p.63).

However, the latest *State of the World's Children* reports substantial increases in vaccination coverage. For example, among countries with very high under-5 mortality rates, figures between 1981 and 1986 reporting on full immunisation of 1-year-old children, show rises from 26% to 46% in immunisation against tuberculosis; from 14% to 27% against DPT; from 7% to 28% against polio; and from 19% to 33% against measles. Amongst pregnant women, figures show a rise from 5% to 11% in immunisation against tetanus (UNICEF, 1989, p.98).

The basic problem is that these figures are not believable. Table 6.8 compares the figures in SWC 1989 and those provided by the staff of the EPI programme *for the same year*. The only case of concordance, Kenya, is where the data come from a survey conducted in 1987. Otherwise SWC (1989) estimates are higher, sometimes substantially, for every country except Egypt.

Table 6.8 Percentage coverage of the Expanded Programme of Immunisation according to UNICEF and the staff of the programme

		TB	*DPT*	*Polio*	*Measles*	*Tetanus**
Ethiopia	UNICEF	28	16	15	13	5
	Henderson (84/86)	12	7	7	10	5
Egypt	UNICEF	72	82	88	76	12
	Henderson (86)	77	80	79	78	9
Kenya	UNICEF	86	75	75	60	37
	Henderson (87)	86	75	75	60	37
Sudan	UNICEF	46	29	29	22	12
	Henderson (86)	22	14	14	11	6
Tanzania	UNICEF	95	81	80	78	60
	Henderson (86)	93	69	65	76	60
Zaire	UNICEF	54	36	36	39	26
	Henderson (86)	52	32	33	39	27

Source: Henderson et al, 1988; UNICEF, 1989. *Pregnant women only

Moreover, the assessment of the effectiveness of the Expanded Programme of Immunisation is sometimes cavalier in similar ways to the antics of those estimating population. For example, an evaluation in Cote d'Ivoire (Shepard, Sanoh and Coffi, 1986) used case fatality rates from Ghana, even though the latter's reported incidence of the target diseases was nearly four times higher.

More detailed studies generate further problems with these data. For example, women may not realise that they have to return for the repeat dose. Goyea (1988) also asked about immunisation. Of the 353 replies from parents, 62% reported immunising their children with BCG, 32% with oral polio and triple vaccine, 27% with measles, and only 8% with tetanus. Of the 114 who had the first dose of polio and triple vaccine, only 83 (73%) returned for the second dose, and even fewer, 59 (52%), for the third.

Figure 6.2 Percentage of children aged 1-2 with diarrhoea and immunised

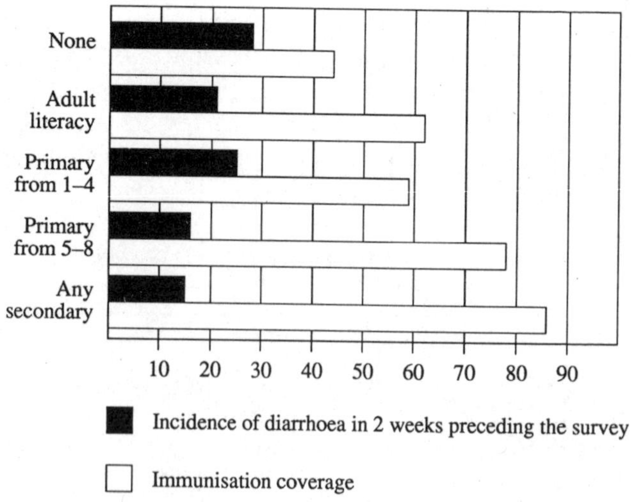

Another study shows how, even if the aggregate figures were accurate, they may not be very useful for policy purposes. De Boer and McNeil (1989) interviewed 1879 women of childbearing age according to a stratified two-stage cluster sampling design in the

catchment area of Chogona hospital in the Meru District of Kenya. They showed how the incidence of diarrhoea decreased and the coverage of immunisation increased with education. Those who need immunisation most are least likely to have received it.

6.5 BIRTHWEIGHT DISTRIBUTION

The distribution of birthweights in a community has been proposed as a sensitive indicator of the level of socio-economic development of a community (Sterky and Millander, 1973; see also Lechtig, 1977). In particular, low birthweight, conventionally defined as less than 2½ kg at birth, is associated with perinatal and later mortality and, in developed countries, with subsequent morbidity and retarded development (e.g. Illsley and Mitchell, 1984). Mean birthweight is less useful, although it may be indicative of the mother's own general state of health and, specifically, of her nutritional status during pregnancy.

In comparison with other indicators, significant volumes of data have been collected in developing countries and results from a selection of the larger studies are given in Table 6.9. These data show wide variations, although in nearly every case, the rates of low birthweight are higher than those typically found in developed countries.

However, collecting reliable data about birthweight distributions is not easy. Apart from any doubts about the feasibility of the data collection process (e.g. time of weighing, accuracy of weighing machines and of recording) under difficult conditions, nearly all these studies are hospital based and subject to selection biases. The problem is universal as one cannot be certain that those who deliver outside hospital would have the same birthweight distribution; and, where a (Western) hospital serves a dispersed (traditional) community, there is every reason to expect such biases. The 'finding' by Sargent et al (1986) that mean birthweight decreases with distance from the hospital and that the rate of low birthweight is 20% among those residing within a 5km radius, against 30% among those living further away, is important here. They speculate that this might be associated with the likelihood of receiving anti-malarial prophylaxis (and

Table 6.9 A compendium of studies in sub-Sarahan Africa of birth weights from the 1960s

Country	*Year*	*Type*	*Sample size*	*Live &/or singletons*	*Mean*	*% LBW*
Angola[m]					2,876	
Burundi[m]					2,730	13.5
Central Af. Rep.	1973	H	19,496		2,873	23 E
Chad	1965	H	3,000		3,114	10.5
Congo	1964	H	943		2,907	15.0
Cote d'Ivoire	1975	H&D	7,154	LS	2,950	14.1
Ethiopia						
Addis Ababa	1964–68	H	8,469	LS	3,132	8.8
Gondar	1966–67	H	500	LS	3,047	13.4
Gabon	1970–72	H	7,032	S	2,979	13 E
Gambia						
Kenaba	1962–63	R	99	L	2,800	
Sukuta	1965	R	100	L	3,038	14 E
Guinea	1963				2,975	18.0
Guinea-Bissau	1977	H	3,239	L	3,229	8.0
Kenya[r]	1975	H	1,595	L		18.9
Lesotho	1969	R	3,129	L	3,012	14.5
Lesotho	1980		1,026		3,050	7.7
Lesotho	1982		829		3,060	7.5
Mali		H			3,049	12.7
Nigeria						
Ibadan[g,h]	1968–72	H	10,839	L	2,920	19.2
Igbo-Ora	1971–75	R	4,334			11.0
Nigeria	1974		1,032		2,870	18.7
Rwanda	1971	R	7,929		2,890	17 E
Senegal	1959	H	8,409		3,115	9.9
Seychelles	1977		1,131		3,060	14.0
Tanzania						
Dar-es-Salaam[m]	1975–76	H	16,532	L	2,991	15.2
Muhumbili					3,300	4.0
Moshi	1960–63	H	2,166	LS	3,040	10.1
Tanga	1966	H	1,000		2,970	11.2
Tanzania	1980		6,140		3,010	10.6
Tanzania	1981	H	2,640	L	3,018	11.0
Zambia	1971–72	H	2,401	L		14.2

Abbreviations: D – Domiciliary deliveries; E – Estimated; H – Hospital deliveries; L – Live; R – Records; S – Singletons.
Notes: g – University hospital, many referral cases; h – Yoruba, high twinning rate; m – low socio-economic class; r – Kenyatta National Hospital.
Source: World Health Organisation, *Division of Family Health,* 1980.

therefore relative debilitation during pregnancy). The more probable interpretation is that because women living further away are, in general, less likely to make the effort to attend the clinic, those who *do* attend are more likely to be those who have problems with their pregnancy.

The difficulties of collecting population birthweight data are immense; in the meantime, results reported from a clinic or hospital setting must be treated with caution.

ANNEX

(A) *The decline in infant mortality rates, 1960–1980–1987*

Table 6A.1 shows the overall decline of infant mortality rates between 1960 and 1980 and between 1980 and 1987 using solely data published by UNICEF.

Table 6A.1 Infant mortality rates, 1960, 1980 and 1987

Country	*1960*	*1980*	*1987*
Angola	208	154	169
Benin	185	125	111
Botswana	119	79	68
Burkina Faso	205	156	139
Burundi	152	127	113
Cameroon	163	107	95
Central African Republic	183	144	133
Congo	143	83	74
Cote d'Ivoire	165	111	97
Equatorial Guinea	188	143	128
Ethiopia	175	154	155
Gabon	171	117	104
Gambia	213	160	153
Ghana	132	101	91
Guinea	208	165	148
Guinea Bissau	188	149	133
Kenya	124	84	73
Lesotho	149	117	101
Madagascar	219	140	121
Malawi	206	170	151
Mali	210	186	170
Mozambique	190	157	170
Niger	191	152	136
Nigeria	190	119	106
Rwanda	146	136	123
Senegal	180	148	129
Sierra Leone	219	173	155
Somalia	175	146	133
Sudan	170	125	109
Swaziland	152	135	119
Tanzania	146	120	107
Togo	182	107	95
Uganda	133	113	104
Zaire	148	112	99
Zambia	135	91	81
Zimbabwe	110	83	73

Source: UNICEF, 1989a, 1989b.

In the UNICEF study Cornia suggested that there have probably been 'increases in infant and child mortality' (AwHF, p.30) during the 1980s, but actual increases have occurred only in Angola, Ethiopia and Mozambique— each involved in a war. In the remaining 33 countries, the infant mortality rate has continued to decrease and in 23 countries (more than two-thirds) the *rate* of decrease has accelerated!

(B) *Determinants of malnutrition*

Haaga, Kenrick, Test and Mason (1985) also tried to predict levels of malnutrition. They examined graphically the relationships between percentages of low weight-for-age and GNP *per capita,* average calorie intake, distribution of income within countries, supply of safe water and percentage of adult women illiterate, and they estimate statistical relationships for:

- GNP per capita (with the percentage below 80% of standard weight-for-age = 162.4 – 21.1 $\log_e$ GNP giving an $R^2 = 0.47$);
- Average calorie intake (with the percentage below 80% of standard weight-for-age = 74.7 – 0.0196 Kcal but allowing for a different constant and slope for South Asian countries, giving an R^2 of 0.80).

They then developed a prediction equation essentially by adding on the child death rate (deaths of children aged 1–4 per 1000) to the equation for average calorie intake, and used this equation to predict the prevalence of malnutrition by WHO region. This is rather a silly exercise, as a prediction equation is most likely to provide good estimates if one can believe the model; yet this equation includes both a cause (food availability) and effect (child mortality) as predictors. Moreover, the equation is only a marginally better internal predictor than food availability alone for the original 24 countries.

7 Adult health and health care

> My approach, however, will be to focus not exclusively on disease but on health as well—that state of social wholeness which indigenous African medicine strives to maintain and which political organisations in some parts of the continent are succeeding in re-establishing... This view of health and health care contrasts vividly with the mechanistic, biomedical, technical definition that seems implicit in Western hospital medicine.
>
> (Wisner, 1976)

Ideally, this chapter would include data on age-specific morbidity and mortality rates, or, at least, life expectancy at, for example, age 20. Unfortunately, these data are non-existent or totally unreliable, apart from mortality from very specific conditions.

As an example: no-one would want to play-down the ravages of the AIDS pandemic in central Africa; but it is important to recall how we now know that AIDS is probably the major killer of young males in central Africa (PANOS, 1989). This knowledge depends upon the identification of people as reacting positive to an HIV test. Given that each *test* costs roughly US$2 and that the average *per capita* expenditure on health care is around US$6 (in most sub-Saharan African countries GNP *per capita* varies between US$200 and US$400 and the proportion of GNP spent on health typically varies between 1% and 3%), monitoring the spread of this pandemic, unless paid for by donors, is completely impracticable.

The changing patterns of the cause of death and, in particular, mortality from AIDS, are crucial. But the lack of such data for countries in sub-Saharan Africa is also pandemic. In this chapter, therefore, only indicative data is provided on the shifting pattern of revealed morbidity; the bulk of the material is concerned with changes in the health care system.

Specifically, the first section shows how patterns of adult morbidity are shifting broadly from infectious to chronic diseases: the second section presents data on maternal mortality, both as a commentary on the risk for women, and as an indicator of the quality of the health care system (Jazeiri, 1976). The next two sections are concerned with provision: the third section presents data on the trends in expenditure on Western style health care; and the fourth section assesses trends in traditional medical practice. The fifth section is concerned with the conflict between comprehensive and selective primary health care, the controversy over user charges and the Bamako initiative; and the final section looks briefly at the wider context.

7.1 MORBIDITY

One is unlikely to be healthy if lacking food. There is extensive adult malnutrition in the same areas and circumstances as childhood malnutrition (see Chapters 4 and 6 above). Seasonal weight changes are the rule among adults in rural areas of developing countries. Teokul, Payne and Dugdale (1988), reviewing the literature, report a difference of 2–5kg between the post-harvest peak and the pre-harvest minimum. The semi-permanent menace of famine and starvation discussed in Chapters 4 and 6 above must not be forgotten.

Data also exist for many conditions specific to the tropics which still ravage developing countries. For example, Mburu and Steinkuller (1983) review the distribution and extent of river blindness and other ocular needs. Here the issue is the extent to which the pattern of disease is shifting, along with the processes of modernisation, away from common communicable diseases and towards chronic conditions (McKeown, 1976).

Chojnacka and Adegbola (1984) studied the pattern of morbidity at Lagos University Teaching Hospital during the 1970s, and observed a pronounced shift away from infectious, respiratory and endocrine diseases, but an increase in the proportion of digestive, gastro, urinary, nervous and blood diseases. Manton (1988) projects 'tremendous increases' in mortality rates from cancer, heart disease and stroke in both developing and developed countries by the year 2000.

Indeed, the emphasis on 'tropical' diseases may already be inappropriate.

(a) Numerically there are currently more chronic disease deaths in developing countries than in developed countries.

(b) As fertility control is disseminated and life expectancy increases, significant population ageing [implies an] even greater proportion of the global chronic disease burden in developing countries.

(Manton, 1988, p.264)

This argument can be illustrated—although the numbers are pitifully small—by the prevalence of hypertension which is a condition typical of the disease pattern in developed countries (see Table 7.1).

Table 7.1 Prevalence of hypertension in subjects aged approximately 40–55 years

				Males		*Females*	
Country		*Year*	*Age*	*N*	*Prevalence*	*N*	*Prevalence*
Ethiopia	rural	1983	30–39	60	3	51	2
			40–49	42	11	31	3
Nigeria (Bendal State)	civil servants	1983	35–39	42	10		
			40–49	49	12		
	policemen	1983	35–39	69	13		
			40–49	38	11		
Tanzania	rural		35–44	88	2	94	2
			45–54	75	3	58	–
Zaire	urban	1983/4	40–49	21	33	34	15
Zambia	rural	1979	35–44	20	5	61	11
			45–54	27	11	32	9

Source: Nissinen, A., Bothig, S., Granroth, H., Lopez, A. D.,1988, 'Hypertension in Developing Countries', W.H.S.Q. 41, pp. 141–154.

7.2 MATERNAL MORTALITY

Maternal mortality, according to the International Classification of Diseases, is 'the death of a woman while pregnant or within 42 days of termination of pregnancy ... [but excluding] accidental or incidental causes'. Despite the latter caveat, it is essentially a 'time of death' definition (Rosenfield and Maine, 1985), with a fairly arbitrary cut off point, and not necessarily the most useful for designing policies and programmes (Maine et al, 1987). In practice, most maternal deaths are not likely to be classified as such unless the pregnancy is well advanced or the death occurs close to the time of the birth.

Maternal mortality is underestimated everywhere. In developed countries, with efficient vital registration systems, the major source of underestimation is the classification of deaths in the early stages of pregnancy. Cates et al (1982) found that maternal deaths not related to induced abortion had been undercounted by about 29% in England and Wales and 33% in the USA.

In developing countries, with incomplete vital registration systems, several studies have revealed huge discrepancies between the officially reported figures and those emerging from detailed enquiries. Countries with the poorest statistical infrastructure are also thought to have the highest levels of maternal mortality (Graham and Airey, 1987), and given that most deaths will eventually be reported—although not linked to the pregnancy—those countries will also have the most undercounting of maternal mortality.

The Population Council has produced data for a dozen African countries (see Annex), but Tietze (1977) estimated that statistics on maternal deaths are available for less than a tenth of the populations of Asia and Africa. As well as the lack of medical certification of cause of death (assuming a certificate has been issued), there are many social, religious and emotional reasons for the selective omission of maternal death. In particular, if the attribution of a cause of death is interpreted as conferring blame on an individual or institution, then there is a tendency to avoid censure by obscuring or omitting the cause. Whilst there are many good reasons for using primary health care workers as information gatherers about morbidity and mortality in general (see, for example, Hill and Graham, 1987), asking traditional birth attendants to record cause of death may not always produce reliable data.

Despite the very weak data, maternal causes are presumed to account for between a quarter and a half of all mortality among women in the reproductive age groups in developing countries, and Fortney et al (1986) demonstrate that in Egypt and Indonesia they are the leading cause of death for these women. Finally, WHO (1986) estimates that between 88% and 98% of maternal deaths in developing countries could be prevented with appropriate health care.

Boerma (1987) analyses a series of studies to assess the probable level of maternal mortality in sub-Saharan Africa. He concludes that national levels of maternal mortality probably vary between 250 and 700 per 100,000 live births. Whilst this is still very high (cf. c.6 for Sweden), it is below the range of 300–1,700 cited in UNICEF (1989b).

Table 7.2 Percentage of mortality among women aged 15–49 due to maternal causes with maternal mortality ratio and crude birth rate

Country	*Source*	*Year*	*Pct of all mortality*	*MM ratio*	*CBR*
Gambia	Marodua and Kenaba	1951–75	29	1,025	55
Kenya	Machakos	1974–78	11	86	44
Mauritius	National	1952	17	306	46
		1962	13	150	39
		1972	13	176	26
		1980	3	108	27
Sweden	National	1951	10	900	
		1980	0.2	6	

Notes:
Pct of all mortality = percentage of all mortality among women aged 15–49 due to maternity associated causes
MM ratio = number of maternity associated deaths per 100,000 live births
CBR = crude birth rate

Current campaigns tend to adopt a family planning approach focusing on the avoidance of births to the high risk categories of mothers (for example, mothers at the beginning and at the end of the reproductive cycle.) But, because those groups also tend to have lower birth rates, the overall risk of maternally associated death is largely independent of age, so that such an approach

> cannot prevent between half and three quarters (depending on the level and pattern of fertility) of all maternal deaths ... [and] it is not 'efficient' since a substantial number of births must be avoided for each maternal death averted.
>
> (Winikoff and Sullivan, 1987)

Moreover, women in the prime reproductive age group—where the greatest number of maternal deaths occur—also have the highest proportion of young children. Instead of targetting resources primarily on the basis of maternal age and parity, a simple alternative would be to use the number of 'dependent' children as a scoring factor in identifying a target group of women (Graham and Airey, 1987).

7.3 ADJUSTMENT AND EXPENDITURE ON HEALTH CARE

> Health for All was launched in 1977 on the basis of two hidden assumptions. The first was that economic growth would continue. Only in the case of Africa south of the Sahara was it thought that economic growth might not rise as fast as the growing population. The second was that richer countries of the world would provide substantially more aid to the health efforts of developing countries.
>
> (Abel-Smith, 1986a, p.202)

As Abel-Smith (1986) comments, for many countries it is only possible to draw inferences from whatever is known about many of the factors which affect health. He proceeds to 'document' trends in income per head (as well as mentioning debt, devaluation and drought), trends in unemployment, poverty and malnutrition, the adverse terms of trade and increases in 'defence' expenditure.

Finally, he correctly says that the 'key question for developing countries is whether expenditure on the health sector per head has been going up or down in real terms'. But because 'very few countries have data in this form ... inferences have to be drawn from other available data.' Table 7.3 shows how health care expenditures have dropped as a proportion of GDP, in contrast to educational expenditures.

Table 7.3 Percentage of national budgets spent on health services in eight countries, 1979–85

Country	*1979*	*1981*	*1983*	*1984*	*1985*
Angola	–	5.8	6.0	6.6	–
Burundi	5.5	5.1	4.7	5.5	–
Chad	–	–	1.63	1.58	1.49[b]
Ethiopia	5.2	7.5	7.6	5.9	–
Mali	7.3	8.2	8.5	8.3	7.8
Mozambique	11.0	11.9	9.6	–	–
Swaziland[a]	10.4	10.6	10.5	9.9	–
United Republic of Tanzania[a]	8.0	7.5	5.9	5.8[b]	

a Financial year starting during the year
b Provisional figures
Source: Abel-Smith, 1986a, Table 6, p.211.

7.3.1 A country example: Zambia

The rapidly shrinking government revenue led to substantial cutbacks in both recurrent and capital expenditure in 1984 and 1985 (Figure 7.1).

Figure 7.1 Trends in real government health expenditure per capita (Zambian Kwacha)

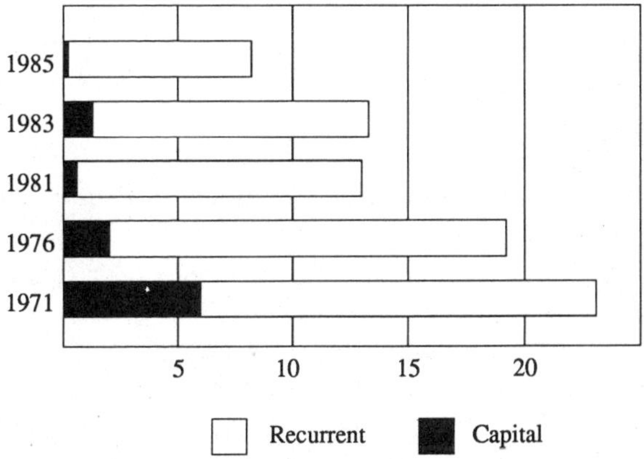

Source: Freund, 1986.

Freund (1986) describes the manpower crisis exemplified by a drop of nearly 40% in the number of doctors. He also says 'There is a growing (sic) shortage of clinical personnel officers', although the *increase* in the latter almost exactly compensates for the drop in the former (see Figure 7.2). Meanwhile, the number of nurses has increased by nearly 40%.

Figure 7.2 Health personnel trends (1981–85)

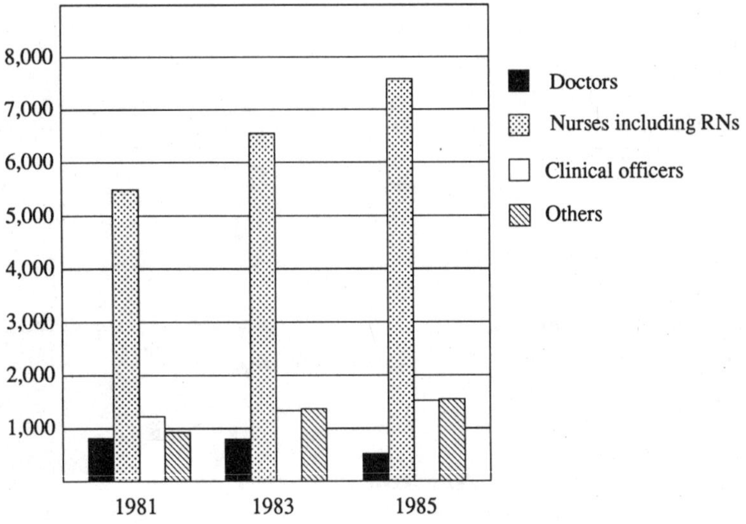

Source: Freund, 1986.

7.3.2 Self-medication

Fassin (1987) studied street sellers of drugs in Pikine, a suburb of Dakar, showing how prices were low and that the typical practice of selling in small amounts is more related to the popular management of money. He calculates a turnover of FCFA32.4 million, almost as high as public drug sales. He also claims it is increasing (p.166).

Self-medication can, however, be dangerous. In a study of 200 urban and 200 rural households in Zimbabwe, malaria prophylaxes were taken by 38 urban and 65 rural respondents (Stein, Gora and Macheka, 1988). Only six urban and 10 rural respondents were aware that chloroquine could have harmful adverse effects, and of the 103 respondents taking prophylaxes, only 16% urban and 31% rural were taking the correct dose. Van der Geest (1987) found 70 drugs on sale 'over-the-counter' in an area of South Cameroon. A local physician considered that 24—including 12 antibiotics, laxatives and suppressants—should be withdrawn because of their risk.

7.4 TRADITIONAL AND WESTERN MEDICINE

The WHO proposes to use African traditional healers as generalists and as 'agents de premiere ligne' after retraining. This is not appropriate: traditional medicine might be *complementary* to modern medicine but it is *different* (cf. Bibeau, 1985; Cumper, 1987). Where both traditional and Western medicine are available, traditional healers are the most popular source of first treatment for some symptoms but not others (Mwabu, 1986). However, choice in this sense is a luxury.

Anyinam (1987) reviews data on the availability and accessibility of African ethno-medicine. He recalls Ademuwagun's 1969 estimate (cited in Harrison, 1979) that 4% of adults in urban areas and 10% of adults in rural areas are ethno-medical practitioners (EMPs) and draws on other authors' estimates for around the mid 1970s to report that 'Ratios of ethno-medical practitioners in other cities include Urban Mathare (Kenya) 1:847; Dar-es-Salaam 1:350–450; and Nairobi 1:403' (Anyinam, 1979, p.804). He also cites his own PhD study of a District in Ghana with a healer/population ratio of 1:224 and a (Western) physician/population ratio of 1:20,625.

Although there are very few (Western) medical practitioners, and those who exist are concentrated in urban areas, one might expect a decline in EMPs. For example, Good (1980, p.33), studying Kenya, observes:

> Traditional healing in Kilungu appears to be undergoing a steady decline as part of a broader pattern of social and economic change. This process is linked with access to formal education; the influence of Christianity; individual and society

perceptions of "modernity"; and, to a limited extent, contact with cosmopolitan health services.

Another study in Botswana indicates that fewer new recruits are entering the occupation. The credibility of the healers is also declining, and the development of bio-medical care is depriving the traditional healers of much of their former prestige and many of their patients (Ulin, 1975). On the other hand, their roots are in the milieu: the occupation is therefore unlikely to atrophy and die through legislation, organisation or regulation.

More data are needed, about not only the age structure of EMPs but also how long they have been practising and the 'drop-out' rate. The few detailed studies that do exist suggest that EMPs are elderly. Thus, Odebiyi and Togonu-Bickersteth (1988) interviewed 98 healers among the Yoruba in Ife-Ife, a University town east of Ibadan with a population of 130,000, in early March 1983. These were a one-in-three representative sample of all those registered with the National Association of Traditional Healers. More than half were diviners, the remainder being split equally between faith healers and herbalists; three-quarters were men and nearly two-fifths were over 50. Whilst the overall numbers (1 per 430) compare very favourably with the number of Western physicians (with the average for Nigeria as 1 per 15,740), it is considerably less than the 4% of adult males estimated by Ademuwagun in 1969. Elsewhere among the Yoruba, Oyebola found that nearly three-quarters of the 156 EMPs he interviewed were more than 40 years old and that 'the number of trainees ... today are fewer' (Oyebola, 1980).

Of course, the crude ratio of healers to population is relatively meaningless unless account is taken of the *distribution, type* and *quality* of services provided. Anyinam demonstrates that there is very little basic data on the geographical distribution of (different types of) EMPs, or their accessibility *in practice,* because of lack of any planning or research effort, despite the apparent increase in acceptability of traditional healing among governments. Equally, whilst there is some suggestion that African EMPs are very adaptable (e.g. Senghor and Diop, 1988), Fassin and Fassin (1988) suggests that this might more plausibly be interpreted as a struggle over sources of legitimation. Despite all these doubts, the relative ratio of healers to population still compares very favourably to that of (Western) physicians to population: so that in rural areas, they are often still the only source of medical advice, and in urban areas they also serve an important pastoral function (Anyinam 1987; Fassin and Fassin 1988).

7.5 USER CHARGES AND CONTROVERSIES OVER PRIMARY HEALTH CARE

Over the last decade, there have been attempts to shift some of the 'burden' of financing health care systems onto the 'consumer' (Gray, 1986). Dunlop (1983) reviews the earlier experiences; a later review (Bennett, 1989) shows how:

- The evolution of essential drug programmes (in Eastern Africa) from national donor-assisted programmes to community-based drug programmes is not easy.
- The 'need' to institute cost recovery is a problem, while the (national) political manifesto guarantees free health care.
- There are problems with starting cost recovery at community level while mid-level and tertiary levels remain free.
- The need for the provision of life-saving drugs at community level cannot be met while professional interests refuse to agree to antibiotics and certain other drugs being prescribed by non-professionals.

The Bamako initiative was launched to counter problems of securing adequate amounts of essential drugs and vaccines which need to be imported and local financing of the costs of health posts and of health workers. The 'vision' was of a system of cost recovery for essential drugs at community level which would finance salaries of community level health workers and maintenance of the centre and which would raise the quality of the services with community involvement (Bennett, 1989).

UNICEF/Somalia (1986) reports on an evaluation in North West Somalia. In 24 villages, the services of the community health workers (CHWs) were used very frequently and health knowledge and practices were significantly better in these villages. The evaluation also showed considerable spillover effects of the benefits of CHWs to the 16 non-PHC villages. In a similar comparison in Uganda, of 30 villages with community-based health care, with 30 other villages, the former had better scores on health knowledge and practices of, for example, immunisation, oral rehydration therapy use, utilisation of health services, and even slightly better nutritional status (Vella and Adkinson, 1987).

The Bank also claims that user charges

- raise *money* to cover (non-salary) costs
- promote *equity* because user fees can be used to extend facilities to the under-served
- enhance *efficiency* because individuals bear the cost of decision to use health services.

Schemes have been introduced in the Central African Republic, the Congo, Rwanda and Zaire. Ellis (1987) reports that the health card scheme in the Central African Republic has been abandoned because it has generated very little revenue; that the scheme in Rwanda generated 5% of the Ministry of Health's 1985 budget; and that the scheme in Zaire generates about 10% of recurrent health costs. Ellis (1987) goes on to propose such a scheme for Kenya based on a set of principles incorporating efficiency, equity and administrative considerations, and in particular that 'Fees should be consistent with patients' ability to pay, and should maintain access to health care' (p. 996). With these provisos, Ellis estimates that between 10% and 15% of the overall budget can be raised and that an appropriate fee-charging scheme would also improve quality of service overall and would direct resources towards the rural areas.

The major snag is that whatever provision is made for exemption or 'forgiving' charges (the latter denoting some form of charity?), use is likely to decline amongst the poorest groups who need it most: indeed, Ellis (1987) *presumes* a drop in 'demand'. Some concrete evidence for this expectation comes from Waddington and Enimayou (1989) who studied the impact of user charges in the Ashanti-Akim District of Ghana. They documented many distortions on the supply side: the focus here is on access. There was a massive drop in utilisation at the two rural health centres when user charges were introduced, although this appeared to follow an already declining trend (see Table 7.4). In the urban health centres, there was also a noticeable drop after the increase in user charge, although rates had recovered by 1987.

Whilst utilisation has increased substantially at Agogo hospital, this does not apparently reflect increased rural demand, as the proportion of rural/urban patients at Agogo did not change over this period. Following group discussions, families reported great difficulties in paying for health services. They persist because they see they have no choice if they are to save their relatives. The greater elasticity of demand in rural areas—rather than suggesting that there was a greater degree of use for minor complaints prior to the introduction of user charges—therefore suggests that families in rural areas were forced more frequently than those in urban areas to make 'impossible' choices between saving their relatives and feeding their children. A study in Zaire of health service utilisation after an abrupt price increase (De Bethune, Alfani and Lahaye, 1989) reaches the same conclusion.

Table 7.4 Ghana: Ashanti-Akim District utilisation: all government and mission health centres, 1984–87, nearest thousand

	Half years	*Rural health centre*	*Urban health centre*	*Agogo*	*Total all facilities*
1984	1	12.0	14.8	37.9	64.7
	2	8.9	12.2	38.1	59.1
1985	1	7.7	13.0	42.8	63.4
	2	3.7	9.1	37.7	50.4
1986	1	1.8	9.1	38.0	48.9
	2	1.6	11.3	40.8	53.7
1987	1	2.3	15.4	51.3	69.0
	2	2.4	15.0	58.7	76.1

Source: Waddington and Enimayou, 1989.

The introduction of user charges follows on from attempts to provide selective primary health care (SPHC) rather than comprehensive PHC (e.g. Walsh and Warren, 1979). Unger and Killingsworth (1986) show that the empirical foundations for SPHC are dubious; the most important factors are political, socio-cultural and economic.

The crucial issue is the confidence the community has in the village health worker (VHW); in turn, this depends upon their command over resources. Thus, evidence from the Mali and Sine Saloum projects suggests that, whilst rural populations will move considerable distances to government health clinics, they are not enthusiastic about a health service filtered through VHWs with minimal training, especially when the VHWs do not have regular access to pharmaceuticals. In contrast, in Ikot-Omin (Nigeria), Amanam (1980) observed that the family health worker could offer a wider range of services at home than the clinic-resident midwives.

Fairly wide PHC coverage can be achieved in many areas at low or even zero marginal *personnel* cost, in a programme or project mode. But if PHC is organised from outside in this fashion and is dependent upon either central or donor funds, the project's logistic support for field workers is vulnerable. The vertical approach of SPHC is not conducive to the attainment of the Alma Ata goals of effective community control over health. Whilst progress is slow, it is clear that the modalities for successful PHC programmes are being learnt (see, for example, Rifkin et al, 1988). A comprehensive primary health care, if adopted and controlled by the rural poor, can improve their living conditions.

7.6 FUTURE TRENDS IN HEALTH

The decreases in infant and child mortality and in maternal mortality over the last thirty years, are encouraging—although the technical debate about the relative importance of 'stunting' and 'wasting' among children seems to ignore all the evidence from the North about the relation between height and health potential (Tanner, 1978). But, even apart from the AIDS pandemic, levels of and trends in morbidity suggest that future improvements are likely to be slow.

Moreover, the shift to the chronic conditions of modernity can only be aggravated by under-development. The stagnation in overall health care expenditure is perhaps depressing but, given the lack of any close relation between the level of expenditure and health, it is probably of much less importance than the nature of provision in the current unhealthy environment. Indeed, one of the more pernicious aspects of current patterns of 'development' is the marketing of health-damaging products. The baby milk scandal is well-known (Campbell, 1984). Trends in cigarette consumption are equally discouraging (see Table 7.5). Tobacco control policies in developing countries have to be based on

> concern for the coming epidemic, the way in which household expenditure on tobacco in marginal survival situations competes with that for food, the drain on hard currency caused by deficit balances of trade in tobacco, and the environmental impact of the industry.
>
> (Chapman, Ball, Gray, Nostbakken and Omar, 1986, p.222)

Table 7.5 Cigarette consumption in selected African countries

Country	*1977*	*1979*	*1981*	*1983*
Burkina Faso	0.6	0.5	0.7	0.7
Congo	0.7	0.8	0.8	na
Cote d'Ivoire	3.5	4.4	4.0	3.9
Ethiopia	1.3	1.4	1.5	1.5
Ghana	3.5	2.6	2.7	2.7
Kenya	3.5	4.4	4.9	5.3
Malagasy	1.9	2.2	2.4	2.5
Malawi	0.7	1.0	1.3	1.2
Morocco	11.3	12.2	13.3	13.5
Mozambique	2.9	3.0	3.1	3.2
Nigeria	11.2	11.4	10.3	10.1
Senegal	2.2	2.7	2.5	2.7
Sierra Leone	1.7	1.6	1.6	1.6
South Africa	24.1	27.6	31.1	32.0
Sudan	1.7	1.7	1.5	1.5
Tanzania	4.0	4.4	4.0	3.6
Tunisia	5.5	5.5	4.9	7.0
Zaire	2.7	3.4	3.9	3.4
Zimbabwe	2.4	2.4	2.7	2.1

Finally, the discussion has so far ignored the socio-economic environment. For example, much of the research on malaria has focused on the problem of vector resistance arising out of the widespread use of pesticide in conjunction with the development of large-scale agricultural projects. Packard (1986), analysing the history of malaria in Swaziland from 1959–78, shows how the parasite load of the Swazi population had been reduced to near zero in 1959; but with the rapid development of the Swazi economy, foreign labour was introduced into the sugar estates and contributed to the re-establishing of malaria parasites among the Swazi population. Packard (1986) concludes that any programme must go beyond purely biomedical responses and that it is also important to take account of changes in agro-econosystems, labour utilisation and settlement patterns, which are also associated with large-scale agricultural development.

ANNEX

Table 7A.1 Maternal mortality rates per 100,000

Country		*1970*	*1980*
Angola	1970	99	23
Botswana	1970	400	180
Ethiopia	1970	2,000	400
Gambia	1970	110	
Ghana	1970	1,500	
Malawi	1970–72	241	194
Mali	1970	200	
Mauritius	1972	171	110
Mozambique	1970	650	
Nigeria -	1970	600	
Cameroon	1970	150	
Senegal	1970	960	

Source: Population Council, Socio-Economic Indicators of Women's Status.

8 Children's education

There are many forms of instruction, both religious and secular, in Africa as elsewhere, all of which play an important part in human development and social reproduction. The focus in this chapter—partly, it must be admitted, for parochial reasons—is on the availability of 'modern' Western schools—formal education—to Africa's youth. Similarly, there are many levels and types of school, but the basic concern is the availability to all of a minimum level of primary schooling.

Table 8.1 School enrolments and enrolment ratios in sub-Saharan Africa, 1960 and 1983

Level	*1960*	*1983*
Primary education		
Enrolment (thousands)	11,900	51,300
Gross enrolment ratio	36%	75%
Secondary education		
Enrolment (thousands)	800	11,100
Gross enrolment ratio	3%	20%
Higher education		
Enrolment (thousands)	21	437
Gross enrolment ratio	0.2%	1.4%

Source: World Bank (1988), Table 1.1, p.13.

There have been substantial increases over the last quarter of a century in the provision of first level formal education. Thus the enrolment ratio around independence at primary level was 38% in the Francophone territories (50% in the Belgian colonies and just 31% in the French) and 40% in the Anglophone. But between 1960 and 1983 there have been substantial increases (see Table 8.1). Over the same period, the number of primary schools in sub-Saharan Africa increased from about 73,000 to roughly 162,000 and the number of primary school teachers from 310,000 to more than 1.3 million. Although the average pupil-teacher ratio remained roughly the same during this period (approximately 39 to 1), the average primary school size almost doubled (from 162 pupils in 1960 to 317 in 1983).

In 1983, 12 out of 39 countries had gross enrolment ratios (GERs) at the primary level equal to or greater than 100%. GERs greater than 100% occur because of the definition, which divides total enrolment by the total population *of school age*. Students outside the official age range are included. The net enrolment ratio, which excludes under-age and over-age children, is preferable, but this information is not generally available, nor very reliable. Moreover, enrolments are usually recorded near the beginning of the school year when they are largest; the numbers actually attending school throughout the year will typically be smaller still.

8.1 RECENT TRENDS IN ENROLMENTS

The push towards universal primary education (UPE) is, however, losing momentum: in a few cases absolute numbers enrolled are dropping. The justification of UPE in itself is discussed in Appendix 3: here we concentrate on the data.

In 19 of the 39 countries, the present estimated growth rate of the school-age population exceeds that of primary school enrolments. If growth in primary enrolments continues at below 3%, by the year 2000 on these estimates, the GER will have fallen back below 70%, the level of the late 1970s. Indeed, it has been suggested that in 20 to 30 years Africa will have fewer people educated than today (Adediji, 1989).

Whilst this alarmism seems a little misplaced given the enormous growths *already recorded*, there has been a slowdown. At the turn of the decade, between 1980 and 1983, first-level enrolments actually fell in four countries—Angola, Mozambique, Somalia and Togo. Further, Table 8.2 suggests that enrolments did 'peak' in several countries in the first half of the 1980s. The largest decreases are for Angola and Somalia, both of which have been torn apart by war.

Mozambique appears anomalous: but the recent SIDA study by Johnston, Kaluba, Karlsson and Nystrom (1987), shows a 20% drop in the gross enrolment ratio between 1980 and 1984 and a further drop of 20% between 1986 and 1987. However, partly because of stricter adherence to age limits (and possibly because all those outside the age limits who wanted to go to school had already gone), the net enrolment ratio (of 7–10 year olds) rose from 31% to 49% between 1980 and 1984 and stayed there. Note, however, that this figure included a large amount of repetition. For example, using 1984 figures, of 1,000 entrants to grade 1 only 718, 506 and 362 eventually entered grades 2, 3 and 4 respectively. The 362 entering grade 4 would spend nearly eight years in primary school and only 196 would graduate.

Table 8.2 Recent trends in primary education in African countries where there has been a drop

		Primary level enrolments		
Country	*Year of maximum*	*Maximum*	*1985*	*% Decrease*
Angola	(82-83)	1,065,025	750,000	–29.5
Benin	–	44,232	–	–
Central Af. Rep.	(84-85)	308,022	294,312	–4.4
Guinea	(82-84)	262,833	246,129	–6.2
Kenya	(83-85)	4,380,200	4,342,300	–0.8
Madagascar	(82-85)	1,731,383	1,625,216	–6.1
Malawi	(81-83)	882,903	847,157	–4.0
Mali	(79-83)	298,697	293,050	–1.8
Nigeria	(82-83)	14,654,798	14,383,487	–1.8
Somalia	(80-83)	271,680	220,680	–18.7
Togo	(81-84)	506,356	462,853	–8.6
Tanzania	(83-85)	3,561,410	3,169,759	–10.9

The World Bank argues that: 'In general, given a country's present enrolment, the rate of its enrolment growth is closely related to its income *per capita*' (World Bank, 1988, p.29). They do not report the analysis leading to that conclusion. The implication—that income growth *per capita* is a good thing—is not borne out by their own data; the correlation between enrolment growth and income growth *per capita* calculated from their tables of 0.081 is not worth writing home about (see the table in the Annex to this chapter). The corresponding partial correlation among more recent (1980 to 1985) data is –0.017, which is in the opposite direction. Moreover, none of the correlations calculated on the recent data are high (see Table 8.3).

Table 8.3 Correlations between economic and educational data (N = 39 countries)

	Rate of growth in enrolments	*Average % change in GER*	*Average % change in educ. expend. as % public*	*Average rate of growth in GNP*
Enrolment 1980	–0.24[a]	–0.26[a]	–0.29[b]	0.08
Gross enrolment ratio 1980	–0.69[c]	–0.59[c]	–0.18	0.05
Educational expenditure as a % public expenditure	–0.01	0.03	–0.24[a]	0.26
GDP 1980	–0.08	–0.03	–0.02	–0.01

a = significant at 10% level
b = significant at 5% level
c = significant at 1% level

Source: Author: own calculations from UNESCO data.

The reductions in enrolment warrant a more serious analysis. Any slowdown would appear first among new entrants. Table 8.4 shows that, for the 30 countries with data, the number of new entrants has fallen in 6 countries but total enrolments have fallen in only 3.

Similarly, the drop-out rates are high: Figure 8.1 summarises the survival rates in 1980 (they were very similar in 1985).

Reductions in enrolment might arise for 'technical' reasons: for example, because of a system of automatic promotion, pupils spend fewer years in school; or for 'statistical reasons', when a country is at or near universal primary enrolments and the problem of early and late entries has been resolved. There may have been a drop in the 'supply' of schooling; more plausibly, the quality of what is on offer may have declined. Moreover, 'demand' may have dropped: children who might have attended school in better times are kept out or pulled out in dire situations, such as the recent drought, because they are needed at home, or because the family is forced to migrate, or because family incomes have fallen just as many countries have introduced or raised school fees.

Table 8.4 Index numbers for 1985 or for latest year of available data of numbers of new entrants and of total enrolments (1980=100)

Country	*New entrants*	*Total enrolments*
Benin	98	117
Botswana	121[c]	137
Burkina Faso	168	194[c]
Burundi	312[c]	257[c]
Cameroon	113[b]	119[b]
Central African Rep.	112	111[c]
Congo	110	122
Cote d'Ivoire	105[b]	115[b]
Gabon	119[a]	115[b]
Gambia	115	159
Ghana	100[b]	106
Guinea	91	105[c]
Kenya	109	120
Lesotho	114	131[c]
Madagascar	75	92[c]
Malawi	110	117[c]
Mali	110	100[c]
Mozambique	40[c]	91
Niger	122[c]	128[c]
Rwanda	131	128[c]
Senegal	131[b]	139
Swaziland	107[c]	127[c]
Tanzania	93	94
Togo	98	101[c]
Uganda	152[a]	144[a]
Zaire	109[a]	111[a]
Zambia	121[b]	131[c]

a = 1983, b = 1984, c = 1986.

Figure 8.1 Survival rates in 1980

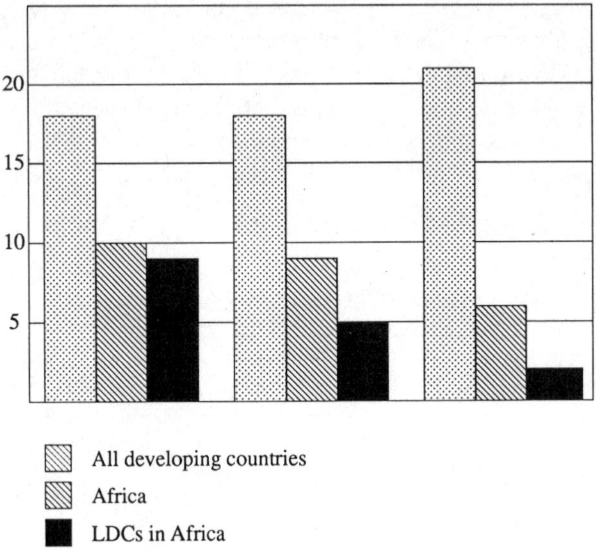

Note: Calculated by the reconstructed Cohort method.

8.2 RESOURCES

On the 'supply side', the World Bank (1988) report shows how expenditure as a percentage of GNP *per capita* at the primary level remained roughly constant from 1970 until around 1983, at about 16%, whilst that at secondary level approximately halved (see their Tables A.17 and A.18). Dougna (1987) provides more recent data based on national reports. He shows how the relative share of education in public expenditure has increased in 14 of the 24 countries for which there are data (see Table 8.5). Except for Angola and Tanzania, the increases have been relatively large. For 23 of the countries, data exist disaggregated by level and, in 11 countries out of the 18 where there has been some reallocation, primary education has benefitted relative to the other levels.

Dougna's analysis for the countries where there has been a substantial drop in the number of enrolments at the primary level, suggests that the governments only reduced places *after* the drop in numbers registering. However, he suggests that the supply of places might have been reduced for other reasons. For example, some countries have become stricter about *entry* procedures or have reduced the number of scholarships; other countries have reduced the numbers of diplomas awarded.

Table 8.5 Evolution of educational expenditure and distribution by level, 1982-85

Country	*Changes in fraction of public expenditure*			*Levels affected by reallocation*			
	1982	→	*1985*	*Up*		*Down*	
Algeria	24.3	D	8.0	-	-	-	-
Angola	6.0	U	6.9	3	-	1	2
Benin	27.8	U	33.4	-	-	-	-
Botswana	10.7	S	10.4	3	2	-	-
Burundi	19.1	D	16.0	1	-	2	3
Cameroon	16.4	D	15.4	3	-	1	2
Cape Verde	-		-	1	2	3	-
Central African Republic	25.0	U	27.0	1	-	3	-
Congo	17.8	D	13.5	2	-	1	3
Cote d'Ivoire	40.2	U	42.3	1	-	2	3
Egypt	9.2	U	10.8	1	3	2	-
Ethiopia	11.0	U	12.1	1	3	2	-
Guinea	16.0	U	18.0	-	-	-	-
Kenya	17.7	U	20.3	2	3	-	-
Libya	24.0	U	37.0	-	-	-	-
Mali	25.0	U	26.0	2	3	1	-
Maroc	18.0	U	23.0	-	-	-	-
Nigeria	9.6	U	12.0	-	-	-	-
Sierra Leone	13.0	S	13.0	1	2	3	-
Sudan	15.0	S	15.0	-	-	-	-
Tanzania	-		-	1	3	2	-
Togo	21.0	D	19.1	1	-	2	3
Tunisia	20.4	U	22.1	3	3	2	-
Uganda	20.7	U	27.3	1	-	2	-
Zambia	12.9	U	13.4	-	-	1	3
Zimbabwe	-		-	-	-	-	-

Source: Dougna (1987) taken from country reports to 40th General Conference of UNESCO and supplementary national sources; Tanzania from UNICEF (1987); Zambia from Kaluba and Karlsson (1987).

Adjustment and educational expenditure: the case of Mozambique

Sometimes, of course, the economy has suffered so much that, whilst the proportion spent on education remains roughly constant, the absolute level has dropped sharply. Mozambique is a good example.

Figure 8.2 Mozambique's expenditure in education, 1980–86 recurrent and investment (billion meticais) in constant 1980 prices

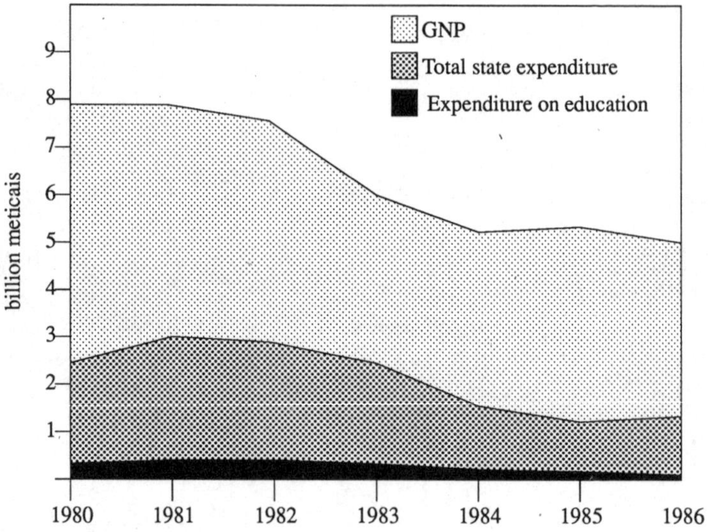

Source: Johnston, Kaluba, Karlsson and Nystrom (1987).

In real terms, GNP has, from 1981 to 1986, dropped by 35%, state expenditure by 58%, and educational expenditures by 45%.

But, in general, the impact of reductions in educational expenditure on primary enrolment will have been indirect: either because parents perceive a decline in governmental commitment to education *overall*, or because the 'quality' of what is offered suffers.

8.3 QUALITY

There have been attempts to use material from the International Association for the Evaluation of Educational Achievement (IEA) as a commentary on school quality in Third World countries (e.g. Heyneman and Loxley, 1983; and also the *Comparative Education Review* for 1979). In such comparisons, Third World educational systems fare badly. The school appears to have a greater influence on achievement relative to background than in the North; hence the emphasis on 'school quality' as a way of improving achievement.

But the apparent importance of school relative to the 'impoverished' environment may simply reflect the difficulty of measuring crucial demand factors like parental ambition for children. For only a proportion of children from each kind of background goes to school—those who are encouraged by their parents in ways which others are not.

Nevertheless, the World Bank argues several times that there has been a *decline* in quality. They also cite cross-sectional studies of the IEA showing poor performance among students in Nigeria and Swaziland, and *ad hoc* studies in Malawi and in a Francophone African country (why so delicate?). They conclude that 'the quality of education in SSA is below world standards' (World Bank, 1988, p.33). This is highly likely: but where is the evidence for a *decline?*

Even apart from caveats about the cultural transferability of the teaching procedures, etc., it is difficult to assess trends. For the typical comparison is between the achievement of the top 1% of the age group rather than of those in school. This assumes that the group in a grade are selected on merit from the population (Wilson, 1984). But where enrolment is not 100%, and selection systems are inefficient, such comparisons using only a fixed fraction of the age group (e.g. Comber and Keeves, 1973; Tuppen and Deutrom, 1982) will make the performance of such an education system and the pupils within it look poorer than they actually are.

8.3.1 Is there a trend?

In the absence of reliable data, there is a tendency to use expenditure data. In general, Governments mobilise all available resources to meet teachers' unions pressure to preserve salaries and relatively low pupil/teacher ratios. Fewer resources are available for materials; some countries are counting on parents to supply teaching materials (Lourie, 1987). However, even the World Bank admit that:

> Much of the evidence is indirect: supplies of key inputs (especially books and other learning materials) are critically low, and the use of those inputs has declined in relation to the use of teachers' time and of physical facilities. Less is known about the output performance of students.
>
> (World Bank, 1988, p.2)

Moreover, even analyses of expenditure and input data do not always give clear answers. Fuller (1986), after discussing the difficulties of measurement of quality, also ends up analysing levels of recurrent expenditure per student and the student/teacher ratio, in relation to GDP *per capita,* government expenditure as a share of nation's GDP (Table 8.6), as well as primary school enrolment rates.

Table 8.6 School quality trends for developing and industrialised nations, 1970-80

	Countries		
School quality indicator	*Low income*	*Middle income*	*Industrialised*
Primary school expenditure per pupil (constant 1980 USD)			
1970	109	127	1,205
1980	75	195	2,343
(Countries reporting)	(11)	(33)	(17)
Pupil/teacher ratio			
1970	44	36	23
1980	45	31	18
(Countries reporting)	(33)	(57)	(18)

His overall comparison of 1970 and 1980 shows how primary school expenditure per pupil has indeed dropped in low income countries in comparison with others, but the pupil/teacher ratio has hardly changed.

His analysis shows, rather obviously, that school expenditure per pupil is associated positively with the share of education expenditure in GDP and negatively with the primary school enrolment rate. He concludes by asking, but not answering, useful questions, such as:

> When countries are forced to cut teachers' salaries in real terms, how does their behaviour change? When allocation for instructional materials are modified, how is instruction within the classroom influenced?
>
> (Fuller, 1986)

Probably, teachers whose real pay has dropped will tend to supplement their income elsewhere, and will pay decreasing attention to their classroom performance. Assuming the number of contact-hours between teachers and pupils increases 'quality', then the classroom 'quality' will have dropped.

Even more crucial is to understand the concrete situation of peasants:

> But it is a naive person who believes that improvements in the quality and relevance of education alone will encourage people to stay in rural areas and farms, or set up small scale industries, and send all their children to school. A more efficient and effective primary education system, a less examination oriented and more work oriented curriculum and minimal conflict between school attendance and agricultural activities will, of course, all help the attractiveness and benefits of school attendance. But amidst the poverty of rural Botswana and the pursuit of greater economic security and improved material comfort, what is really needed is the means to realise greater primary benefits from schooling, [otherwise] parents and children alike will continue to look to the formal education system as the way to an urban job.
>
> (Allison, 1983, p.274).

8.4 DEMAND

Bowman (1984) shows the wide range of factors which have to be taken into account in analysing demand. Dougna provides some detailed analysis for Benin, Kenya, Nigeria and Togo. In Benin the decrease is concentrated in three of the most flourishing agriculture regions (Zou, Borgou and Oueme). In Kenya, the decrease is concentrated in the coastal regions where there is a flourishing cocoa trade. In Nigeria, the largest decreases since 1981–82 are in Kavo (–38%), Rivers (–37%) and Banchi (–25%), the two latter, together with the six other states showing a decrease, are either on the coast or in the regions of the Niger. In Togo, it is once again the agriculturally fertile regions which are showing the largest decreases.

8.4.1 Economic factors

Dougna presents data for Benin, Mali and Togo, showing how even the relatively small amounts that parents are asked to contribute are a substantial proportion of GNP *per capita* (Table 8.7).

Kaluba and Karlsson (1987) show how in Zambia the average annual amounts paid by parents for education in each region vary between 50 and 100 Kwacha in the rural areas and around 200 Kwacha in the urbanised areas. Given that the minimum wage is K4 per day, families will be paying a substantial amount of their yearly money income on education.

These difficulties have been compounded by characteristics of the labour market. The rapid expansion of the educational system over the last quarter of a century has led in many countries to difficulties of employing educated manpower. There has been a drop in expectations about the private return to educational investments because of the reduction in numbers of jobs in the modern sector for educationally qualified personnel. This has led to a 'brain drain'; but it has also led to the 'diploma disease' whereby the qualifications required for any particular job have increased, which, in turn, increases the pressure for expansion of upper levels of the school system whilst making terminal first level education unattractive.

Table 8.7 Parental costs at the primary level in three countries in 1986 in French Francs

Type of expenditure	*Benin*	*Mali*	*Togo*
Registration fee, parents association, etc.	50–100	70	24–50
Materials	40–80	40–100	40–80
School uniform	30–70	–	36–70
Total	120–250	110–170	100–200
Share (%) relative to GNP *per capita*	7.6–16.0	12.2–18.8	7.2–14.4

Sources: Benin: Arni Toure, 'Le problematique de financement de l'enseignement de base en Republique Populaire de Benin' (Term Paper IIEP, June 1987);
Mali: Ministere de l'Education Nationale Direction de la Planification de l'Education, 'Le financement de l'education', mimeo;
Togo: Author's own estimation.

8.4.2 Socio-cultural factors

In the North, the primary school has been the main instrument for social integration of our children and formal education is therefore almost universally accepted as of central, fundamental value. But, in Africa, it is a 'Western' invention: it does not, in general, serve the same integrative function; indeed, in many areas, the 'modern' school has been viewed as antagonistic to religious (and secular) traditional values. It is only because the school appeared, correctly, to be the best means of social advancement, that 'modern' schools expanded so rapidly everywhere after independence. When the expected advantages of scholarisation begin to disappear, the principal motivation for attending school becomes much less powerful. Indeed, instead of asking why there has been enrolment stagnation in the African primary school, given present rates of (disguised) youth unemployment in the North, one might more legitimately ask whether parents will continue to encourage their children to stay on at a dead-end school in our countries.

Analysis of disparities in educational provision throws more ligh on the factors affecting take-up of enrolments. According to Dougna's data, presented in the introduction to this section, it is the agriculturally fertile regions which show the largest decrease suggesting a rather instrumental view of school. In Zambia, the urbar areas show the largest decrease (see also Appendix 3).

8.5 WHAT IS TO BE DONE?

The problem for an educational planner concerned to institutionalise UPE (or more) is therefore to motivate demand. It is important to recognise that, from a parent's point of view, high repetition rates are very discouraging and, in particular, that the introduction of parenta charges imposes a relatively high cost on families who may well no be very enthusiastic in the first place. Is there any scope fo improvement?

Lee (1988) examines the prospects of achieving UPE by the yea 2000. He argues that without an improbably large rate of growth in GNP there has to be either a very large increase in national effort (the proportion of GNP devoted to primary education) or a reduction in recurrent unit costs.

The recession has clearly imposed constraints on educationa expenditures, and, given the relative power of teachers' associations in maintaining their employment (if not their real salary levels), othe inputs (textbooks, etc.) suffer; but provision at the primary schoo level is much cheaper than at other levels, and should not be reduced.

It is accepted that the 'rate of return' to primary education is highe than to either secondary or tertiary education (Psacharopoulos, 1984) yet there are very large per student subsidies in higher education in terms of *per capita* GNP. In countries for which data were available the median was *four times per capita* GNP around 1979–80. Minga and Tan (1985) set out to show what a cut in subsidies to post-primar education could achieve in terms of expanding primary schoo enrolments. They present simulations for two alternative shifts awa from post-primary education towards primary education (i) 100% cu in higher education student subsidies (ii) 100% cut in higher an secondary student subsidies plus 100% recovery of all highe education operating costs (Table 8.8).

Table 8.8 Simulations for gross enrolment ratio (GER) around 1979-80 at primary level

Country	*Current GER with current patterns of subsidies*	*Potential GER with potential patterns of subsidies* Cut (i)	Cut (ii)
Central African Republic	68	76	81
Cote d'Ivoire	76	94	100
Mali	27	33	43
Niger	23	25	31
Senegal	48	58	73
Togo	100	100	100
Upper Volta	20	24	30
Malawi	59	64	95
Tanzania	100	100	100

If present policies are continued, those most in need are most likely to be excluded. But, as Lourie says, 'The development of a privileged urban class at the detriment of rural and poor suburban children ... may well spell the inability of these countries to mobilize the intellectual and creative resources of tomorrow' (Lourie, 1987, p.16).

ANNEX

Table 8A.1 World Bank data on GNP growth rates and primary school enrolment

Country	*Income per capita 1984* (a)	*GNP per capita Av. ann. growth rate 1965-84* (b)	*Primary GER 1970* (c)	*Primary AGR 1960-1980* (d)	*Total AGR 1960-1980* (e)
Mali	140	1.1	22	7.8	8.6
Burkina Faso	160	1.2	13	6.6	7.0
Niger	190	–1.3	14	11.4	12.0
Gambia	260	1.1	24	9.6	9.5
Somalia	260	–	11	13.2	13.6
Chad	–	–	35	6.2	6.6
Ethiopia	110	0.4	16	11.9	12.4
Zaire	140	–1.6	88	5.1	6.4
Malawi	180	1.7	36	5.4	5.4
Guinea-Bissau	190	–	39	7.4	7.3
Tanzania	210	0.6	34	10.5	10.4
Burundi	220	1.9	30	3.3	3.7
Uganda	230	–2.9	58	4.8	5.0
Togo	250	0.5	71	8.3	9.3
Central Af. Rep.	260	–0.1	64	6.7	7.5
Madagascar	260	–1.6	90	5.5	5.9
Benin	270	1.0	36	7.5	8.4
Rwanda	280	2.3	68	5.0	5.0
Kenya	310	2.1	58	8.4	8.8
Sierra Leone	310	0.6	34	6.4	6.9
Guinea	330	1.1	33	5.0	6.5
Ghana	350	–1.9	64	5.3	5.7
Sudan	360	1.1	38	7.5	8.1
Senegal	380	–0.5	41	6.1	6.7
Mozambique	–	–2.0	47	5.9	6.1
Mauritania	450	0.3	14	11.0	11.9
Liberia	470	0.5	56	7.0	7.9
Zambia	470	–1.4	90	6.6	7.1
Lesotho	530	5.9	87	3.0	3.4
Cote d'Ivoire	610	0.8	58	7.4	8.4
Zimbabwe	760	1.5	74	4.8	4.8
Swaziland	790	4.0	87	6.1	6.9
Botswana	910	8.4	65	8.1	8.6
Mauritius	1,090	2.7	94	0.7	2.2
Nigeria	730	2.7	37	8.1	8.7
Cameroon	800	2.9	89	5.6	6.2
Congo	1,140	3.7	130	6.3	8.2
Gabon	4,100	5.9	85	5.1	5.9
Angola	–	–5.7	75	13.5	13.6

Sources: Columns (a) and (b) World Bank (1988), Table B.1.
Column (c) World Bank (1988), Table A.7.
Column (d) World Bank (1988), Table A.1.
Column (e) World Bank (1988), Table A.6.

9 Literacy and adult education

Literacy is presumed to be essential for economic growth; for many it is also the first step to raising political consciousness. All African countries pay at least lip service to the importance of literacy. The data are considered in Sections 9.1 and 9.2.

There is still a long way to go before universal literacy. Many (e.g. Coombs, Prosser and Ahmed, 1973) have seen adult education programmes as providing a 'second chance' to those who had missed out in the explosion of primary school enrolments, and as providing post-literacy exposure to written materials for those likely to relapse into illiteracy. The available data—even more patchy than most discussed in this book!—are analysed in Section 9.3.

9.1 ADULT LITERACY

The 'bottom line', as they say, for assessing the 'success' of an educational system, is the rate of adult literacy. Apart from the difficulty of making precise population estimates, the definition and measurement of literacy is not easy. UNESCO's Statistical Office has produced a manual for national statistical offices but it is rarely adhered to: by its very nature, there are very unlikely to be any institutional records of illiteracy, and *ad hoc* local surveys, even if they are being conducted, are rarely reported.

Nevertheless, the consensus is that less than 10% of the populations of many countries, including the Gambia, Cote d'Ivoire and Senegal in West Africa and Tanzania and Somalia in East Africa, were literate at the time of their independence. According to estimates by national authorities, literacy rates have climbed steadily throughout the 1970s. Since these estimates are mostly based on extrapolations from primary school completion rates and those have risen, one would expect these illiteracy rates to continue to fall (see Table 9.1).

Table 9.1 Years of schooling and literacy rates in sub-Saharan Africa, 1965, 1983

Economic status	*Median estimated number of years of schooling*		*Median literacy*	
	1965	*1983*	*1960*	*Latest year*
Low income semi-arid	0.1	0.9	2	15
Low income other	0.5	2.9	10	41
Middle income oil importers	1.3	4.2	19	72
Middle income oil exporters	0.7	3.6	16	56
Linguistics				
Francophone	0.5	2.4	7	40
Anglophone	1.2	3.4	18	58
Sub-Saharan Africa	0.5	3.3	9	42

Source: World Bank, 1988.

The overall pattern is one of increases during the 1970s and then stagnation during the 1980s recession. Other factors have also intervened. For example, in Mozambique, the primary equivalent programme for those who did not go to school has seen a constant decline from its heyday in 1980, when the census registered 579,500 participants. In 1984, despite all the problems of insurgency, a declining economy and simply lack of access, there were still over 180,000 registered, but by 1987 the number had declined to about 83,000.

On the other hand, whilst illiteracy rates have dropped steadily for both men and women since 1970 in nearly every country (Table 9.2), in most cases male–female differentials have shown a steady increase (Table 9.3). The exceptions are Burundi, Cape Verde, Central African Republic and Malawi. It is likely that this trend will be reversed—at least in these data—as the impact of the relative equalisation between boys and girls in primary school enrolments spreads through the adult population.

9.2 RETENTION OF LITERACY

It is assumed that 4–6 years of primary schooling are required for retention of literacy. In fact, there have been very few studies of the retention of literacy by those who have left school. Wagner et al (1990) report on a longitudinal follow-up of 72 adolescents in Morocco. They found females retaining more than males, the urban subsample more than the rural subsample. As they suggest, young adults with higher skills may be kept out of the workforce due to gender, ethnic, regional or other biases.

Table 9.2 Illiteracy rates in the population aged 15 years and over in 20 LDCs (1970–85)

Country	*1970* %	*1975* %	*1980* %	*1985* %
Benin	84.7	78.7	72.1	74.1
Botswana	58.0	48.5	38.9	29.2
Burkina Faso	92.1	90.3	88.6	86.8
Burundi	81.1	76.3	73.2	66.2
Cape Verde	69.2	63.9	56.2	52.6
Central African Rep.	84.6	76.3	67.0	59.8
Chad	89.4	84.0	79.2	74.7
Ethiopia	93.7	92.3	a	37.6
Gambia	89.3	84.4	79.9	74.9
Guinea	85.7	80.3	79.9	71.7
Guinea-Bissau	90.4	87.0	81.1	68.6
Lesotho	37.8	33.7	30.2	26.4
Malawi	70.9	67.4	63.7	58.8
Mali	92.8	89.6	86.5	83.2
Niger	96.2	93.2	90.2	86.1
Rwanda	68.2	58.4	50.3	53.4
Somalia	96.8	95.4	93.9	88.4
Sudan	83.0	79.7	74.1	
Uganda	58.9	53.0	47.7	42.7
Tanzania	67.6	62.1	b	

a The Ministry of Education estimates that at the end of the third phase of the national literacy campaign (October 1980) the percentage of illiterates in the population aged 10 years and over was reduced to less than 65%.

b According to the 1978 census, 26.5% of the population in the 10 to 50 age group were illiterate in continental Tanzania.

Source: UNESCO Office of Statistics.

Table 9.3 Illiteracy rates by sex in 20 LDCs in 1970, 1975 and 1980

	Difference in the illiteracy rate of female and male (in % points)			
	1970	*1975*	*1980*	*1985*
Country	*F% – M% diff in %*	*F% – M% diff in %*	*F% – M% diff in %*	*F% – M% diff in %*
Benin	10.3	18.6	23.2	21.0
Botswana	–2.5	–1.4	0.3	3.1
Burkina Faso	10.8	12.4	13.4	14.6
Burundi	19.0	22.2	23.5	17.1
Cape Verde	20.9	21.3	19.2	22.8
Central Af. Rep.	19.9	25.4	29.1	24.7
Chad	17.5	22.9	26.6	29.6
Ethiopia	4.6	6.1	–	–
Gambia	9.7	13.9	17.5	20.5
Guinea	14.0	17.8	20.4	22.5
Guinea-Bissau	7.2	8.3	11.2	28.9
Lesotho	–25.0	–24.4	–23.5	–22.1
Malawi	24.0	23.4	22.5	21.4
Mali	7.1	9.2	10.4	11.9
Niger	3.4	6.0	8.2	10.8
Rwanda	21.7	22.6	22.0	28.5
Somalia	3.9	5.6	7.9	11.9
Uganda	22.0	23.5	24.1	24.4
Tanzania	29.6	29.5	–	–

Source: UNESCO Office of Statistics.

They tested for retention of Arabic, French, Maths. After two years, their sample recorded gains in scores in Arabic and French and losses in Maths. They suggest the latter may be due to lack of notational practice rather than to a loss in arithmetical skills. Equally interesting, they observed that French literacy is retained after only *three* years of schooling: frequent practice is more than sufficient to compensate for less formal teaching.

A more relevant study—because it is concerned with adults—is by Carron, Mwiria and Righa (1989) in Kenya. They interviewed in 1986 a sample of those who had obtained their literacy certificate in 1981, 1983 or 1985 in four rural locations and part of Nairobi; and tested them on the 3 Rs. Extracts from their results are given in Figure 9.1.

The results vary wildly by location, although Carron, Mwiria and Righa show how both local living conditions and the quality of the local literacy services are associated with these variations. More immediately, as the scores for those who graduated in 1981 and 1983 are better than those who graduated in 1986, they provide no support at all for the supposition that there is a rapid relapsing into illiteracy.

Figure 9.1 Kenya: percent of learners with average global mastery level by location and mean test results by year of literacy certificate

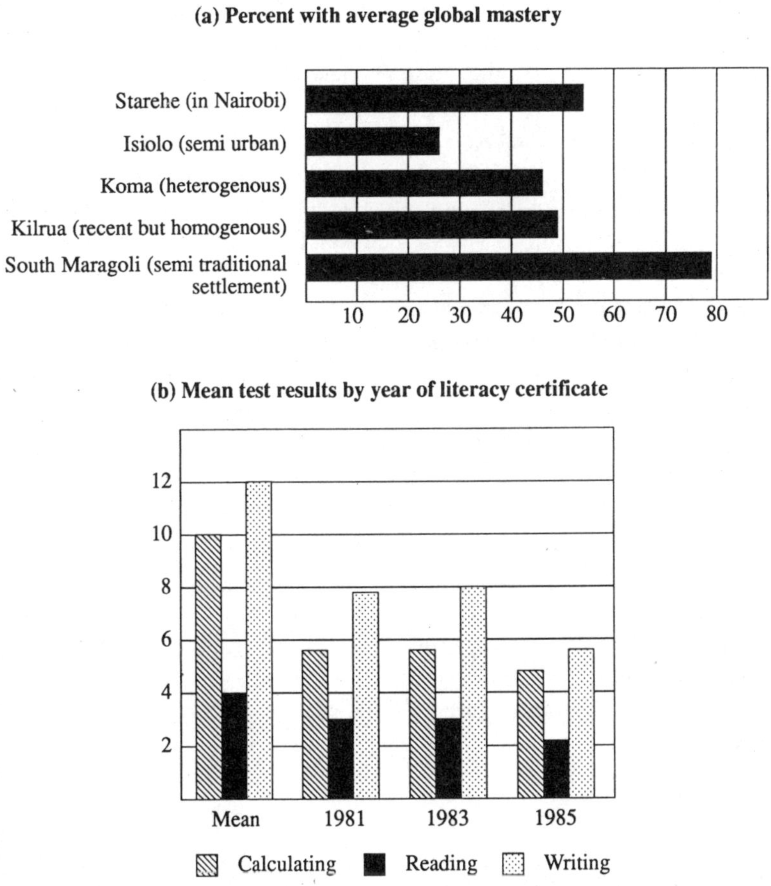

Source: Carron, Mwiria and Righa (1989).

The overall picture is mixed: literacy almost certainly is increasing but we could do with many more (local) longitudinal studies to provide a sounder base for assessment of the trends; and the disparity between men and women is large. However, the worries over retention appear to be misplaced: if literacy skills are (seen as) useful, they are, rather obviously, used.

9.3 ADULT EDUCATION

It has become commonplace to remark upon the development and diversification of out-of-school educational opportunities over the last couple of decades. For some, nonformal education is *better suited* than the regular school for the achievement of educational objectives; hence the promotion of lifelong education encompassing a variety of flexible, individually-tailored pedagogical forms such as vocational retraining programmes, health education programmes, cultural activities, etc. For others, non-formal education programmes have been, or should be, introduced in the face of *escalating costs;* although it has also been argued that adult education tends to retract in recession because it is marginal (Lewin, 1987). Finally, there are some who have argued that 'innovative' non-formal education—such as youth training programmes—have been introduced as a *cheap substitute* to 'cool-out' the educational aspirations of the poor.

The diversity and presumed explosion in various directions means that it is extremely difficult to capture and count the volume, let alone categorise and classify its various components, whether by the degree of formalisation (Coombs, Prosser and Ahmed, 1973), or according to the modes of learning (La Belle, 1982). In particular, the statistics available from official sources are limited to those courses where the student has completed a registration document and where the course organisers make some return to the national authority. The remainder of this chapter draws on Carr-Hill and Lintott (1985), who analysed those data.

9.3.1 Enrolments

The index of participation (enrolments per 1,000 adults) varies between 1 in Botswana and 401 in Tanzania. The latter figure seems high even given the massive adult education campaign in Tanzania, and Kweka (1989) confirms that some of the enrolment is fictional. Instead, the more surprising figures are for Botswana, the Central African Republic and Zimbabwe (all around 1 per 1,000). Whilst none of these countries were engaged in a mass campaign at the time, one suspects that the coverage of the data may refer to only part of the programmes of adult education. Variations in the proportions of females enrolled between the countries are not negligible: the two countries with the lowest proportion of females, Central African Republic and Guinea Bissau, are in West Africa, although it is hard to say what that may mean.

Some recent data were available for 16 countries in sub-Saharan Africa. Full tables are given in the Annex to this chapter; only those countries with trend data are included in the text tables.

According to the trend data (Table 9.4), there seems to have been a tendency for enrolment ratios to rise in the course of the late 1970s, and to fall thereafter from a peak around 1979. The exceptions are Guinea-Bissau, Mozambique and Somalia, where the opposite seems to have happened (but the tendency is weaker). The proportion of women amongst enrolees declined in the two countries with the highest and lowest proportion initially but increased in the three countries when the initial proportion was around 40% (Table 9.5). It may be—and this hypothesis is confirmed by the comparison of adult education with regular education (see Table 9.6)—that where countries have adopted a strategy of active government intervention and planning of economic development, an emphasis on adult education is likely to be part of that strategy (almost regardless of 'failure' or 'success'). In the face of recession-related factors which lead elsewhere to declines in adult education, adult education enrolment may then be less affected because it is cheaper!

9.3.2 Types of adult education

Carr-Hill and Lintott (1985) analysed the data by level and field of study. The data were classified according to the International Standard Classification of Education (ISCED), in which the categories defined are deliberately modelled on the regular school system of education. Given that one of the major characteristics ascribed to non-formal education (organised education outside the school system including

Table 9.4 Trends in enrolment in adult education per adult

Country		*Base year*	*1976*	*1977*	*1978*	*1979*	*1980*	*1981*	*1982*	*Enrolment in base year*
Benin	MF	1977		100	91	152	91	56		15,448
Botswana	MF	1976	100	141	153					119
	F	1976	100	144	211					46
Burundi (Q)	MF	1977		100	115	170	138	121		5,107
	F	1977		100	108	123	101	99		4,492
Guinea-Bissau	MF	1977		100	80	92	99	102		13,086
	F	1977		100	74	77	86	84		2,941
Mozambique (Q)	MF	1980					100	103	65	411,063
Somalia (P)	MF	1976	100	39	35	27	28			65,927
	F	1976	100	55	46	31	28			26,891
Sudan	MF	1977		100	67		94			99,169
Zambia	MF	1976	100	55	66	73	42			42,276
	F	1976	100	58	65	81	46			14,389
Zimbabwe	MF	1976	100	118						1,821

Note: The symbol 'P' indicates that the data have come from a pilot study; the symbol 'Q' that the data are from the reply to the questionnaire sent out by the Division of Literacy, Adult Education and Rural Development (UNESCO).

nearly all adult education; NFE) is its non-hierarchical character in *contra*-distinction to regular, school education, breakdowns by level are highly suspect and are not discussed here. The Annex presents the breakdown by field of study.

Table 9.5 Trends in proportion of women enrolled in adult education

Country	*Base Year*	*1976*	*1977*	*1978*	*1979*	*1980*	*1981*	*1982*	*% of women among those enrolled in base year*
Botswana	1976	100	102	138					38.7
Burundi	1977		100	93	72	73	81		88.0
Guinea Bissau	1977		100	93	84	86	82		22.5
Somalia	1976	100	140	129	115	103			40.8
Zambia	1976	100	105	104	111	111			34.0

Source: Carr-Hill and Lintott (1985), Table 5, p.24.

The point is that the various components have arisen in different contexts for different reasons with different social referents. One should distinguish, at least, between:

- *Parallel education* provided for groups who did not attend or failed to complete the school programme. Is modelled on school.
- *Private tutoring* intended to compensate for a schooling perceived to be inadequate or to give comparative advantage to children of richer parents. The content is entirely determined by the school curriculum.
- *Professional and vocational education.* This is the 'classic' NFE providing training supplementary to the school-based curriculum.
- *Popular education.* Courses intended to conscientise, to empower, to foster participation, explicitly directed towards the poorest of the poor. Some literacy campaigns in Africa have started out like this.

- *Leisure and cultural NFE,* where education is considered as consumption good. Only really relevant to richer groups in Africa.
- *Autodidactic learning.* People learning from each other.

The forces making for comparison or retraction of each component are different. Without a detailed study in a particular country, it is almost impossible to comment on a reported pattern or on the trends.

9.3.3 Resources for adult education

These data on the extent and nature of participation are better appreciated against the background of the level of resources devoted to adult education. The rare data available suggest both a very low level of commitment and wild variations (Table 9.6). The only other data available are on the number of teachers. As both students and teachers are liable to be part-time, the simple ratio (see Annex) is difficult to interpret: ideally, one would need data on student-hours and teacher-hours.

Table 9.6 Expenditure on adult education in relation to GNP units spent

Country	*Expenditure on adult education (local currency – thousands)*	*GNP (local currency – millions)*	*Units spent on adult education per million units GNP*	*Year*
Egypt	583	24,525	24	1982*
Liberia	5,301	972	5,453	1980
Sierra Leone	1,279	1,101	1,162	1980
Sudan	604	4,018	150	1980

Source: Carr-Hill and Lintott (1985), Table 13, p.51.

*Literacy programme only.

9.3.4 Adult and regular education

One of the 'hidden agendas' in the discussion and promotion of adult (or other out-of-school) education is the comparison of its effectiveness (in terms of learning outcomes) and efficiency (in terms of cost) with the effectiveness and efficiency of regular (in-school) education. We cannot compare learning outcomes and cost comparisons are fraught with difficulties, but we can attempt to compare enrolments (Table 9.7). There are several problems with this comparison: variations in age structure; full-time and part-time involvement; differences in levels and types of study.

Table 9.7 Enrolment in regular and adult education

Country	*Year*	*Enrolment in regular education (000s)*	*Enrolment in adult education as % of enrolment in adult and regular education*	*Notes on coverage*
Benin	1981	564	1.9	
Botswana	1978	165	0.1	
Burkina Faso	1981	251	16.8	
Burundi	1981	228	2.9	
Central African Republic	1977	281	0.4	
Guinea-Bissau	1981	95	13.0	
Liberia	1980	166	6.0	
Mozambique	1982	1,443	16.2	
Nigeria	1976	10,748	1.8	Regular education data for 1977
Sierra Leone	1980	329	3.4	
Somalia	1981	321	7.2	Regular education data for 1980
Sudan	1980	2,028	4.8	
Swaziland	1978	155	1.8	Adult education = rural educational centres and Swaziland International Education Centre
Tanzania	1977	3,037	54.5	
Zambia	1980	1,152	1.7	
Zimbabwe	1979	900	0.4	Adult education = African Adult Education Trust Fund

Source: Carr-Hill and Lintott (1985), Table 15, p.17.

With all these caveats, there still seem to be real variations. Tanzania stands out with enrolment in adult education nearly half the total—and Burkina Faso, Guinea-Bissau, Libya, and Mozambique all show percentages above 10%. This suggests that in countries with a strong emphasis on central government planning of economic development there may be more (recording of?) adult education.

The difficulty with interpreting trends is that adult education programmes have grown up for different reasons and in different social contexts. The data presented in this section are more useful for prompting questions than for reporting on involvement in adult educational activities.

ANNEX

Table 9A.1 Enrolment in adult education as a proportion of the adult population (15+)

Country	*Year*	*Adult education enrolment*	*Population 15 and over (000s)*[a]	*No. of adult students per 1000 population 15 and over*[b]
Benin	1981	9,719	1,959.3	5
Botswana	1978	192	386.8	1
Burkina Faso (Q)	1981	50,680	3,934.0	13
Burundi	1981	6,770	2,523.3	3
Central African Republic	1977	1,152	1,241.1	1
Guinea-Bissau	1981	14,160	356.6	40
Liberia	1980	14,660	1,023.8	14
Mozambique (Q)	1982	278,561	6,206.6	45
Nigeria	1976	201,332	35,859.2	6
Sierra Leone (P)	1980	11,643	1,949.5	6
Somalia (P)	1981	24,815	2,717.8	9
Sudan	1980	101,336	10,269.4	10
Swaziland	1978	2,896	288.9	10
Tanzania (P)	1977	3,567,544	8,904.3	401
Zambia	1980	19,787	3,052.0	7
Zimbabwe	1979	4,065	3,777.6	1

a As estimated by the United Nations (assessment made in 1980).
b Figures given to nearest whole number for ease of comparison.

Note: The symbol 'P' indicates that the data have come from a pilot study; the symbol 'Q' indicates that the data are from the reply to the Questionnaire sent out by the Division of Literacy and Rural Development (UNESCO).

Source: Carr-Hill and Lintott, 1985, Table 2, p.6.

The basic data on enrolment in adult education in Africa are presented in Tables 9A.1 and 9A.2. These have been commented on in the text.

The breakdown by field of study is given in Table 9A.3. Whilst participants in Liberia, Libya and Sierra Leone concentrate on literacy programmes (level I), in Swaziland and Zambia humanities programmes are more popular.

Finally, Table 9A.4 presents the (rather unbelievable) data on student–teacher ratios.

Table 9A.2 Proportion of women enrolled in adult education

Country	*Year*	$\frac{F}{\% M + F}$
Botswana	1978	53.1
Burundi (Q)	1981	71.7
Central African Republic	1977	17.7
Guinea Bissau	1981	18.5
Liberia (P)	1981	45.4
Sierra Leone (P)	1980	35.1
Somalia (P)	1981	42.4
Tanzania (P)	1977	52.0
Zambia	1980	37.5

Note: The symbol 'P' indicates that the data have come from a pilot study; the symbol 'Q' indicates that the data are from the reply to the Questionnaire sent out by the Division of Literacy and Rural Development (UNESCO).

Source: Carr-Hill and Lintott, 1985, Table 2, p.6.

Table 9A.3 Percentages of adults enrolled in different fields of study

Country	*Year*	*I*	*II*	*III*	*IV–VI*	*VII–VIII*	*IX*	*Total enrolment*
Central African Republic	1977	–	25.8	–	25.5	42.2	6.5	1,152
Liberia (P)	1981	30.6	17.3	2.0	26.6	22.7	0.8	14,660
Sierra Leone (P)	1980	66.0	2.6	6.3	13.2	10.9	1.0	11,643
Somalia (P)	1981	–	5.4	25.0	7.5	7.9	54.2	24,815
Sudan	1980	–	25.0	–	1.3	73.8	–	101,336
Swaziland	1978	4.1	–	35.4	22.2	34.2	4.0	2,896
Zambia	1980	–	–	95.7	–	0.1	–	19,787

Source: Carr-Hill and Lintott, 1985, Table 7, p.31.
I Literacy programmes; II Agriculture, forestry and fisheries; III Humanities (and general education); IV Science and technology; V Trade, craft and industry; VI Business and commerce; VII Health and other services; VII Home economics; IX Other fields.

Table 9A.4 Number of students, number of teachers and student teacher ratio

Country	*Number of students (a)*	*Number of teachers (b)*	*Student teacher ratio (=a/b)*
Botswana	192	24	8
Central African Republic	1,152	93	12
Liberia (P)	14,660	958	15
Libya (P)	94,470	4,983	19
Sierra Leone (P)	11,643	774	15
Somalia (P)	24,815	1,560	16
Sudan	68,355	3,343	20

Note: The data are from the same year as in Table 9A.1.
Source: Carr-Hill and Lintott, 1985, Table 12, p.46.

10 Urbanisation

According to Ankerl (1986), the proportion of the population living in urban areas in 1980 varied considerably between Eastern Africa (16%), Western Africa (22%), and Middle Africa (34%). The largest capital cities in tropical Africa were Kinshasa (Zaire) with 3.09 million, Lagos (Nigeria) with 2.50 million, Accra (Ghana) with 1.41 million, Nairobi with 1.28 million and Dar-es-Salaam with 1.08 million; but two other Nigerian cities (Ilorin and Ado-Ekiti) and Kananga in Zaire also had more than 1 million population.

10.1 THE URBAN PROBLEMATIQUE

In the 1950s and 1960s, urbanisation was blamed on unemployed peasants who 'flooded' the cities in search of jobs and caused 'over-urbanisation' (Davis, 1965). A mechanical argument was developed: the village 'pushed' and the city 'pulled'. Lewis (1965) emphasised the economic non-absorption, the social marginality and the physical isolation of the urban poor and saw migrants as trapped in a 'culture of poverty'. Hoselitz, a leading modernisation theorist, drew attention in the 1950s to apparently pathological features of urban growth in the Third World: unemployment; urban destitution; a division between what were later termed the 'formal' and 'informal' urban economic sectors; and overall, indications of over-urbanisation (Singer, 1977, p.14).

In the 1970s, the stereotypical picture of a typical African country was of a modern sector where urban elites and wage earners derived extravagant privileges from high incomes, government services and political influences,and a vast undifferentiated rural sector where the peasant lived in poverty and produced the wealth to pay for those privileges. Between the two was a dimly perceived growing population of peri-urban squatters, drawn by the magnet of high wages and 'bright lights', living in increasingly miserable conditions around the cities (Peattie, 1975). These were later to be called the 'informal sector'.

Rural–urban migration was then explained in terms of the rate of urban unemployment and the urban-rural income gap, also rather mechanistically (Todaro, 1969). But empirical work rapidly (Knight, 1972; Levi, 1973) showed this to be nonsense, partly because none of the three variables involved were or are directly measurable. Instead, urbanisation is no longer seen as a pulling process running in parallel to industrialisation, but as a consequence of changes in the rural production structure resulting in increased numbers of landless. Kiray (1970) calls this 'depeasantisation'.

The shift of approach corresponded to a changed terminology to describe housing in the peri-urban communities, moving from squatter housing and shanty towns to autonomous housing, spontaneous housing and popular settlements. Correspondingly, housing policies have moved away from mass demolition and resettlement in medium rise flats, and in the direction of squatter upgrading and new semi-serviced plots, although the appropriate financial and management systems have not been developed.

According to Western theorizing, 'The impact of urbanization (Western style) upon society is such that society gives way to urban institutions, urban values, urban demands' (Riessman, 1964, p.154). Wirth (1938) postulated an opposition between primary and secondary kinship groupings, the replacement of traditional customs with modernity and rationalism, and a move from homogeneity to heterogeneity. The relevance of these theories has been questioned:

> most of these studies ... report that rapid migration has not produced the alienation, anomie, psychological maladjustments and other symptoms of disorganization held in the Wirthian model to be hallmarks of rapid urbanization.
>
> (Berry, 1973, p.83)

The model of rural–urban continuum needs to be modified for the African context (Salau, 1979); whilst,

Kinship ties continue to exist. The extended family served as a source of shelter as well as providing for the economic, religious, legal and recreational needs of its urban members.

(Aldous, 1962)

10.2 UNCONTROLLABLE GROWTH?

The proportion of the population living in urban areas grew substantially between 1960 and 1980 (Table 10.1), and although the estimated rate of urban growth at around 6% is double the estimated rate of overall population growth, current projections of the proportion of population living in urban areas by the year 2000 are between 35% and 45% (according to the author consulted!), which are still low on a world scale.

Table 10.1 Urban population: 1960, 1980

Country	*Estimated total population (millions, 1978)*	*Urban population as percent of total*	
		1960	*1980*
Mozambique	9.9	4	9
Upper Volta	5.6	5	9
Malawi	5.7	4	9
Tanzania	16.9	5	12
Uganda	12.4	5	12
Kenya	14.7	7	14
Ethiopia	31.0	6	15
Madagascar	8.3	11	18
Guinea	5.1	10	19
Mali	6.3	11	20
Nigeria	80.6	13	20
Angola	6.7	10	21
Zimbabwe	6.9	13	23
Sudan	17.4	10	25
Senegal	5.4	23	25
Zaire	26.8	22	34
Cameroon	8.1	14	35
Ghana	11.0	23	36
Cote d'Ivoire	7.8	19	38
Zambia	5.3	23	38
Sub Saharan Africa	291.9	12	21

Source: Gilbert and Gugler (1981), *Cities Poverty and Development: Urbanization in the Third World,* p.6.

Moreover, some of this growth is a statistical illusion:

> The myth of mass rural–urban migration is fostered by three statistical illusions. First, a city, physically expanding with natural increase, often 'swallows' villages without changing their character. Second, natural increase pushes many communities across arbitrary urban–rural borderlines ... Third, two nearby villages, expanding with natural increase, may become contiguous, and thus acquire the status of a single community above the urban borderline.
>
> (Lipton, 1980)

The impact of changes in boundary definition is illustrated in Table 10.2 for the Kenyan case. Some of the growth is undoubtedly due to in-migration, but the adjective 'phenomenal' is perhaps more appositely applied to the growth in the number of new urban centres (nearly sixfold) than to the growth in the proportion of population living in urban areas (threefold).

Table10.2 Growth of Kenya's urban centres, 1948–79

	1948	*1962*	*1969*	*1979*
No. of urban centres	17	34	47	98
Total urban population 000s	286	671	1,080	2,309
Urban pop. as % of total pop.	5.1	7.8	9.9	15.1

Note: Urban centre defined as a gazetted settlement with a minimum of 2,000 inhabitants.

Source: G. C. Macoloo, 1988, Table 1, p.160.

Although urban growth is perhaps not so large as believed (World Bank, 1988), the proportion living in miserable conditions is. In principle, one distinguishes between slums (highly congested residential areas of residential housing which have deteriorated) and shanty towns (a section of a city or town comprising constructions intended to be temporary), but this distinction is not easy to make. In either case, rent is a problem (see Annex, Table 10A.1).

Some data are produced by the UN World Housing Survey (1973) and the UN Economic Commission for Africa (1976, p.78). Data are available, although rather ancient, from UNCHBP: *The Improvement of Slums and Squatter Settlements* (New York, 1971), from the UN Documentation of the Conference in Vancouver (New York, 1976) and from Granotier (1977), and these are presented in the Annex (Table 10A.2). They differ: for example, for Lusaka, the UN World Housing Survey estimates that 48% live in slums and uncontrolled settlements, while Granotier estimates it at 27% for the same year (1967).

Trends have been estimated for only a handful of cities: these data, presented in Figure 10.1, are compiled from Ankerl (1986).

Ankerl (1986) concludes:

> By way of general conclusion, the first task for Tropical Africa is to collect systematically at least basic data in order to constitute time series and inter-regional comparisons (p.27).

Figure 10.1 Percentage of population living in slums (and uncontrolled settlements): trend data

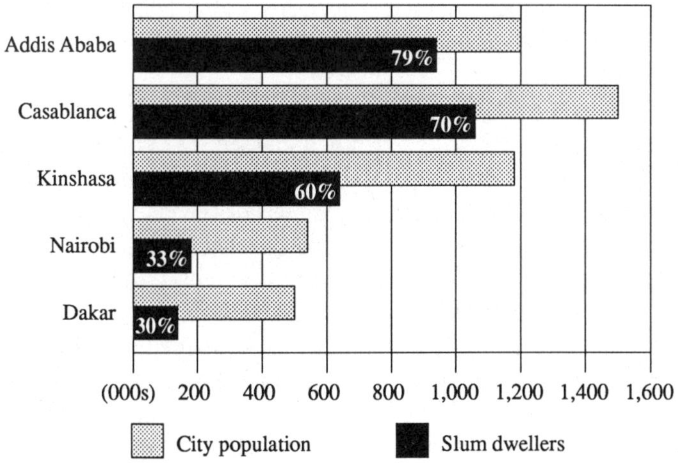

Source: Ankerl (1986).

10.3 THE URBAN BIAS

Many have argued that there is an 'urban bias' both in the provision of services and in our assessment of economic and social conditions in sub-Saharan Africa. Thus, Lipton (1977, p.13) argued:

> The most important conflict in the poor countries of the world today is not between labour and capital. Nor is it between foreign and national interests. It is between the rural and the urban classes. The rural sector contains most of the poverty … the urban sector contains most of the articulation, organisation and power.

Fifteen years later, Lourie remarks that the expansion of post-primary levels of education also increases inequity as'rural-based primary school-age children are neglected in favour of secondary and higher education students who are essentially urban-based and represent an articulate and … vocal constituency close to the centres of political power.' (Lourie, 1987, p.12).

These arguments are usually premised upon the notion of a relatively clear rural–urban divide. Indeed, in the late 1960s and 1970s, general theories were put forward which claimed to explain economic progress in the Third World by prevailing rural–urban relationships.

But, just as there is a modern sector and an informal sector in most urban areas, the rural sector is not homogenous. We have already shown how the physical separation of rural from urban is not that clear-cut. In addition, different groups of producers may have different, and conflicting, interests; and distance from the capital city leads to differences in both the objective interests and the political power of the rural population considered.

Further, Chambers (1983) points to six kinds of bias which make rural poverty systematically invisible to outside observers.

(1) *Spatial biases:* urban, tarmac and roadside. 'Most learning about rural conditions depends on vehicles … the hazards of dirt roads, the comfort of the visitor, the location of places to visit and places for spending the night, and shortages of both time and fuel

dictate a preference for tarmac roads and for travel close to urban centres.'

(2) *Project bias:* where visitors are directed towards rural areas where something is being done. Investment by donors draws research after it and funds it, which, in turn, gives the project high profile and so into a cycle of public relations management.

(3) *Person biases:* rural development tourists, local level officials and rural researchers tend to meet the less poor and more influential, men rather than women, users of the service rather than non-users, the active and fit rather than the apathetic and weak.

(4) *Dry season biases:* for those depending on cultivation, 'the most difficult time of year is the wet season, especially before the first harvest (see Chapter 6 and Appendix 2). But many rural areas, especially those which are remote and poor, are quite simply inaccessible by vehicles during the rains. The worst times of the year to the poorer people are thus those that are the least perceived by urban-based outsiders. Chambers (1983) quotes from a manual of rural appraisal:

> once the jeeps needed for transporting the interviewers were recalled for a month during the few precious months of the dry season.

(5) *Diplomatic biases:* politeness and prudence variously inhibit the awkward question, the walk into the poorer quarter of the village, the discussion with working women.

(6) *Professional biases:* specialisation makes it harder for observers to understand the linkage of deprivation.

Whilst both the urban bias and the ignorance of rural poverty can be demonstrated, the basic issue is the relative incomes. This is considered in the next section.

10.4 RELATIVE INCOMES IN RURAL AND URBAN AREAS

A corollary to 'theories' of migration and to the postulated rural–urban bias is that the proportion of workforce in agriculture has declined and that incomes in rural areas have dropped relative to incomes in urban areas. In fact, for 1950–67 in Africa as many countries recorded significant rises (over 1%) in agricultural shares of workforce as recorded similar falls. However, there probably has been a shift in the composition of the workforce. But Jamal and Weeks (1988) argue that the real wages of the urban poor have fallen over the last 20 years, in some cases dramatically (see Table 10.3), and that the security and stability of formal sector employment has diminished.

In particular, for Tanzania, Jamal (1982) estimated a 9% increase in real incomes of farmers from 1973–75 to 1980 whilst wage earners' real income fell by nearly 50%. The minimum wage which, in real terms, rose by about 30% from 1965 to 1974, declined steadily to about 75% of its 1965 value by 1981 and, over the next five years, was reduced to a quarter of its 1965 value. This is a grim commentary on Knight and Sabot (1982) who had lamented the allocative efficiency of stability of employment in urban Tanzania, because of 'wages high in comparison with incomes outside of the modern sector' (cited in Jamal and Weeks, 1988).

Table 10.3 Trends in real urban wages in Nigeria, Sierra Leone, Tanzania and Uganda (1970=100)

Year or contiguous year	*Nigeria*	*Sierra Leone*	*Tanzania*	*Uganda*
1958	–	118	–	26
1965	82	118	90	103
1970	100	100	100	100
1975	119	126	108	32
1980	94	66	52	5
1985	51	81	35	8

Source: Jamal and Weeks (1988), various tables.

For Uganda, the picture is even more dramatic. Trends had indeed shown an 'urban bias' in the 1960s. Whilst in 1957 the minimum wage would have bought only 3/5 of a typical family's food supply, by 1972 these could be bought for only 3/5 of the minimum wage. But, during the 1970s, Uganda not only shared with other African countries the negative repercussions of the recession in the West, oil price shocks and disastrous weather conditions, but Uganda has had to adjust to the break-up of the East African Community, to a war with Tanzania—and to General Idi Amin as the supreme economic planner and political overlord. His most important step was the War of Economic Independence launched against the Asian community in 1972. This crippled the economy so that, by 1984, the minimum wage would have bought no more than a week's supply of food.

Jamal and Weeks (1988) conclude that the urban wage-earning class has ceased to exist as a distinct entity. Households re-established links with the countryside reversing the labour force stabilisation process of the 1960s and also began to grow their own food in the towns. With substantial reductions in their real wages, workers spent less time at their job and took up trading. Distinct classes—which had existed briefly in these countries—began after the mid 1970s to coalesce into a hybrid class of 'traders-cum-wage-earners-cum-shamba-growers': though urban incomes fell quite sharply, total earnings from trade, wages and own farming kept most households above basic food poverty.

Their evidence also suggests that the income gap between urban wage earners and the rural population has narrowed considerably (Table 10.4). For example, in Nigeria, although the average gap between urban and rural households has widened, the gap between unskilled wage earners and rural households has narrowed. Whilst, during the oil boom, there was a tremendous increase in urban incomes, little of this filtered down to the majority of workers. In Sierra Leone, the picture is distorted by the (diamond) mining sector. Without these workers the ratio of rural:urban income dropped from 4.6 to 3.0 over the 1970s. But, relative to average wage income, average income in urban areas rose. A declining urban–rural income gap does not necessarily imply an improvement in income distribution.

On this basis, Jamal and Weeks (1988) argue that the primary dynamics of distribution is between rich and poor within both urban and rural sectors. The poor include wage earners (particularly the unskilled), informal sector operators and peasants in smallholdings. However, they also argue that migration from rural to urban areas has not abated, so that the simple Todaro model is inadequate. It continues as part of a struggle of the rural poor to survive as best they can. For many migrants, even the deplorable urban setting provides opportunities lacking in the rural areas (Peattie, 1975).

Table 10.4 Rural versus urban income

		(a) Nigeria 1973/4	1978/9 (1977/8 prices)	*(b) Sierra Leone*	1970/71	1980/81 (1980/81 prices)
Rural	1. Average family income	733	725	1. Agricultural average income	58	71
Urban	2. Average family income	2,520	3,378	2. Average income	352	247
	3. Average unskilled wage	780	741	3. Non-mining	264	211
				[Average wage income	77	42]
Ratios	row 3 to row 1	1.1	1.0		4.6	3.0

Source: Jamal and Weeks (1988), Table 1, p.278 and Table 3, p.280.

10.5 HEALTH AND INDUSTRIALISATION (AND MODERNISATION AND URBANISATION)

> A comprehensive measurement of industrial health costs should also include an assessment of the impact which industrial development and the creation of an industrial workforce has had on ecological relationships, environmental conditions and patterns of sickness and health in areas surrounding industrial centres.
>
> (Packard, 1986, p.476).

Industrial health problems in Third World countries are often presented as unintended 'hidden costs' of industrial production or as the inevitable consequence of industrial production within a Third World context. However, with current knowledge about the health risks associated with various industrial processes and patterns of development, and adequate economic and manpower resources, the health costs of industrial production could be largely eliminated.

Packard (1986) argues that reducing the burden of health costs borne by workers and peasants entails forcing capitalists to adopt health and safety measures which reduce their profit margin. Packard goes on to argue that the dependence of African states on international capitalists' interests places restraints on their governments' ability to respond positively to the interests of workers and peasants even when they want to. (Note that the same kind of argument could be equally applied to the North.)

The magnitude of the health problems of the urban poor is usually masked in city health statistics (Harpham, 1986). This is partly because squatter and slum inhabitants do not appear in the statistics (because they are not 'official' residents) and partly simply because they are lumped together with the better-off groups. Basta (1977), drawing on several studies, shows that whilst many of the major cities of the developing world report infant mortality rates (IMRs) of between 75 and 90 per 1,000 births, the rates are two to three times higher amongst their urban poor (see also Donohue, 1982).

Studies which have compared the health of rural and urban populations have usually found more severely malnourished children in low-income urban populations than in rural populations (Kerejan and Konan, 1981; Brink et al, 1983; Pickering, 1985). Nelson and Mandl (1978) show how, in contrast to South East Asia and Latin America, where rural labourers often depend largely on their landlords for food, many rural African families own—or can use the produce from—a small plot. Whilst salaries are higher in the city, so are costs, and the urban poor have only a small proportion of their miniscule income to spend on food.

Coulibaly (1981) reported that whilst the average rate for tuberculosis infection was 1.5%, this varied from 0.5% in the rural areas to 2.5% in Abidjan. Benyoussef et al (1973) found that one-third of a peri-urban sample were positive for ascaris (roundworm), while only three cases were found in a sample of 400 in a rural area.

Traditionally, cities have benefitted from a disproportionately large share of resources available for health care; that is partly why most developments in low-cost primary care have been in the rural areas. But there has then been a rapid growth of the urban poor and the state-provided curative services cannot cope. Consequently:

> the urban poor are at the interface between underdevelopment and industrialisation and their disease patterns reflect the problems of both. From the first, they carry a heavy burden of infectious disease and malnutrition, while from the second they suffer the typical spectrum of chronic and social diseases.
>
> (Rossi-Espagnet, 1984).

One other consequence is that the urban poor continue to appeal to traditional practitioners and practices in many cities (Gelfand, M. et al, 1981; Mehaniah and Kimpianga, 1981; Odejide et al, 1977, Senghor and Diop, 1988). As Imperato (1974) suggests, folk medicine has survived in apparently modern urban centres, not only because large numbers of people have faith in it, but also because the state-provided services have often not changed since colonial times, whilst folk medicine has adapted itself to the new urban scene.

There have been some developments: neighbourhood health programmes, the training of urban community health workers; and more 'rational' use of available local health facilities rather than rushing to the main hospital. UNICEF (1984), reviewing nine case studies of urban projects, conclude that, contrary to those who assume lack of social organisation and apathy among the urban poor—a community based approach is viable.

10.6 EPILOGUE

No-one would want to advocate equality of emiseration. But conflicts between urban and rural sectors are not good for either. Gakou argues for 'putting an end to the rural exodus and reducing urbanisation to a level low enough "not to divide economic and social policy overall ..." [to] be achieved by creating the conditions for a massive *voluntary* return to the countryside' (Gakou, 1987, p.84, my emphasis).

The emphasis on the voluntary means that conditions in rural areas have to be made sufficiently attractive so people *want* to remain.

ANNEX

Table 10A.1 Percentage of income spent on rent according to income

	Income groups (Kenyan shillings)			
% of income	*0–1499*	*1500–2999*	*3000–4999*	*5000+*
< 15	52	30	43	25
15–20	21	28	22	38
21–35	19	38	27	33
35	8	4	7	4
Nos of households surveyed	134	194	81	48

Note: A substantial proportion spend more than the official figure.
Source: Macoloo (1988), data collected in early 1980s, Table 5, p.167.

Table 10A.2 Percentage of city population living in slums (and uncontrolled settlements)

City	*Year*	*%*	*Year*	*%*	*Number of inhabitants in 1970 (thousands)*	*Population growth between 1960 and 1970*
Yaounde	1970	90			178	(198)
Douala	1970	80			250	144
Ibadan	1971	75			725	125
Lome	1970	75			150	(182)
Mombasa	1970	66			256	158
Kinshasa	1969	60	1964	40	1,370	269
Abidjan	1964	60			1,190	180
Dakar	1971	60	1969	30	559	150
Accra	1968	53			754	190
Ouagadougou	1966	52			100	160
Blantyre	1966	56			148	(150)
Dar es Salaam	1970	50	1967	34	375	229
Monrovia	1970	50			–	–
Nairobi	1970	48			550	238
Lusaka	1967	48	1967	27	299	(265)

Note: Data in brackets refer to the period between 1970 and 1980.
Source: Ankerl, 1986, Table 8.

11 The impact of state violence and warmongering

This chapter presents data on the 'blacker' side of life. Populations everywhere and throughout history have suffered at the hands of those in authority over them and because of wars. This should be remembered when interpreting the levels and trends which will appear high.

Threats to national and international security extend beyond external (and internal) military threats. Obvious non-military dangers are the degradation of the environment and of resource depletion; but the focus here is on potentially violent attacks on the individual.

Four issues are considered: first, the extent of repression and torture; second, the committment of resources to the war machine; third, the numbers of war deaths; and fourth, the numbers of refugees. A brief annex departs from the practice in the remainder of the book by focussing on South Africa—and, in particular, its impact upon the SADCC countries.

11.1 REPRESSION AND TORTURE

Whereas dictatorships were rare in the mid–1960s, they are now very common. By 1980 there were over 50 governments in the Third World dominated by the military, of which the great majority were described as 'repressive' in the source (i.e. using torture, summary execution)—and that number does not include the many *civilian* regimes which are hardly democratic on any definition (Seers, 1973, p.6).

Whilst the extent of dictatorship cannot be measured directly, the extent to which human rights have been abrogated in various countries is at least partially documented in successive Amnesty Reports. Table 11.1 presents a summary of their 1980, 1986 and 1988 reports. There is little obvious amelioration over the decade.

Table 11.1 Violations of human rights

	'Civil war'/ mass killings	*Detention, torture and killing of political prisoners*
Angola	MPLA-UNITA throughout	Many prisoners held for alleged membership of UNITA throughout, also members of Tocoist Church in 88R; reports of torture 80R; 14 killed in '85, 100 in '87.
Benin		At least 100 prisoners (mostly students) throughout; many tortured 86R and 88R; 100 killed in 80R after attack on Cotonoy, 2 in 88R.
Burkina Faso (not included in 1980 report)	Coup in '86	Some detained in '86R; 70 in '87; reports of torture in both years; 1 killed in '86R, deaths in '88R.
Burundi	Hutu-inspired rebellion in '72, 80,000 dead; Bagaza deposed '87	Leading members of Hutu detained in '79, prisoners of conscience held since; both groups tortured, some released by Buyoya; no reports of killings after '72.
Cameroon	Army killed 50-200 in Dolle in '79; coup in '84	Approx. 200 pol. prisoners in 80R, 50 held without trial since '76; 250 arrested after '84 coup; 50 executed and 40 still held in 88R; also refugees from Chad detained in 88R; 51 executions in 86R after 84 coup; no reports of torture.
Central African Republic	Bokassa killed 100 schoolchildren and students in Bangui '79	MLPC leaders detained in '79, around 100 arrested in '85, several prisoners of conscience in '88R; in '86R reports of torture by National Gendarmes; executions in Pauva area and 4 deaths in prison in 86R.
Chad	Civil war throughout; 1000 killed in '80, 100s in '86R, many in '86	Hundreds disappeared in '86R and reports of beatings and torture since then; many deaths in '86 (see special Amnesty Report).
Comoros		76 opponents held after unfair trial in '86R, 20 still held in '88R when a further 40 were arrested; reports of torture throughout; and a few deaths in '86R and '88R.

Note: 80R = 1980 Amnesty Report; 86R = 1986 Amnesty Report; 88R = 1988 Amnesty Report.

	'Civil war'/ mass killings	*Detention, torture and killing of political prisoners*
Congo (not included in '80)	Small numbers killed in demonstrations	In '86R at least 20 political prisoners, also refugees and members of religious sects, and a further 60-70 arrested in '87; reports of torture of all groups.
Cote d'Ivoire (not included in '80 or '86)		At least 15 trade unionists were arrested in '87.
Djibouti (not included in '86		In '88R refugees and asylum seekers forcibly returned to country of origin; in '80R reports of torture.
Equatorial Guinea	Execution of President Nguema after 11 year rule of mass killings	One prisoner under death sentence in '86; six in '88 after unfair trial; total of 11 executions between Sep. '79 and Aug. '86 (see Special Amnesty Report).
Ethiopia	Large scale in '80R; ongoing conflicts in Eritrea, Tigray	Several hundred Orama arrested in '80, by '86 some held over 11 years; a further 30-50 members of the DFSS since '86; large scale torture throughout; 60 executed in '74, several civilians since then.
Gabon		Prisoners of conscience tried in '88R, criminals and alleged illegal immigrants tortured at CEDOC; first execution in '86R.
Gambia (not included in '80 or '88)		In '86R death sentences commuted and some political prisoners detained without trial.
Ghana		'House cleaning' exercise in '80R with 100 wealthy businessmen arrested and heavy sentences; many arrested and detained without trial in '86R; 8 prisoners of conscience arrested and 30 held without trial after unsuccessful coup in '88R; torture reported in '86; in '79 8 executed; in '86, 58 sentenced to death with 16 executed by firing squad.

	'Civil war'/ mass killings	*Detention, torture and killing of political prisoners*
Guinea		500 political prisoners disappeared '79-80; about 60 former officials of Toure still imprisoned in '86R when given unfair trial and sentenced to death; torture alleged '80 and '86; 30 associates of Toure killed in 86R, 20 others in '85.
Guinea-Bissau (not included in '80)		50 detained in '86R, 40 still there in '88R; torture reported; total of 7 deaths in custody reported in '88.
Kenya (not included in '80)		Hundreds arrested in '86, many members of Mwakenya arrested in '87, of whom 39 tried and found guilty after torture; 12 air force involved in '82 coup executed in '86R; many deaths in custody (see special Amnesty report).
Lesotho	50 killed by PMU in '80R	Detention without trial in '80R; suspected LA sympathisers held '86R; torture; 17 deaths in custody in '86R; 3 in '88.
Liberia	40 died in 'rice riots' of '79, a further 27 killed in '80 coup	300 detained without trial after '80 coup, prisoners of conscience detained without trial in '86R; reports of assaults in '86R; 13 public executions in '79, a further 30 after '80 coup.
Madagascar	20-60 people killed in '86R who belonged to martial arts clubs	Prolonged pre-trial detention throughout; RC church members and Kung Fu members detained in poor conditions in '86; 38 arrested in '85, still in custody in '88.
Malawi		Long term detention without trial of poets, political prisoners, prisoners of conscience, and Jehovah's Witnesses throughout.
Mali (not included in '86)	15 students killed in '79 demos	40 students arrested in Nov. '79; 300 young people detained in Feb. '80; 6 of 27 political prisoners detained since '78 still in Taoudenit in '88; many tortured; 2 dead in Taoudenit.

	'Civil war'/ mass killings	*Detention, torture and killing of political prisoners*
Mauritania		Improvements of human rights reported after new government in '84; in '88R 17 political prisoners remain after unfair trial in '86, a further 40 imprisoned after protesting at above; and another 51 detained for conspiracy; alleged torture; 3 of 51 executed.
Mozambique	FRELIMO vs RENAMO many thousands killed	Many released in '80R, but many remain; series of unfair trials between '79 and '83; about 4,000 arrested in '84 for supporting armed opposition groups; many still held in '88; torture reported in '86R; 16 executions in '80R.
Namibia	SADF vs SWAPO, many civilians killed	270 refugees and SWAPO detained at special camp in '80R; 40 evangelists detained in Ovamboland in '86R; prisoners of conscience; torture alleged throughout.
Niger (not included in '80)		20 opponents detained without trial in 86R; amnesty of 100 political prisoners detained since '76 in 88R; also 7 out of 12 members of Tuareg ethnic minority group.
Nigeria	19 killed in religious clashes in Kafanchan	Imprisonment of prisoners of conscience in 86R; 20+ trades union leaders arrested and released within 2 weeks in 88R and 24 prisoners killed after assault on prison officer in Benin City in 88R.
Rwanda (not included in '80)		Prisoners of conscience had been released in 86R, but about 300 others were convicted in '86, although they were released in '88R; 50 political prisoners who had disappeared in 1970s confirmed as killed in prison.
Senegal (not included in '80)	17 injured in clashes with riot police in Dakar	200 arrested after '84 disturbances in Casamence region in 86R; a further 150 arrested for supporting separatist movement in 88R; many of latter tortured and persistent reports of torture.

	'Civil war'/ mass killings	*Detention, torture and killing of political prisoners*
Seychelles (not included in 80R)		Imprisonment of prisoners of conscience in 86R.
Sierra Leone		42 detained during strikes in '85; 50 arrested for conspiracy 88R.
Somalia		100 political prisoners in '79, 2,658 prisoners released in '80; many prisoners of conscience still detained in 86R; hundreds of Ethiopian nationals held at secret camp and a further 70 for religious activities in 88R; reports of torture 86R, 88R; 100 executions in '85, 4 in '87.
Sudan		250 officials and politicians detained in 86R, but most released; 120 prisoners remained under death sentence in 88R; torture alleged throughout, also amputation and flogging in 86R and 88R.
Swaziland (not included in 80R)	S.A. exiles killed	Prisoners of conscience in 86R; members of Royal Family held in 88R.
Tanzania		100 released in '79; 18 charged with treason in 86R; 2 prisoners of conscience in 88R; torture of several hundred in '75 and '76, and allegations in 86R.
Togo		Detention of government opponents in 86R, sentences considered in 88R; torture alleged throughout; several deaths.
Uganda	100,000 or more killed under Amin in 80R; many executions by army etc. (86R)	5,500 political prisoners in 80R, many reported in '84; torture alleged throughout.
Zaire	215 killed by troops at Mbuji-Mayi (80R); civilians executed in Kiwu region (88R)	100+ political prisoners released '79; many UDPS supporters and 40 prisoners of conscience detained in 88R; reports of torture in 86R and 88R; deaths in custody in 86R.

	'Civil war'/ mass killings	*Detention, torture and killing of political prisoners*
Zambia (not included in 80R)		Detention without trial in 86R, 50 Angolan refugees and 12 others in 88R, reports of torture in 88R.
Zimbabwe	Nkomo alleges 375 disappearances (86R)	8,000-15,000 arrested under martial law Oct. '79, most released in '80; during '85 at least 200 detainees at Stops camp; epidemic torture in '79, reports in 86R and 88R.

Note: The term prisoners of conscience refers to those detained for reasons of belief, colour, sex, ethnic origins, language, or religion who have neither used nor advocated violence.

However, it is reasonable to suppose not only that the accuracy of their data has increased over the years, but also that their capacity to find out has also improved over the years. One might therefore find grounds for qualified optimism in the relatively flat picture painted in Table 11.1.

11.2 RESOURCES FOR WAR, HEALTH AND EDUCATION

The development of human resources is becoming the watchword of development agencies. Whilst no single indicator can reflect changes in human resources, an indication is the balance between armed forces and social services in a country. The numbers in the armed forces of the various African countries in 1979, 1982, 1985 and 1988 compared to the numbers of educational and health care personnel in the same years are given in Table 11.2. They present a depressing picture.

11.3 WAR DEATHS

The numbers of war deaths in African countries over the last thirty years are given in Table 11.3. There is no clear trend.

Table 11.2 Human resources in armies, education and health, thousands

	Armed Forces			*Physicians*			*Teachers*		
Country	*1979*	*1982*	*1985*	*1979*	*1982*	*1985*	*1979*	*1982*	*1985*
Angola	40	38		.4	.5		40	34	
Benin	2	3		.2	.2		8	14	
Botswana	1	3		.1	.1		6	7	
Burkina Faso	4	4		.1	.1		4	5	
Burundi	5	5		.1	.1		5	6	
Cameroon	8	7		.6	.6		31	38	
Central African Republic	1	2		.1	.1		5	5	
Chad	5	3		.1	.1		5	6	
Congo	7	9		.3	.3		10		
Cote d'Ivoire	5	5		.5	.6		31	43	
Equatorial Guinea	2	2		–	–		1	1	
Ethiopia	222	250		.5	.4		40	55	
Gabon	2	2		.2	.3		4		
Gambia	–	–		.1	.1		2	3	
Ghana	20	15		1.5	1.7		80	85	
Guinea	9	10		.3	.1		10	12	
Kenya	12	17		1.5	2.3		107	132	
Lesotho	1	–		.1	.1		6	7	
Liberia	5	5		.2	.2		8	10	
Madagascar	11	21		.8	.9		31	35	
Malawi	5	5		.1	.1		12	16	
Mali	4	5		.3	.3		10	12	
Mauritania	9	8		.1	.1		2	3	
Mauritius	na	–		.4	.6		10	10	
Mozambique	24	22		.3	.4		19	23	
Namibia	na	–		na	.2		na	9	
Niger	2	2		.1	.1		6	8	
Nigeria	193	138		6.6	8.6		339	597	
Rwanda	4	5		.2	.2		10	14	
Senegal	8	10		.4	.5		13	16	
Sierra Leone	3	3		.2	.2		11	14	
Somalia	46	63		.3	.3		10	10	
Sudan	63	58		2.2	2.2		58	65	
Swaziland	1	–		.1	.1		4	5	
Tanzania	52	40		1.0	.6		80	91	
Togo	3	4		.1	.1		12	14	
Uganda	21	5		.5	.6		40	51	
Zaire	21	26		1.9	2.1		133	156	
Zambia	14	14		.7	.8		24	28	
Zimbabwe	22	63		1.0	1.2		26	50	

Table 11.3 Wars and deaths, 1960–82

				Number of Deaths (000s)	
Country	*Years*	*Intervention*	*Invasion*	*Civilian*	*Soldiers*
Angola	1961–	Portugal, 61–75; 76– Cuba 76–78	S. Africa,	48	7
Burundi	1972–73			50	50
Chad	1968–81	France, 68–70,78,79; Libya 71–81		na	na
Ethiopia-Ogaden	1961–	Cuba 77–78	Somalia 61–	10	15
Ethiopia-Eritrea	1962–	Cuba 78		na	30
Ghana	1981			na	na
Guinea-Bissau	1962–74	Portugal		na	na
Mozambique	1964–75	Portugal		na	na
Nigeria	1967–80,81			1,000	1,000
Rwanda	1960–65			62	3
Sudan	1960–72			450	250
Tanzania	1978–79	Libya	Uganda	na	17
Uganda	1966			na	2
West Sahara	1975–		Morocco	na	na
Zaire	1960–66	Belgium 60; UN 60–64; UK 64; Sudan 65		10	100
	1978	France		na	na
Zimbabwe	1965–79	Zambia 77		13	12

Notes: Intervention by foreign forces or by UN signifies overt action and irritation by a recognised government. It is usually identified with a civil war.
Invasion is a hostile intrusion by a foreign country and includes air and missile attack, whether or not accompanied by land invasion. An intervening or invading country is identified in this table only when it was the first to take such action and when the action was overt.

11.4 REFUGEES

Out of a total of 14,421,800 refugees throughout the world, 4 million are African. Since 1981 the estimated number of African refugees has increased by over 1 million people, a 40% increase.

A number of problems exist when trying to count the exact number of refugees living in Africa. The various organisations which collect data on refugees, such as the United Nations High Commission for Refugees (UNHCR), individual African governments, and international agencies, use different definitions to classify refugees, and collect their data from different sources. Moreover, distortions are bound to occur when the funding body is also a source of data collection such as the UNHCR.

Difficulties arise over the distinction between registered and unregistered refugees. Refugees who have not been officially registered will not be counted in total figures collected, although they are living in the host country. Where some refugees have been resettled into a host country's society, many figures do not state whether resettled refugees have been included or excluded in the total number. In the World Refugee Survey 1988, a table headed 'Principle Sources of the World's Refugees in need of protection and/or assistance' does not include populations considered to be living in refugee-like circumstances. The 'notes' to this table also state: 'sources vary significantly in numbers reported'.

The politics and administrative procedures of a nation will affect the counting of refugees. Some organisations/sources report certain aliens in a country as meriting international recognition as refugees, while others term them illegal migrant workers. It may be in the political interest of a government to understate its refugee population, or in other instances, to report inflated numbers. Individuals who could be classified as refugees through virtue of their circumstances but are admitted to a country under other classifications are not counted. Asylum seekers whose applications have been denied, but who are allowed to remain in a country, will probably not be counted as refugees. International assistance is sometimes provided to individuals who do not meet the international refugee definition per se, but who are deemed to be living in refugee-like circumstances, and these numbers too may be included in refugee counts.

The following discrepancies illustrate the many anomalies which arise:

> *Algeria* has hosted a large concentration of long-staying Sarhawi refugees since 1975. The exact number is in dispute. The Algerian Red Crescent estimates that there are 165,000 in four settlements and thousands more living outside the settlements. The US Government estimates a 50–100,000 refugee population.
>
> In the north of *North Angola* many displaced persons have lived in the bush for years, avoiding the towns for fear of being captured or accused of being a rebel. Their numbers are impossible to determine. 5,000 new arrivals in 1988 from Namibia makes current 1988 tables immediately out of date (1988 table quotes 92,100).
>
> In *Burundi* there are an estimated 76,000 refugees. The government of Burundi estimates a number three times that amount, but their figure includes more than 140,000 Rwandans who have been fully integrated into their society, both economically and socially.
>
> In *Cameroon* some 35,000 to 45,000 Chadian refugees have not sought refugee status but have, on the whole, been integrated into the local economy.

There are similar anomalies in many other countries; one might also be suspicious of rather strange shifts in the pattern of refugees funding in different countries. For example, in Mozambique, the amount of funding per refugee has decreased by a factor of 12; in Ethiopia by half; whilst there has been level funding in Somalia (see Table 11.4). With all these caveats, the growth in the estimated number of refugees is given in Table 11.5.

Tables 11.6 and 11.7 give an idea of the flow of refugees into and out of different countries.

The main producers of refugees in Africa in the late 1980s have been Ethiopia and Mozambique. From a total of 2.5 million (Table 11.6), 57% of the refugees came from Ethiopia and Mozambique (701,500 and 757,000 respectively). Somalia and the Sudan were the next largest producers, with 350,000 and 330,424; followed by Angola, Burundi and Chad.

Table 11.4 Patterns and/or oddities in refugee funding and movements

Country	*No. of refugees 1980*	*Amount of UNHCR funding relief and other assistance (000s US dollars) 1981*	*No. of refugees 1988*	*Projected 1989 financial requirements from UNHCR (000s US dollars)*
Ethiopia	11,000	1,745.8	685,000	54.4 million
Mozambique	100	1,423.4	385	417,000
Somalia	1,540,000	55,173.7	834,000	30,000

Table 11.5 Estimated totals of African refugees as at 31st December 1974 – 31st December 1981

Year	*Number*	*Percentage increase*
1974[1]	1,032,000	
1975[2]	1,119,850	8.5
1976[3]	1,212,630	8.3
1977[4]	1,636,515	34.9
1978[5]	2,232,125	36.4
1979[6]	2,715,977	21.7
1980[7]	3,589,340	32.2
1981[8]	2,923,000	–18.6
1988[9]	4,088,260	39.9

Source:

1) Report of the UNHCR: General Assembly Official Records:Thirtieth Session, Supplement No. 12 (A/10012), New York, 1975.
2) Report of the UNHCR:General Assembly Official Records: Thirty–first Session, Supplement No. 12 (A/31/12), New York, 1976.
3) Report of the UNHCR:General Assembly Official Records: Thirty–second Session, Supplement No. 12 (A/32/12), New York, 1977.
4) Report of the UNHCR:General Assembly Official Records: Thirty–third Session, Supplement No. 12 (A/33/12), New York, 1978.
5) Report of the UNHCR:General Assembiy Official Records: Thirty–fourth Session, Supplement No. 12 (A/34/12), New York, 1979.
6) Report of the UNHCR:General Assembly Official Records: Thirty–fifth Session, Supplement No. 12 (A/35/12), New York, 1980.
7) UNHCR News from the UNHCR No. 1/January–February 1981.
8) Preliminary Report of the UNHCR United Nations Economic and Social Council: Second Regular Session E/1982/29, 1982.
9) World Refugee Survey 1988, p.33, Refugees in Need of Protection and/or Assistance (this figure includes 500 South African refugees).

Table 11.6 Receptions of refugees to African countries, 1966–88, thousands

Country	*1966*	*1972*	*1981*	*1988*
Angola	–	–	73	92.1
Benin	–	–	–	1.1
Botswana	–	4.5	3.4	1.1
Burkina Faso	–	–	–	0.3
Burundi	79	42.1	234	267
Cameroon	–	–	263	51
Central African Republic	31.5	20.5	7	3.1
Congo	315	–	10	–
Cote d'Ivoire	–	–	–	0.8
Djibouti	–	–	42	1.5
Egypt	–	–	5	–
Ethiopia	5	16.1	11	685.2
Gabon	–	–	30	–
Ghana	–	–	0.2	0.1
Kenya	–	2.5	3.5	–
Lesotho	–	–	10	4
Liberia	–	–	0.2	0.3
Malawi	–	–	–	627
Morocco	–	–	0.5	–
Mozambique	–	–	0.1	0.4
Nigeria	–	–	110	5.2
Rwanda	3	4	10.2	20
Senegal	55	82	5	5
Sierra Leone	–	–	0.4	0.1
Somalia	–	–	1,540	834
Swaziland	–	–	10	29.4
Sudan	–	56.5	424	–
Tanzania	28	98	150	–
Togo	–	–	–	3.4
Uganda	145	165.4	112.4	–
West Sahara	–	4	–	–
Zaire	–	490.8	400	–
Zambia	6	24.8	25	143
Zimbabwe	–	–	–	100
Others	1	4.5	52	–
Total	668.5	1,015.7	3,528.9	2,875.1

Note: Inconsistencies between sums of column entries and column totals in original.

Source: For 1966: N. Rubin, 'African Refugees and the OAU' in *The New African,* October 1967
For 1972: W.T.S. Gould, 'Refugees in Tropical Africa' in I.M.R. Vol VIII, No.3, Fall 1974, p.415.
For 1981: All figures from UNHCR, News from the UNHCR, No.1, January–February 1981.
For 1988: All figures from UNHCR, No.43, January–February 1988.

Table 11.7 Refugees from African countries, 1966–88

Country	*1966*	*1972*	*1981*	*1988*
Angola	253	421.3	215.0	98.0
Burundi	3	58.0	144.0	60.0
Central African Republic	–	–	15.0	–
Chad	–	–	349.0	60.7
Congo	65.5	–	–	–
Equatorial Guinea	–	–	48.0	–
Ethiopia	–	52.0	1,953.8	701.5
Ghana	–	–	–	3.0
Guinea–Bissau	55	82.0	–	–
Mozambique	15	64.4	–	757.5
Namibia	–	1.0	52.5	69.3
Rwanda	161	151.0	101.0	–
Senegal	–	–	–	4.8
Somalia	–	–	–	350.0
South Africa	1	0.9	28.7	21.1
Sudan	115	128.4	11.0	330.4
Uganda	–	–	189.5	–
West Sahara	–	–	52.0	–
Zaire	–	43.8	68.0	22.5
Zambia	–	–	1.8	–
Zimbabwe	–	0.8	–	0.5
Others	–	12.4	299.6	165.4
Total	668.5	1,016.0	3,529.9	2,644.7

Note and Sources as for Table 11.6

Due to the harsh political and economic situation in Eastern Africa, several countries have both produced and received refugees. For example, in 1981, a total of 98,000 people left *Angola* for Zambia whilst 92,000 people entered Angola—69,000 from Namibia, 9,600 from South Africa and 13,500 from Zaire. Similarly, in 1988 a total of 701,500 people left *Ethiopia*—700,000 Ogadenia Ethiopians went to Somalia and 1,500 to Djibouti. At the same time, 685,000 refugees entered Ethiopia—350,000 Somalis and 330,224 Sudanese.

When there are data for more than one year, the tables also show how there have been very large changes in the numbers of refugees. For example, in *Angola*, the numbers leaving have declined from 421,000 in 1972 to 215,000 in 1981 and to 98,000 in 1988. But in *Ethiopia* no people were registered as leaving in 1966 whilst, in 1981, 1,932,800 left for Somalia and the Sudan and, in 1988, 700,000 left for Somalia and 1,500 went to Djibouti; similarly, in *Mozambique* 15,000 were registered as leaving in 1966 whilst in 1988, 757,500 people left to settle in Malawi and in *Sudan*, the numbers leaving have oscillated from 128,000 in 1972 to only 11,000 in 1981 but jumped again to 330,400 in 1988. However, it looks as if the total number of refugees has dropped substantially.

ANNEX

Infants and children under five killed by war in Angola and Mozambique: 1980–88

In 1979–80, it appeared likely that Angola and Mozambique would, within five years, reduce their infant and under-five mortality rates to levels comparable to Tanzania's. They had adjusted to the traumatic transition from Portuguese rule to independence and had articulated health, education, water and food strategies.

Over 1980–85, no such convergence of mortality rates occurred. Tanzania's continued to decline—albeit more slowly than before. Angola's and Mozambique's rose to levels which wiped out the 1975–80 gains.

The cause—the basic difference in context and performance—was the escalating effects of war and destabilisation in Angola and Mozambique.

The impact of war and economic destabilisation on under-five deaths can be estimated by comparing the probable difference in under-five mortality in Angola and Mozambique with that of Tanzania in 1985. There were an estimated 325 to 375 deaths of children under five years per 1,000 live births for the two war-ravaged States and 185 for Tanzania. The difference is 140 per 1,000 live births if the conservative mortality estimate of 325 is used.

In 1985, there were around 406,000 births in Angola and 602,000 in Mozambique. Applying the 140 'excess' of war-and-destabilisation caused infant and child death rates gives 56,840 deaths of Angolans and 84,280 of Mozambicans before the age of five which would not have happened in the absence of war. Adjusting for the base year of population data, 1985, under-five war-and-destabilisation deaths were 55,248 in Angola and 81,920 in Mozambique.

To estimate 1980–88 total infant and child war-and-destabilisation deaths, it is assumed that:

- the mortality rates would have converged with Tanzania's gradually over 1981–85
- there were no war-and-destabilisation related infant and child deaths in 1980
- 1986, 1987 and 1988 under-five mortality rates remained in the 325 to 375 range rather than rising

Therefore, the 1986, 1987 and 1988 'excess' death estimates rise at 2.6 per cent a year parallel to population and birth estimates.

These assumptions lead to the following estimates (Table 11A.1).

Table 11A.1 Estimates of war-and-destabilisation related deaths of infants and children (thousands)

Year	*Angola*	*Mozambique*	*Total*
1980	0	0	0
1981	10	15	25
1982	20	30	50
1983	31	46	77
1984	42	63	105
1985	55	82	137
1986	56	84	140
Total	214	320	534

Source: *UNICEF (1987) Children on the Front Line,* New York, p.31.

12 The status of women

This chapter focuses on data specific to the situation and status of women. In part, this is because, for some of the data presented in the previous chapters, it was not always possible to provide data disaggregated by gender. Moreover, the problem with population data is exacerbated when disaggregating by gender. Baster (1981) demonstrates the difficulty of using census data: as Fetter (1985) says,

> Male statistics suffer from undercounting of adult men because of labour migration and flight from tax collectors, while female statistics inflate the number of women and underestimate that of girls.

These kinds of biases need to be borne in mind when interpreting aggregate data on the social conditions of women of the kind presented in the Annex to this chapter.

The role of women in development has been the subject of a considerable literature. Most empirical studies focus on women's labour-force participation, women's education and the growth of female-headed households, and these are the main themes considered in this chapter. However, given the importance of non-market labour in sub-Saharan Africa, the participation of women in the modern sector labour force is only a very partial representation of their activity and so the first sections consider the inordinate length of their working day as well as women's labour-force participation.

The next two sections consider two other major trends which may affect the status of women: the increase of education enrolment and attainment among women; and the increase of female-headed households and consequent marginalisation. The chapter ends by considering the impact upon women's health and, briefly, the potential conflict between the advantages—and oppression—of the extended family, and the benefits—and disadvantages—of liberation.

12.1 A LONG, HARD DAY

The length of their working day is, of course, only one element in understanding the conditions of women. Other important variables include 'practices related to household income generation and maternal budgeting … and the distribution of food and child care responsibilities within the home' (Piwoz and Viteri, 1985). But the pattern of women's working day provides a stark contrast with men.

Time allocation studies are most reliable for estimating the total numbers of hours spent working, less so for estimating time spent on specific activities in part because of the problem of recording joint activities. Table 12.1, drawn from Leslie (1989), summarises various studies in African countries, selecting only those with moderately large samples.

Comparative time allocation studies have shown that women work longer hours than men in developing countries, that low-income women work longer hours than better-off women, and rural women work longer hours than urban women (Birdsall and McGreevey, 1983). A low-income woman in the rural areas of developing countries may be working an average 18 hour day (Sivard, 1985).

A picture of the woman's typical working day is given in Table 12.2, and Table 12.3 presents data from two studies which have explicitly compared men and women. The total work time per day in the Cote d'Ivoire study including illness was 6.9 hours for men and 9.8 hours for women; and in the Burkina Faso study it was 7.6 hours for men and 9.8 hours for women. As the latter study counted activities over a fixed 14-hour day, the ratio of work:free time can be compared: it was 1.2 for men, 2.5 for women.

This heavy burden puts the UNICEF child survival and development revolution (CSDR) in a different perspective. For the presumption of the CSDR is that mothers will have no problem finding the time to incorporate each of the new health and nutrition technologies into their lives. Yet even a marginal increase in the typical 10-hour day of low-income rural women may have an important effect on a mother's decision to adopt or participate in what must appear to be essentially discretionary health behaviour. We must look at the opportunities and problems of caring for children through the eyes of the mother.

Table 12.1 Time studies of woman's daily work (hours)

Reference		*Country*	*N*	*Food processing and cooking*	*Hauling fuel/water*	*Agricultural production*	*Child care illness and health care*	*Other work*	*Total*
Bono	1984	Cote d'Ivoire	720	5.10	na	na	na	6.90	12.00
Mueller	1984	Botswana	957	3.00[ab]	1.10	0.63[c]	1.06	0.43	6.22
Kamuzora	1980	Tanzania	105	3.02	na	4.96	1.19[d]	0.59	9.76
Fryella	1985	Sudan	8 vills.	2.39	3.05	2.98	2.00	3.24	13.66

a Includes handicrafts, marketing and other work.
b Cooking and housework combined.
c Measures during the slack agricultural season.
d Includes attending funerals.

Table 12.2 A typical woman's working day in three African countries

	Tanzania	Upper Volta	Togo
4			Get up
5		Peeling millet	Get water in large numbers
6	Get up and prepare ugali	Water duty	of round trips between home and source
7	Go to work	Cooking	Cleaning, meal
8	in the field		preparation
9		Departure for fields	Collect wood,wash clothes
10			Field work
11			
12	Return to		
13	prepare lunch	Meals to the fields	Cooking midday meal
14	Three hours	Restart work in fields	
15	cleaning beans, firewood		Grinding millet
16	collection and	Stop work	(16.30) Rest
17	return to fields	(17.30) Water duty	Collect water
18	Preparing supper	(18.30) Cooking	Cook evening meal
19	Fetch water		
20	Talk and pray	Meal	
21	Go to bed		

Source: Centre for Development Research, 1989; Togolese Federation of Women in the Legal Profession, 1986; Gisson cited in Conti, 1979.

Table 12.3 Comparison between men and women; hours spent

	Cote d'Ivoire		*Upper Volta*	
	Men	*Women*	*Men*	*Women*
Farm work	3.2	5.3	3.3	5.2
Domestic work	1.5	3.7	0.1	2.5
Non farm work and illness	2.2	0.8	4.2	2.1
Total work time	6.9	9.8	7.6	9.8
Social activities	1.7	1.8	6.4	3.9
Total	8.6	11.6	14.0	13.7

Source: For Cote d'Ivoire, Schwartz, 1983; for Upper Volta, McSweeney cited in Piwoz and Viteri, 1985.

Leslie (1989) reviews the time cost of breast feeding, immunisation, growth monitoring, and oral rehydration therapy (ORT). Tentatively (because of the very limited information available), she concludes that the time costs of breast feeding are probably not seen as a deterrent (Uyanga, 1980); that under-utilisation of vaccination services is almost certainly related to the opportunity cost of maternal time which has been underestimated by planners (Haaga, 1986); that the low participation rates in growth monitoring programmes are almost certainly due to time constraints; and that effective ORT programme implementation depends on factors—such as lack of fuel to boil water and time to administer the solution—which have been ignored by planners (AED, 1985).

UNICEF has paid progressively less rather than more attention to the burden placed on mothers by the child survival and development revolution. Their 1985 report did indeed discuss the additional demands made on women's time, energy and knowledge by the child survival technologies, and emphasised the need for practical support to women, in the form of labour-saving technologies and greater participation by other members. But the 1986 report only had a single chapter entitled 'The benefits for women', emphasising the savings in time, money and energy for women accruing from long-term reductions in child illness; and the 1987 report no longer had a separate chapter, but a subsection on 'Support for Mothers', which did not even acknowledge the demands made upon mothers by the 'child survival' revolution (Leslie, 1989). The 1989 report contains only a table of data on women.

The implications of the CSDR for women must be taken more seriously—apart from an exhortation to parents to look after their children.

> The advantages to women remain hypothetical and long term: moreover, any savings in time, money or energy are unlikely to be attributed by women to the child survival technologies.
>
> (Leslie, 1989, p.11)

12.2 WOMEN'S LABOUR-FORCE PARTICIPATION

Women's involvement in the agricultural labour force has consistently been undervalued because of the non-recognition of women's role in household and subsistence production (see, for example, Haper, 1981), as well as in cash crop production. Estimates drawn up through the US Bureau of the Census (1985) indicate the importance of women's role in agricultural production (see Table 12.4), with women constituting over 90% in nearly half the countries. At the same time, it should be recognised that on or near the breadline, women (and men) will turn their hand to anything. Thus Coughenour et al (1985) investigated the production and income of women farmers in North Kordofan (Sudan) in 1982. They reported that the number and variety of sources of sustenance was remarkable: mariisa (beer) production and mat weaving were common, each involving about one fifth of households; one out of six worked as an agricultural labourer; one third sold agricultural products. Eicher and Baker (1982) suggest that this pattern is common throughout sub-Saharan Africa. Recent research by the author in an urban community of Dar es Salaam and three villages in Tanzania found the same diversity of income sources.

Table 12.4 Percentage of women in agricultural labour-force

Mali	1976	91%
Niger	1960	98%
Benin	1961	21%
Ghana	1970	54%
Cote d'Ivoire	1975	81%
Liberia	1974	88%
Sierra Leone	1973	61%
Cameroon	1976	91%
Rwanda	1970	96%
Ethiopia	1968/71	90%
Madagascar	1966	91%
Mauritius	1977	39%
Tanzania	1960	98%
Angola	1960	47%
Botswana	1971	95%
Lesotho	1976	50%
Malawi	1977	96%
Mozambique	1970	94%
Zambia	1969	39%

Source: US Bureau of the Census, Women of the World in Sub-Saharan Africa, 1984.

Additionally, the proportion of women in the modern sector work force is increasing. Aggregate estimates are given in the Annex to this chapter. Figure 12.1 presents comparative data from censuses in Sudan in 1973 and 1983.

Figure 12.1 Percent female to males in selected occupational classes; Sudan

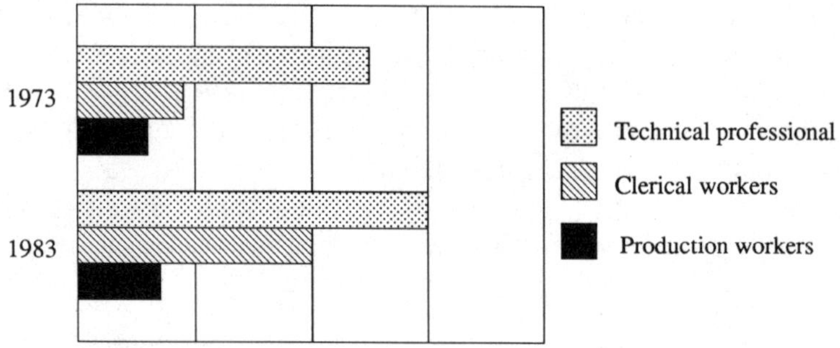

Source: Ministry of Labour and Social Security (1982, 1984) from Mohammed El Murfada Mustafa, 'Women Work and Development: a View From Sudan', The Afhad Journal, 2, 1, June, pp.39–45.

However, the status and condition of women and children will tend to be associated not only with the amount and type of labour that women contribute, but also with the control they can exert over the disposition of the product. Accordingly, in agriculture-based economies, their status will tend to be low in dry-land ploughing regions where their labour is perceived to be ancilliary or marginal, but higher in wetter climates with economies based on hoe-cultivated crops where their labour is essential. Murdock (1967) suggests that this explains why African societies that give dowry as the prevailing mode of marriage wealth exchange (or as a supplementary mode with bride wealth), are all clustered in the dry-land environment, especially in north-east Africa, whilst in wet West Africa, bride wealth is the prevailing mode.

These inter-household exchanges of bride wealth and dowry correlate well with gender-specific mortality rates by ecological region, as well as with participation in education and differences in the dominant religion. In Table 6.1 above, for both Mauritania and the Sudan, mortality aged 2–3 was substantially higher among females (even though the differentials in infant mortality in favour of females were, if anything, higher than elsewhere); it was also noticeable that the largest differences between female and male illiteracy rates in Table 9.3 were among the low-income semi-arid countries. The remainder of the chapter examines these conditions directly.

12.3 EDUCATION, LITERACY AND LIBERATION

For many (see, for example, the review by Piwoz and Viteri, 1985) maternal (not paternal) education is crucial because it is associated with decreases in child mortality and improvements in family health. Caldwell (1982) postulates that the education of women significantly alters the balance of power in the home, making women less fatalistic and giving them greater confidence to take decision-making into their own hands. An educated woman, he claims, will allocate a larger share of the household's resources to feeding and caring for her children.

Indeed, much of the primary health care policy literature on child mortality statistics concentrates on female education and literacy. Figure 12.2 shows the usual pattern.

Figure 12.2 Percentage of adults literate, by sex and level of infant mortality

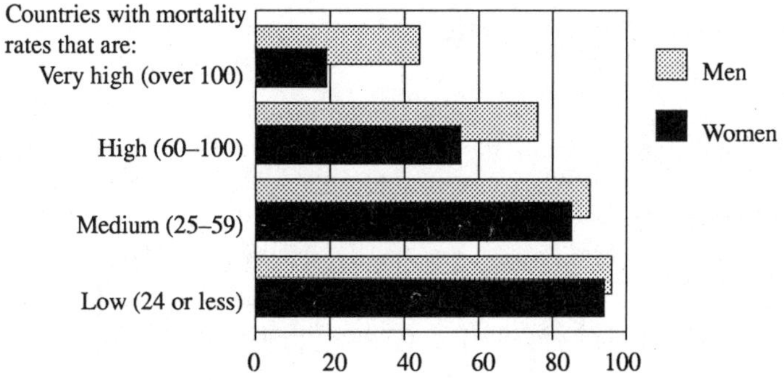

On this basis, the World Bank uses the rates of female literacy in making projections of child mortality rates and thence rates of population growth. But the evidence from micro studies is less clear: whilst maternal education is clearly important, so are several other factors. For example, a study in Nigeria showed women's education is highly correlated not only with husbands' education, but also with area of residence, source of water and use of refrigerator (see Appendix 2). The implication is that children have a better chance of survival in better-off families, whether or not the mother has reached a certain level of primary schooling.

It is important to avoid inferring that increased female literacy causes a decline in child mortality rates from an observation of a statistical association. MacCormack (1988) comments:

> It is a marvellous skill for everyone, and one would wish all women to have as much education as they can absorb. It will, *ceteris paribus,* enhance their social power. But little schooling is not necessarily the *cause* of high child mortality. Both may result from underlying features of the ecology and the economy which we need to understand before being confident that a policy/programme has some chance of success.

Moreover, the impact of formal education upon women can be two-edged:

> Since formal education was neither significantly helping the schoolgirls' trading knowledge nor providing skills likely to land them jobs, it was of questionable use. It took away the benefits of full-time apprenticeship without substituting those of either a full-time wage job or alternative self-employment for a group that must be self supportive.
>
> (Robertson, 1984, p.657)

There is, however, no doubt that more girls are going to primary school than ten or twenty years ago (see Chapter 8, Table 8). The World Bank argues that this can be closely related to GNP *per capita,* but Robertson (1984) has argued that the expansion of female primary school enrolments in African countries between 1950 and 1980 was not associated with GNP or income *per capita* but with the degree of urbanisation. She also reported a negative correlation of 0.4 between the percentage of the population that is Muslim and the 1980 percentage of girls in African schools. The participation of girls in school is shaped not only by economic conditions but also by patriarchal ideologies which mean that girls are less likely to have career aspirations and are more likely to be withdrawn from school.

Most authors (e.g. Stromquist, 1988) presume that, because more girls are going to school, there is a narrowing of the disparity between men and women in terms of illiteracy. For most countries in sub-Saharan Africa, the reverse has happened since 1960 (see Table 9.3 above), which is puzzling, given the rapid growth in primary school enrolments.

A possible explanation is that when a new, valued good or service (such as education) is first introduced, there is a tendency for provision to be adsorbed first by the most favoured groups so that sharp inequalities appear; but that as the overall level of access or provision increases, inequalities gradually decline. Literacy and schooling are relatively new in Africa, so this general tendency may account for the observed pattern.

A detailed study of literacy retention in Kenya (Carron, Mwiria and Righa (1989) supports this: where global mastery is low, inequalities are large; in South Maragoli, where global mastery is highest, inequality has disappeared (see Table 12.5).

Table 12.5 Percent of learners with average global mastery level by location and mean test results, by sex, by location

	Percent with av. global mastery	*Mean test results (M/F)*		
		Calculating	*Reading*	*Writing*
Starehe (in Nairobi)	54	6.9/4.8	2.7/1.8	8.8/5.8
Isiolo (semi–urban)	26	4.2/4.0	2.5/1.6	6.6/3.6
Koma (heterogenous)	46	7.0/4.2	2.8/2.3	7.0/6.8
Kilrua (recent but homogenous)	49	5.6/4.3	2.9/3.0	7.3/5.6
South Maragoli (dense traditional settlement)	79	5.2/6.6	2.4/3.0	8.6/9.1

Source: Carron, Mwiria and Righa, 1989, Table X.13.

This hypothesis is supported by the pattern of disadvantage by age group for the five countries for which recent census data are available (Table 12.6). If there were a general decrease in inequality as literacy increased from zero, one would expect a gradual widening of the gap among older age groups: in fact, this only occurs among countries with already lower levels of illiteracy (Egypt, Swaziland, Tanzania). Countries where the illiteracy rate is high show a peaked pattern, suggesting that when literacy was first introduced, the gap first widened and then began to shrink.

Table 12.6 Illiteracy disadvantage from the late 1970s, by age group

Level of illiteracy		*Date of courses*	*Age groups*				
			10–14	*15–19*	*20–24*	*25–34*	*35–44*
83.5	Benin[a]	1979	25.0	27.3	25.9	21.0	9.8
61.8	Egypt	1976	–	22.6	27.4	34.0	35.2
80.0	Guinea–Bissau	1979	33.7	37.2	32.9	31.6	25.5
90.6	Mali	1976	–	12.4	14.0	7.6	5.7
72.8	Mozambique[b]	1980	13.4	34.1	42.3	37.2	23.9
44.8	Swaziland	1976	3.9	0.3	2.4	7.2	8.0
68.6	Togo[c]	1981	20.4	33.6	39.1	34.6	29.3
53.7	Tanzania	1988	3.9	23.5	29.5	38.6	41.2

Source: UNESCO Compendium of Statistics on Illiteracy, Statistical Reports and Studies, No. 30, Paris, UNESCO.

Notes: The older age groups vary slightly
a = 25–29, 30–34
b = 25–34, 35+
c = 25–29, 30–44

This would also explain the overall pattern of widening over the last 25 years, observed for most countries of sub-Saharan Africa in an earlier chapter (see Table 9.3): for the declines in inequality are only recent and so far affect only a minority of the population. The prospects, however, are good.

12.4 FEMALE-HEADED HOUSEHOLDS AND MARGINALISATION

Differing family systems, for example, as between polygamous and monogamous households will have different impacts on the economic dependence of women. In particular, there is growing recognition of the growth in the number of female-headed households, in part because of labour migration (Section 12.4.1).

The numbers given in Table 12.7 are probably underestimated because of inadequate counting of *de facto* rather than officially female-headed households. Brekke estimates that in the early 1980s, 40% of total households in Kenya, Botswana, Ghana and Sierra Leone were female-headed households. They are becoming progressively marginalised (Section 12.4.2).

Table 12.7 Percentage of women-headed households

Country	*Year*	*%*	*Year*	*%*
Burkina Faso	1975	5.1		
Mali	1976	15.1		
Ghana	1970	28.7		
Liberia	1974	14.9		
Rwanda	1970	16.5	1978	25.2
Ethiopia	1970	12.4		
Mauritania	1972	18.8		
Madagascar	1975	15.5		
Sudan	1973	22.1		
Botswana	1970	–	1981	45.2
Malawi	1970–72	28.8		
Kenya	1969	29.5	1979	32.1
Mauritius	1972	18.8		
Tanzania	1970	25.0		
Zambia	1974	26.4		
Lesotho			1980	40.0
Nigeria			1980–81	14.3
Sierra Leone			1980	20.0

Source: The Population Council Socio-Economic Indicators of Women's Status in Developing Countries 1970–80, May, 1986, and US Bureau of the Census: Women of the World 1984.

12.4.1 The impact of labour out-migration

The absence of adults for long periods leads to neglect of important work in the village such as the clearing of new land or maintenance of irrigation systems because of lack of time for those who remain. Long-term production of food is likely to suffer.

In Southern Africa in particular labour migration is the main factor creating female-headed households. Palmere estimates that, in

Lesotho, 40%–60% of married women are managing households. A 1976 survey in Swaziland revealed that 35% of all households did not have a resident male over 16 years old, and that 75% had at least one absent male.

Kossoudji and Mueller (1983) examined variations in income and capital among a sample of households in rural Botswana, distinguishing between households with a male head who was present (MH-MP: 49%), a male head but not present (MH-NMP: 8%), a female head but with an adult male present (FH-MP: 13%) and a female head with no adult male present (FH-NMP: 28%). Households with no adult males present had fewer members but almost twice as many children to support per adult. Yet their assets and income were much lower. Kossoudji and Mueller (1983) calculated the income and value of livestock for households with a female head and no adult male present, as being under half that of households with a male head who was present. Moreover, whilst female-headed households sometimes received remittances from husbands, their overall income was still less than half that of male-headed households (see Table 12.8); and such remittances often came via other males (95% in their case), thereby increasing dependence.

Table 12.8 Income levels and percentage composition of income by household category; Botswana

	MH–MP	*MN–NMP*	*FH–MP*	*FH–NMP*
Average income, excluding transfer income (rands)	857	749	645	354
Average income, including transfer income (rands)	903	802	749	434
Average total income per adult equivalent (rands)	178	188	142	36
Sources of income (% of total)				
Crops	13.1	8.6	6.7	8.7
Animal husbandry	46.7	69.1	39.6	32.2
Wage labour	20.0	3.2	23.4	22.8
Other	13.7	8.1	15.8	15.6
Transfers	6.4	7.2	15.5	20.6

Source: Kossoudji and Mueller, 1981; in Palmer, 1985.
Note: 'Other' includes manufacturing, trading, services and construction, hunting and fishing, gathering.

Further, according to the Rural Income Distribution Survey, female-headed households netted 7.9 Rand profit per acre, as compared with 11.6 Rand for male-headed households. The lower net returns are evidence that women are not able to spend as much time on their crops as can women in male-headed households.

Figure 12.3 Per capita net income for households, by sex of head, El-Obeid area, 1981

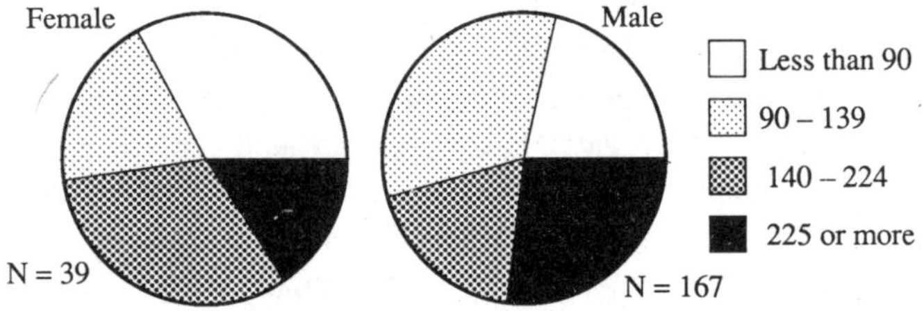

Source: Coughenour et al, 1985.

Coughenour et al (1985) gave figures for the total value of production and other income for 206 households in Sudan and after deducting estimated costs. The largest differences between male- and female-headed households occur between those receiving less than 90 Sudanese pounds. They conclude, 'the net "income" of women farmers in 1981 was low both in absolute terms and relative to the men farmers around El-Obeid.'

The growth of this 'underclass' is not only a rural phenomenon: for example, Ei Nagar (1988) reports a changing pattern of street trading in the Sudan with more young, single and married corresponding to a rise in female-headed households.

12.4.2 Monetarisation and marginalisation

As exchange is monetarised, resources tend to be drained away from the mothers. Whilst domestic roles are not necessarily a constraint on other roles,

> Mothers do not necessarily face incompatibilities between work and childcare, for childcare may be mainly done by others, such as the aged or the older children.
>
> (Oppong, 1987)

But women need to control food production, the food path and distribution of food within the family (Mueller, 1977).

Thus, if monetarisation takes the form of cash-cropping, food production will suffer because of limited labour resources in the critical season. Women have less time (and perhaps less land) to grow food and to feed their children. Cash gives access to town products which are expensive and which give prestige, but which do not compensate for the drop in food production.

A case study from Ghana illustrates the role of the export economy in crop patterns and food production. Initially the introduction of cocoa had created a division of labour with men moving into cocoa cash-crop production and women becoming wholly responsible for food crops. As prices of cocoa began to fall the role of the woman as food producer became increasingly important. By the 1950s, male out-migration was occurring. A survey in 1976 indicated that 50% of households were headed by women. In over a third of households there were no males over 15. Women decided to switch from the traditional yam crop to the less nutritious cassava because it took less time to cultivate. Kwashi-or-kor was first identified in huge numbers of children being fed cassava as a weaning food.

Schwantz (1985) summarises studies during 1972–79 in various parts of Tanzania in a context of government directives in village development aimed at reducing women's workload. Women worked longer hours in the fields, were responsible for planting crops twice a year and for cultivation of yams and potatoes outside the village on separate plots two or three times a year. Open land cultivation had greatly increased work and a greater number of food crops were being grown. The introduction of coffee production had introduced cash into households. However, if women increased their cash incomes, men ceased to make a financial input—a frequent cause of divorce.

In the Ujaama villages, women had the right to be registered as independent members of the village association. However, married women were discouraged from joining; and single women were looked down upon. The main obstacle remained the right of women to own their own land, being dependents with no permanent share in the wealth they earned.

Involvement in development projects has also had a negative impact on women's productive activities. In Sierra Leone where women are the main source of unpaid labour for both cash and food crops, the government's promotion of swamp rice farming resulted in an increased workload for women of 4% in the first year and of more than 10% in the second year. At the same time, mechanisation through use of tractor hire schemes reduced male labour. Similarly, in fish processing, where women had played a major role after 1974, they were forced to buy from large-scale concerns with reduced profit margins (Oppong, 1987).

In Upper Volta, resettlement schemes (AVV) designed to produce cash crops and grains increased women's workloads and resulted in the loss of the economic independence which they had had through their own plots. Under the scheme, where plots were allocated to men, women had little right to their share of their wage equivalent. Before the scheme, 71% had their own economic activity. Nearly all women spun cotton in their spare time. With the advent of the scheme, 42% managed to retain some activity but at much reduced input: once a month rather than once a week in their villages. Only 29% were practising spinning. Overall, women's economic activities were reduced by 50%. They also lacked milling facilities in the AVV villages which they had enjoyed in their former villages and had to walk further for water—estimated between 16 and 32 kilometres a day in the dry season and (8–16 km in the rainy season) (Conti, 1986).

12.5 THE IMPACT UPON HEALTH

These conditions all affect women's health. For example, during 1984–86 1029 women were interviewed in the Rural Woman's Health Survey in Zimbabwe. Only 43 reported no illness. Thirteen per cent of women were ill for 4 months or more before treatment was sought, compared to only 2% of men.

In the 1930s, the 'crisis' of Africa was seen in terms of social reproduction; and malnutrition and high rates of infant and child mortality were seen as the social product of a radically changing economy. Hence the focus on the mother–child dyad, but also the isolation of the problems of reproduction (Vaughan, 1989). Whilst this is important for women, their own health also matters.

In this section, therefore, we consider malnutrition and nutritional anaemia, trends in production and breast feeding.

12.5.1 Marginalisation, malnutrition and levels of nutritional anaemia

Wisner (1980) showed the connection between marginalisation and poor nutritional status in Kihir and Meru Districts of Kenya. Eco-demographic pressure in the high potential areas of Kenya has led to marginalisation (Wisner, 1980, p.1) through the migration of agriculturalists into 'marginal' lands.

Ferguson (1986) studied one such area with a higher than average dependence on women. A standard household-level questionnaire was administered in 524 households in Kibwiri Division, Kenya. Figure 12.4 shows how women in marginal areas are spending much more time than men carrying water and that men are able to use mechanical aids more often. Labour demands are heavier than before and the spread of primary schooling taking away young children only exacerbates that. The majority of women were undernourished, being shorter by 2 cm than in a contiguous area and with nearly half seriously underweight (a Quetelet Index under 2.0).

Additionally, WHO reports that the prevalence of anaemia among pregnant women in Western Africa seems to be higher than in Eastern Africa (see Table 12.9).

Figure 12.4 Water and women: Kenya

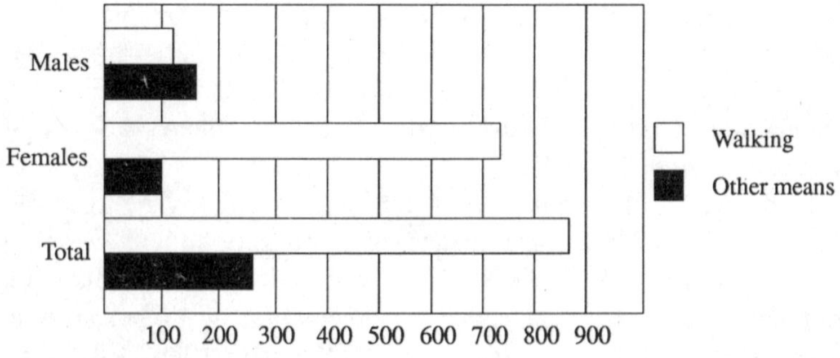

Source: Ferguson, A. (1986), 'Women's Health in a Marginal Area of Kenya', Soc. Sci. Med., 23, 1, pp.17–29.

Table 12.9 Nutritional anaemia among pregnant women

Guinea Bissau	1952 – 99%	1957 – 85%		
Mali	1964 – 50%	1973 – 65%		
Nigeria	1959/60 – 90%	1965 – 50%		
Ethiopia	1958 – 33%	1968 – 7%	1972 – 5%	1976 – 6%
Mauritius	1957 – 70%	1960 – 80%		
Tanzania	1961 – 77%	1971 – 79%	1971 – 59%	1974 – 80%
Zambia	1966 – 65%	1970/71 – 60%	1972 – 50%	

12.5.2 Breastfeeding

The Oxfam campaign against Nestlé's aggressive marketing of baby milk is well-known. But Nestlé still has factories in Cote d'Ivoire, Ghana, Kenya, Madagascar, Nigeria, Senegal and Zimbabwe, producing infant cereals and milk powders. Berg (1975) reports that in Cote d'Ivoire and Ghana in the mid 1970s, it was estimated that breast feeding an infant for 2 years could save a family US$642, with additional savings from the health benefits. This is larger than GNP *per capita* in both countries. In Kenya the estimated annual loss of breast milk in the early 1970s was US$11.5 million, equivalent then to two-thirds of the annual health budget (Berg, 1975).

There have been significant changes (for a broad historical review, see King and Ashworth, 1987). In the early 1950s, a study in a large town in Western Nigeria found only 13% had ever used artificial milk. Partial bottle feeding increased and, among elite mothers, the duration of bottle feeding became shorter. Whilst most mothers still breastfeed till 12 months, artificial milks have become more widely used in urban areas, with a slight trend towards earlier introduction. When urban and rural data were disaggregated, there was less use of artificial milk and later introduction in rural areas. These trends are associated with the reduction in the duration of sexual abstinence over the 1970s (Table 12.10).

In Zaire, a shorter duration of breast feeding (and shorter birth intervals) was reported in the 1950s among wives of 'redistributed' mine and plantation workers. Most mothers still feed to 12 months, and even up to 1984, relatively few mothers used artificial milk.

Table 12.10 Age of child at cessation of sexual abstinence, Nigeria, 1975 and 1982

Age of child in months	*1975* %	*1982* %	*NFS* %
0–6	6	17	24
7–12	10	26	27
13–18	35	36	16
19–24	25	18	20
25+	16	2	8
Non response	8	1	5

Note: NFS = Nigerian Fertility Survey; fieldwork during 1981–82
Source: Olukoya, 1986, Table 2.

Finally, Dettwyler (1987) studied 136 infants from 117 compounds in a peri-urban community in Mali. She shows how breastfeeding is a complicated variable process defined and circumscribed by culture. The cultural norm for weaning was at 24 months, in fact the average age was around 21 months, with the first-born being weaned earlier than later-born. Whilst, in rural Mali, post-partum sex taboos are still strong, in this community women no longer routinely practised post-partum sexual abstinence until the child was weaned; instead when they became pregnant again, they weaned the previous child.

Winikoff and Laukaran (1989) examine the factors affecting bottle- or breast-feeding in four Third World cities. They show that whilst modernisation has hardly affected the *initiation* of breast-feeding, it has obviously affected their awareness of the possibility of artificial feeding and it has influenced mothers' perception of whether or not they will have sufficient milk, in particular, they show the critical importance of the health care system as a mediator between the commercial activities of infant food manufacturers and changes in mothers feeding patterns.

Note that breast-fed babies are not always healthier. Scott-Emuakpor and Okafor (1986) interviewed 401 Benin City mothers in 1981 and found a higher incidence of malnutrition among the breast-fed infants before the second year of life, which they attribute to inadequate dietary supplementation. It may equally arise from selection.

12.6 FUTURE TRENDS?

Modernity is no panacea in other ways. For example, some argue that rape is not only a problem for Western feminists (Olusanya et al 1986). Women are likely to be especially affected by the tobacco invasion. Thus, whilst WHO (1973) estimated that 'In most groups, less than 5% [of women] are smokers', their own database in the late 1970s gave a figure of 21% for Nigerian students.

> Women's options are diminishing, while seeming to widen. Their domestic labour, especially in an urban milieu, is devalued at the same time that their work in the formal sector is becoming increasingly mandatory.
>
> (Hale, 1985, p.39)

In the rural milieu, traditional land rights in parts of Africa have guaranteed some independent access to land for women, albeit on a reduced scale (either through being allocated smaller plots of land in the first place, or through forfeiting their land if they have lost their husbands). Even these have been undermined by colonial land policies, and by the allocation of land to men in development projects.

The collapse of the joint household has important consequences for women. Thus, the more women there are in a household, the less time each has to spend on household chores. Each spends correspondingly more on social and leisure activities, but not on agriculture (Table 12.11). This 'space' is disappearing.

Table 12.11 Average time spent per woman-day on each activity

No. of able women in household	*Time spent (hours)* Water collection	Other household work	Agricultural work	Social activity	Total
1	33	537	34	238	842
2	10	478	70	291	849
3	15	375	44	376	810
4	7	287	94	524	912

Source: Feachem, 1980.

At the same time there is some movement towards sharing of domestic labour between men and women. Bedri (1988) reports on data obtained in 1976–77 from 140 married couples in Omduoman, Sudan, about their domestic division of labour and the employment of wives outside the home. She observed a shift from traditional norms regarding roles of wives: for example, only 23% adhered to the practice of segregated eating; and 71% agreed that a wife with a good education should work. However, only 17% of wives actually had a regular job outside the home. Callaway (1984) argues that, in societies when women have been secluded in some cases, the seclusion of women may have led to an 'ambiguous social polarisation—physically and legally subordinate and socially almost invisible; but they are almost tenaciously self-determining' (p.448). If women then seize upon the independence of employment outside the home, their 'liberation' may be broader, fuller and deeper than in Western societies.

Section 3: Improving the Knowledge Base

The purpose of this section is to suggest ways in which better data for monitoring social conditions can be produced about Africans by Africans and for Africans. Whilst no-one would suggest that producing data should substitute for activities to improve conditions, many aid programmes are premissed upon a fragile knowledge base and inappropriate theory.

13 Monitoring social conditions, top-down

Few now disagree that social programmes should be considered, independently of economic restructuring efforts. Economic development should serve human and social goals. In a statistical context, the emphasis must shift from counting products and things, to counting people, their activities, and what happens to them.

For many authors, the problem is to provide a *framework* into which data about the inputs, processes and outputs of social programmes can be slotted. But this is over-ambitious: our theories are too weak. So that, whilst we know the *kinds* of factors which are important in affecting the state of, or change in, social welfare, we do not know *how* or *when* each factor is important, nor, often, how it relates to other factors. Sometimes we do not even know how to specify the factors in terms of measureable indicators.

In these circumstances, the presentation of data within such a framework is misleading as it suggests that some of the factors *explain* the others. Thus, it is obviously sensible to present data on corporate or government activities—such as GNP or government expenditures—as *the context of* the state of, or changes in, social welfare; but variations in the former should not be taken as *the explanation for* variations in the latter. Baster (1985) reviews many of the proposals and also cautions against:

> grandiose schemes, which attempt to capture socio-economic reality as an integrated totality, because they push more urgent and more useful exercises in statistical bridge-building between sectors out of the limelight.

But, even without making assumptions about causality, the design or maintenance of a particular statistical framework is not a neutral, technical procedure. For the way decision makers interpret current 'reality' and trends and conceive their future information needs itself depends upon the existing framework of data collection and presentation. But the perceived appropriateness of a statistical framework for monitoring also depends on the particular social organisation. For example, 'capitalist' states use the System of National Accounts, and 'socialist' states use the Marginal Product System; whether or not statistics are broken down by gender depends on the recognition of women; a land register in a desert without oil could be superfluous; and so on.

Neither can the choice and definition of what to measure and how to report it be treated as a technical issue. For example, one could argue, on practical and technical grounds, that nutrition status measurements may well be the most reliable and cost-effective source of information about social and economic conditions in countries where the health and social and statistics systems are inadequate—and that comment refers equally to many developed countries with (over-developed) administrative statistical systems. But the promotion of nutritional status as a major indicator is also a political judgement: it may be much easier to achieve a consensus in favour of using nutritional rather than socio-economic status as a basis for comparing needs, regardless of the (undoubted) value of the indicator.

These political influences upon the collection and interpretation of statistics must not be ignored. At the same time, judgements that statistical offices make are not themselves neutral:

> The series a statistical office chooses to prepare and publish exercise a subtle and pervasive and lasting influence on political, social and economic development. This is why the apparently dull and minor subject of statistical policy is of crucial importance.
>
> (Seers, 1975, p.3)

There has to be a theory of social reporting (Johansson, 1976) designed to produced indicators which are relevant for human development (Miles, 1985).

13.1 A FUNCTIONING SYSTEM OF SOCIAL STATISTICS

Several 'sets' of indicators have been proposed for monitoring development and progress over the last 25 years (for example,

UNRISD, 1964; McGranahan et al, 1972). Stewart's treatment in AwHF is taken as the focus here as it is both comprehensive and recent.

Stewart (1987) suggests the following features of an 'ideal' child monitoring system:

(a) Data to be available regularly and speedily.

(b) Provision of indicators of the *status of the population* at large and *of vulnerable groups,* broken down by major socio-economic category and by region, to record how vulnerable groups are being affected by changing economic circumstances and by policies.

(c) Provision of indicators of the *immediate* as well as *underlying causes* of the changing status of the various groups.

(d) A well-functioning system for the *timely reporting, aggregation, analysis,* and *diffusion* of the information collected.

(AwHF, Chap.14, pp.259)

All of these are very important, as she demonstrates, and the discussion below is intended only to draw attention to some of the difficulties which need to be faced before an 'ideal' child monitoring system can be developed.

(a) *Regularity and speed*

It has been recognised for many years now that the (official) statistics available to monitor human welfare status are badly deficient in most countries (OECD, 1970; McGranahan et al, 1972; UNESCO, 1979; UNRISD, 1977). This is due as much to a bureaucratic concentration on the development and maintenance of existing systems of administrative statistics as to any (intellectual or political) reluctance to consider what kind of measures would be most appropriate for monitoring human welfare status.

Whatever the principal cause, however, the deficiencies of the official data are not easy to remedy.

Stewart (1987) comments that, for each of the ten country case studies in UNICEF's study of the impact of recession, there is 'a considerable amount of bitty data' and that 'with a big effort it was possible to arrive at a description and diagnosis of the changing situation of vulnerable groups *which is, probably, pretty reliable*' (AwHF, 1987, Chap.14, p.261, my emphasis). The companion volume to AwHF (Cornia, Jolly and Stewart, 1988) provides an impressive set of ten pictures of the Third World in Decline; but the uniformity of the picture is, in fact, rather suspicious. It is as if data are presented in order to *demonstrate a case* for the Third World in Decline rather than with a concern to present what is often a confusing panorama. As for the town drunk leaning against the lampost when returning home at night, statistics have been used for support rather than for illumination.

It is worth recalling Carlson's conclusion about population data after reviewing data from 52 selected developing countries:

> given the limited potential of measuring infant mortality trends on an annual basis, worldwide progress in reducing infant mortality could meaningfully be reported only once every 3 or 4 years.
>
> (Carlson, 1985)

In other words, whilst rapid feedback is important, so is precision. If we demand that a statistical system be able to monitor sensitively the fine detail of changes, we are likely to overlook the biases and distortions due to inadequate data collection procedures. There is, of course, a danger in over-emphasising the difficulties of data collection and our ignorance, but too many recent publications have erred in the opposite direction (e.g. de Kadt, 1989).

(b) *Status indicators*

Stewart, of course, was only concerned with status indicators for children. She proposed the following list:

1. Prime indicators of health and nutritional status are: (a) Infant mortality rates (b) Child death rates (c) Indicators of nutritional status for the under-5s* (d) Low birth weights* (e) Indicators of morbidity (disease prevalence and incidence).

2. Indicators of educational status are: (a) Literacy levels (b) Primary school completion rates (c) Drop out rates* (d) Repetition rates.

3. Additional indicators of child welfare are: (a) Rates of child labour (b) Number of street children*.

(The asterisk indicates that the indicators will show deterioration in a short time frame, and are therefore especially relevant for monitoring adjustment.)

(Stewart, AwHF, Chap.14, pp.261–2)

Data for many of these indicators have been presented in earlier chapters. We have also demonstrated the difficulty of accurate collection of many of the educational, health and nutritional data. Assuming, however, that these difficulties can be overcome, the proposed list is an interesting commentary on the claim that statistical series can be fitted into a causal framework relating adjustment policies to the impact upon children. For some of the suggested indicators might be *more* appropriate for adults. For example, low birth weight rates are mostly used as indicators of the health and nutritional status of women of child-bearing age (Sterky and Mellander, 1973; Tanner, 1982), rather than as indicators of the child's own status; indicators of morbidity are clearly relevant for both adults and children, but certain conditions and diseases are life threatening for children but not for adults, and vice versa; and literacy levels are, surely, more appropriate as indicators of adult status rather than of child status.

Of course, in the present context, we are concerned not only with children but with adults as well, so that all these indicators are relevant. The issue is whether they should be interpreted as a *direct* commentary upon child status. In certain circumstances, the promulgation of too definitive a framework might lead to inappropriate policy recommendations.

Other indicators which are specific to adults' well-being are:

Health and nutritional status

- height relative to average height of tallest 10% or of wealthiest group in society

- indicators of morbidity (already included)
- mothers giving birth to low birth-weight children (already included)
- adult mortality rates (adjusted for age and sex distribution).

Educational status
- literacy levels (already included)
- primary school completion levels (already included).

Economic security and welfare
- adequate resources
- numbers of dependent children.

Participation in community
- crucial but only sensibly measurable at each local level. Indices have been developed for use in specific community projects (see next chapter).

Finally, there should be some overall sense of demographic trends. For example, it is estimated that almost three-quarters of the increase in the population aged 65 and over by the year 2025 will occur in developing areas of the world. The increases are particularly marked in developing countries. For example, in Nigeria, the population aged 60 and over is projected to increase from 1.3 million in 1950 to 16.0 million by 2025, whilst the increase in the USA is relatively much smaller, from 18.5 million in 1950 to 67.3 million in 2025 (Kalache, 1986).

These status indicators, to be useful, need to be disaggregated in various ways. Rather obviously, for indicators to be useful to the local community, data have to be available on that level. More generally, the concern with the status of particular 'vulnerable' groups means that the data need to be available for each of those groups. For example, one might want to compare the following health-related indicators for boys and girls:

- immunisation coverage for boys and girls
- PHC clinic attendance records sampled to give proportion of boys and girls seen
- nutritional status of boys and girls by age groups
- girls and boys in school by level.

It should be emphasised that, from a basic needs perspective, the issue is not relative inequality as such, but the lower and unacceptable status of certain groups. Some of the ratio measures proposed for inequalities in health—usually in developed countries—recall angels dancing on the head of a pin rather than information that can be used as a basis for policy recommendations. The emphasis should be on simplicity as in the above examples.

(c) *Causal indicators, process and input indicators*

In AwHF, the exposition by Mosley and Chen (1984) is postulated as a model linking process and input variables to changes in status. Stewart suggests choosing only a small subset of indicators; those which

(1) are of the greatest importance—in magnitude—in determining child status;

(2) may be amenable to special policies for the protection of vulnerable groups; and

(3) are affected by changes in the economic environment and macro adjustment policies.

The last criterion is clearly important from the perspective of macro-economists advising UNICEF; it is less clear that it is the most important in any absolute sense. The second criterion ensures policy-relevance. But the first is optimistic: we simply don't know enough to choose which indicators are most likely to reflect crucial changes.

For example, Stewart's choice of process indicators jumbles up 'behavioural' indicators with those effective only at a community level. Thus, on what basis are prevalence of breastfeeding, distribution of oral rehydration, immunisation level, availability of potable water, health service access rate, and primary school enrolment rate put on the same level? Whilst most are 'behavioural' and informed by culture, some are entirely independent of the individual, such as the availability of potable water, the distribution of oral rehydration and—mostly—immunisation levels. This does not make for clarity.

Her emphasis on the importance of monitoring change is, of course, a central focus in this book. But her particular concern with changes consequent upon economic recession, adjustment and policy interventions, is restrictive: we are concerned with any change in basic needs status.

Her choice of input indicators is much more contentious. The focus on real incomes and real government expenditures would be almost irrelevant in some subsistence economies. This is recognised in earlier chapters of AwHF (see Cornia, 1987, p.26)—and in the chapter discussed here—by the acknowledgement that 'real income data are often deficient'. Stewart recommends using 'other, more accessible, data on basic food prices, levels of money income or expenditure in money terms, and employment and unemployment' (Stewart, AwHF, Chap.14, p.263).

More sensitive and useful indicators can be developed, but they depend on the particular context. Whilst we might all agree on the kinds of things that ought to be measured, the precise definitions of indicators and the importance attached to specific data series will differ. The discussion in the text has provided several illustrations of this: for there are debates about the relative importance of the expansion of adult education and of primary schools for literacy, or of stunting and wasting, or of the appropriate form of irrigation, and these debates will be reflected in the kinds of indicator we generate.

At the same time, there are structural conditions which affect the possibility of making progress towards the attainment of basic needs. This has arisen at various points in the text: for example, the importance of changes in ecology and the environment, probably out of the control of most African populations, has been mentioned (see Chapters 4, 5 and 6); the relative accessibility of ethnomedical practitioners and of (Western) primary health care and the resource base for adult education depend upon national and international policies and provision (see Chapters 7 and 9); and we must also not forget the actual and potential impact of war (see Chapter 11).

As with the status indicators, it is important to devise indicators of inequitable state inputs. Thus we would want to monitor:

- the relative proportion of educational expenditure on the different levels of education;

- the relative proportions of health care expenditure on primary health care or on the hospital system.

Similarly, we would want to compare conditions between rural and urban areas and between men and women. As MacCormack (1988) comments:

> a dynamic historical perspective would add weight to any analysis, but how is one to bridge the gap between inadequate, male-based statistics and informants who are very vague about the past?

There can be no universal blueprint. For the form in which data should be aggregated in order to best serve a basic-needs oriented local development policy, will depend on the precise choice of priorities made by the community. For example, different preferred household structures will lead to different kinds of data being collected and combined in different ways. Whichever data series are chosen, they should, once again, be disaggregated to the smallest possible unit.

(d) *A well-functioning system to analyse and give feedback on the data collected*

Stewart cites this as one of the major stumbling blocks; developing country statisticians could reasonably reply that much of their time is occupied in completing regular questionnaires from the international agencies.

Stewart is correct in pointing to the organisation of data collection and the publication of the results as 'one of the most difficult tasks' (AwHF, Chap.14, p.264). It was emphasised at a conference on *Statistical Policy in Less-Developed Countries* held at the Institute of Development Studies 10 years ago (Dasgupta and Seers, 1979); it cannot be repeated too often.

There is, however, a question as to the appropriate level of analysis and discrimination. The preference here is for this structure to be as close as possible to the community providing the data. Whilst the attempts by UNRISD to develop a local area monitoring system have not spread, the general approach is correct (see Chapter 14). Officials record information about and from villagers and then collate the data in a form for onward transfer; they should also be able to provide a minimum interpretation back to the community, on the basis of their report, without waiting for 'the Ministry'. Lourie (1987) also comments that the studies and surveys which do exist of the learning process and of motivation 'need to be published and disseminated' (cf Lourie, 1987). They also need to be synthesised.

There are, of course, many conditions for which a local response is not adequate. Whilst a national surveillance system such as that of Botswana or Indonesia is ideal, it cannot always be replicated, or, if it could in principle, there are frequently practical obstacles. In this kind of situation, it is worth investigating the possibility of obtaining an overall view by other methods.

13.2 SURVEILLANCE THROUGH SURVEY

For many (Wunsch, 1983), where there are no existing sources of data, an integrated approach through a multi-visit survey is the answer. The World Bank, through its *Living Standards Measurement Study,* has been promoting household surveys for over a decade. One is entitled to suspect their motives: a household survey may be the most cost-effective way of obtaining information for social control purposes; compare an assessment of the OECD social indicator programme (Anon. 1979).

Being charitable and leaving those suspicions to one side, the first question is whether they are practicable? They depend upon an adequate infrastructure, well-structured questionnaires, well-trained staff and properly monitored fieldwork. Several reviewers (Carlson, 1985; Nordberg, 1986) are doubtful that this capacity can be generated in the short term.

Second, they depend, crucially, upon a sampling frame. Bondestam, quoting from instructions given to enumerators in Ethiopia in 1968, provides a cautionary tale:

> The first stage sampling will consist of selecting two subdivisions with probability proportional to their administrative population counts (i.e. proportional to the

> hopefully true population), *or some other suitable measure of size if available, otherwise with equal probability.*
>
> (taken from Bondestam, 1973, p.6, his emphasis)

The review of population data (Chapter 3 above) suggests that little has changed since then.

Third, will the answers be reliable? Before modern fertility surveys were first fielded in the United States, it was widely predicted that respondents' modesty, embarrassment, etc. would invalidate the responses. It was later triumphantly reported . . . that the apprehension was unfounded: surveys found that American women were far more reluctant to reveal, say, family income than details about 'intimate behaviour'.

Bleek (1987) asks 'Are things different in Ghana? First, respondents who are *not* reluctant may still lie: second, surveys, with guaranteed anonymity, *are* a familiar cultural practice in the United States but not in Ghana.' Even anthropological knowledge is predominantly based on what people *say* they do, not on what researchers *see* them doing. As a Tiv informant reported:

> When I read what the white man has written of our customs, I laugh, for it is the custom of our people to lie as a matter of course to outsiders, especially the white man. We ask, 'Why does he want to know such personal things about us?'
>
> (A Tiv informant, quoted in Salamone, 1977)

Lucas (1982) in reviewing Casley and Dury (1981), brings a note of realism. He points to

> the steady growth of 'data graveyards' . . . largely attributable to a wildly optimistic view of what probability sample surveys can achieve. . . . If the aim is to 'find out about' a given situation or process, the probability sample survey is often the least useful approach.

13.3 RAPID RURAL APPRAISAL

In the absence of a functioning statistical system and when a survey is not seen as a plausible option because of resource or time constraints, there often seems to be no alternative to the 'expert appraisal'. But this has produced bizarre results: in a manual for assessing rural needs, Ashe (1979) warns of an experience when 'once the jeeps needed for transporting the interviewers were recalled during the few precious months of the dry season'(p.26). Given these and many other known biases of rural development tourism (Chambers, 1983), various techniques of rapid rural appraisal have been promoted.

Collinson (1981), working for CIMMYT, suggested grouping or zoning farmers into homogenous sub-groups, evaluating local circumstances, a rapid description and appraisal, and a verification survey. Hildebrand (1981), writing for ICTA, has developed an ingenious and quick 'technology generating system' involving a field trip by five social scientists paired together with five agricultural scientists who spend a week discussing with farmers in different pairings each day. At the end of a week, the many three-cornered discussions have produced proposals for improved farm practice.

It is often argued that a rapid assessment by an experienced observer could replace big statistical surveys which may take years to grind through their long agonies and come to the same conclusion (e.g. Chambers, 1983, p.65). But often, we only know *which* of the many 'experienced observers' to believe after we have done the grinding! More important, the reliance on 'wise men' pushes the promotion of local data collection and monitoring into the background.

Chambers also describes the work of Senaratne (1978) whose team of ten graduates each studied a village in different regions of Sri Lanka to provide 'a window into their respective regions' (p.5). The researchers and their institutions could then be used to respond 'off the cuff, within a day or two, a week at the outside [to] planners' to problems, such as 'the failure of incentives and the unpredictability of peasant response to urban logic' (ibid. p.4). He recounts how his team were able to provide 'a much needed correction in the form of a micro perspective' (ibid. p.9).

This is obviously an improvement on the experienced observer: but the 'representativeness' of the graduate observers is obviously crucial and the subordination of knowledge to the artificial imperatives of a planning cycle is objectionable.

13.4 AN EXCESS OF ESTIMATES, A DATA DROUGHT

Finally, the demand for data sometimes seems never ending. Where, one might reasonably ask, does it stop?

It has been recognised for some time, at least by 'decision-makers', that there is a problem of information overload which needs to be reduced through a focus on *relevant* items and supporting data. This was, precisely, one of the motivations for the 'social indicator movement' which focused on the problem of selecting a small set of data series.

The issue of whether a data set is adequate or appropriate is vast:

> it touches on the fields of philosophy of social science, including both pragmatic/sociological accounts of the construction and development of theories and the formulation of decision analysis, on the history of the development of scientific disciplines and writing on science policy, as well as on accounts of the design and funding of research.
>
> (Carr-Hill, 1987, p.762)

The fundamental point which should be self-evident is that the collection of data is not an end in itself: it ought to be collected to answer some questions. But there are considerable pressures to extend the nature and range of data collected, including the growth of research specialisations which have meant the generation of new sets of questions (however trivial). Second, the spreading functions of the (international) state implies an extension of administrative activity and therefore the generation of extensive data bases.

Moreover, in a world of extensive computer power and gigantism, where there are rapidly increasing possibilities of collecting and storing large amounts of data, both qualitative and quantitative—there seems no *a priori* reason to impose constraints or limits.

It is, of course, true that the request for further data or further research is often a means of delaying positive social action. At the same time, it is important to recognise that the possibilities of gigantism do not obviate the need to think. Doubtful evidence proliferates whilst crucial data are not collected.

Stewart's own arguments illustrate these points. Discussing data from Ghana, she says 'official estimates based on fertility surveys put the IMR at around 70 per 1000 at the end of the 1970s. However, estimates based on life tables suggest considerably higher rates, perhaps 120' (AwHF, 1988, Chap.14, p.260). The context implies that there has been a substantial rise in the IMR over the last 10 years. In fact, the estimates from the life tables are based on 1960s data. If there is any inference to be drawn, it is that there has been a substantial *drop* in the IMR over the 1960s and 1970s; we can say *nothing* about the 1980s.

The frequent claim in AwHF that 'complete agnosticism and inaction pending the collection of better data is not justified' (p.260) remains strange: are they suggesting that high rates of IMR, low rates of literacy, etc. are tolerable so long as they are not getting worse? This fixation with arithmetical growth as good, stability or decrease as bad, is part of our problem in the North (Schumacher, 1973), not part of their solution in the South.

No-one would dispute that social conditions in much of Africa are appalling, and that every effort, both national and international, should be made to improve them. But global forecasts of further doom and gloom from outside based on macro-estimates of unknown reliability are of little help in formulating appropriate policies. In the short- and probably medium-term, it would be better to devote some statistical resources to building up a picture based on reliable evidence from local studies, rather than to continue to proliferate international guesstimates.

In the long term, the development of a comprehensive national statistical framework could, in principle, provide appropriate data. But disputes over what is an appropriate pattern of growth mean that for the foreseeable future, the elements of such a system would be imposed from the centre. In the short term, local-level monitoring with community participation is a realistic and potentially more democratic approach, and that is the subject of the next chapter.

14 Monitoring basic needs at the local level

The purpose of this chapter is to examine the possibilities of monitoring distance from and progress towards 'meeting basic needs'at the local level. On the basis of the critique of the statistical evidence presented in the body of the book a number of basic principles can be proposed and these are elaborated in Section 14.1. An 'ideal' system can be specified, quite easily, *on paper;* but that specification raises a number of issues about aggregation and about the nature of the indicators required which are discussed in Section 14.2. Section 14.3 discusses the development of local level monitoring over the last thirty years, and the final section considers the problems of introducing community control over this (or any) statistical system.

14.1 SOME BASIC PRINCIPLES OF INDICATOR CONSTRUCTION FOR DEMOCRATIC MONITORING

First, data are *produced* not *collected:* they depend on underlying *concepts* and on a *system* of processing in which different agents have different interests and tasks. Equally, the historical and social context of measurement is important: for example, the ready access of quantitative measures and techniques for aggregates of things has dominated the way in which statistical systems have developed. In sum, measurement work and statistical work are not socially or theoretically autonomous activities.

Consequently, the activity of measurement itself is a potential agent for change. Indeed, the potential of data measurement to influence policy often leads to its suppression, even when no-one disagrees about the concepts or definitions. For example, Gordon (1979) gives a graphic account of her experiences as Director of the Bawku Applied Nutrition Programme in Ghana over a five-year period. She shows how information had to be used in a political way to arouse public opinion to put pressure on leaders, etc. She concludes, ruefully, that 'conventionally trained nutritionists and doctors are not always skilled in presenting their case to the right people' (Gordon, 1979, p.8). We also have to recognise the political role of information.

Second, everyone might agree that a particular phenomenon is worth measuring, but the actual indicator chosen would vary according to the clientele. Consider, for example, school attendance, which everyone wants to know something about. The government planner, typically, will be interested in enrolment, repeater and drop-out ratios, pupil–teacher ratios, construction costs and so on; people would be more interested in access to different types of educational facilities, what they can learn in different 'institutional' contexts (it need not, of course, be a building, or even a formal programme): and concerned pedagogues in the type of resources that are needed to impart the type of knowledge which is socially useful.

Third, the same indicator can be *used* in various ways. Thus, an indicator of individual well-being may reflect a current *condition,* membership of a *risk* group, or a *trend* in the causative factors. Accordingly,

> a change in the use of an indicator from, for example, the diagnosis and treatment of malnutrition in the individual, to the quantifying of risk for families or communities, or to the analysis of trends and changes, requires a change in definition and significance of that indicator. This dependence raises fundamental questions about the procedure for defining indicators, about who should be involved in the process, and about the role and objectives of research.
>
> (Dowler et al, 1982, pp. 101–2).

In general one must be very wary of how an index is used, as opposed to how it was developed.

Finally, since social change can only be carried out by people, measures and statistical activities should be on the human level and, as far as possible, organised around their possibilities for change. In principle, this means that we have to understand how people develop their own goals in their social environment and how they develop their own measurement criteria. In practical terms, many authors have remarked that the validity of data depends upon the extent to which the informant understands and agrees with the motivations and objectives of those collecting the data, and at least consents to the use to which the data will be put. Even this pragmatic approach imposes severe constraints on the viability of surveys which are centrally designed and executed.

A corollary is that measures and statistical procedures should be transparent. That is, although it would be silly for everyone to become a statistician overnight, however sophisticated the procedures used (and I would usually question their utility), the assumptions, and the results and the consequences of varying the assumptions, should be clear to everyone. The obvious example here, is the ease with which an economic statistician slips from talking about economic welfare to measuring GNP *per capita,* without explaining the limitations of using the latter as a proxy for the former.

14.2 AN APPROPRIATE LOCAL INFORMATION SYSTEM

The basic proposal is not, in principle, complex, assuming agreement on the political level about what are minimum standards. It would include the following:

(1) Agreement on the political level about what are minimum standards and about statistical specification of these standards. The same people, of course, might be involved in both the political debate and the technical development.
(2) An accurate picture of the present situation. This is not easy, as exemplified in this book. But the information needs to be presented in a form which is digestible but not pre-digested (already interpreted according to a particular schema). Unfortunately, present statistical skills are not oriented towards the task of presentation: it is not only a task of instigating numeracy among the non-numerate; it is equally important for the data manipulator to learn how to communicate.
(3) A documentation of appropriate resources. This is by far the most difficult because of the lack of substantiated theory as to what kind of resources (of land, labour and capital) are most effective

> with different social organisations in attaining which levels of welfare for individuals. We have a general idea as to which resources are necessary, but not those which are sufficient to attain desired ends.

Overall, the statistical system would resemble more an inventory of opportunities for activities and of possibilities for attainment of basic needs, than a recording of current stocks and flows of products and services.

14.2.1 The nature of the data

The most appropriate form of data collection will vary. Thus, finding out what are people's objectives is, at best, organised collectively. Relevant background data would be made available, and new data might be required; but the appropriate method cannot be decided in advance. Even in a less than ideal system, I would envisage that informal appraisal, inspection, or the interviewing of 'key' persons would be more appropriate than an attitude survey.

There are two difficulties with the traditional survey approach: first, the answers to questions of the form 'which of the following do you think are the most important? ...' when asked by a project team with a specific interest, are almost certainly biased. For example, Faniran (1986) reported on a survey of rural households' perception of water quality in three rural communities, one around Ibadan, the other in Oyo state, and the third around Ilorian. When asked, he not unnaturally found that people gave highest priority to the provision of potable water among their preferred amenities: and 80% gave water as first and second choice (see Figure 14.1).

Second, the answers to general questions about objectives and political strategies for attaining them are open to a wide variety of interpretations. Consider, for example, the assessment of whether or not communities really have control over the decisions which affect their daily life. People usually do have quite clear perceptions about the extent to which they have control over their daily lives although their perceptions may not, of course, tally with those of the researcher. But they are conditioned, and sometimes informed, by the external constraints upon them, and despite the sophistication of the various scales which have been developed by social psychologists purporting to measure autonomy, control and fatalism, these are related to the individual and not to their social context nor to the collectivity which is the issue here. Moreover, there is no obvious way in which communities can express their lack of control other than by affirming it—often in very banal ways (although a modest proposal is annexed to this chapter).

Figure 14.1 Amenity preferences: Ibadan fieldwork, 1980

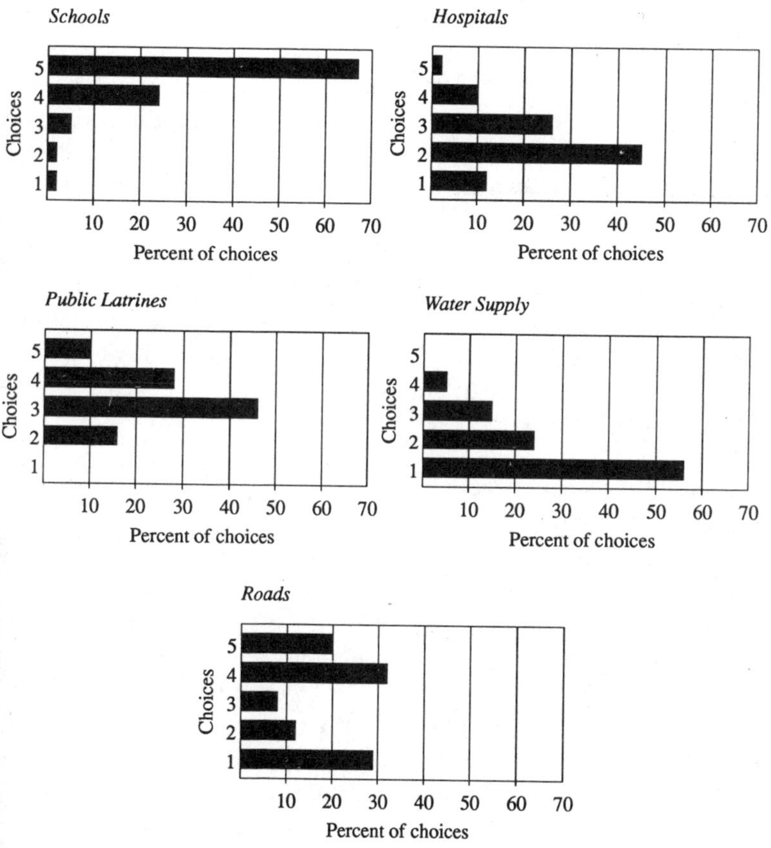

We can be more specific with the next two stages. An assessment of the present situation requires a household survey carefully designed at the local level. An informal appraisal could be wildly erroneous, and administrative data are likely to be systematically biased. Finally, an inventory of existing and potential resources would basically rely on collective discussion at a local level supplemented by household survey data. The only role for administrative records would be in providing background data on the existing situation and for an inventory of possibilities in respect of the more macro objectives such as the equalisation of disparities between population groups.

Much of the data required by such a statistical system need not be very sophisticated. Far too much effort is often invested in both developing and developed countries to obtain precise numerical information about a state of affairs where nominal data would do. For example, it is interesting to know how well someone can cook, but what is important is that we will not be poisoned by what we eat. Similarly, the well-known tendency for the qualifications required for a given occupation to be upgraded over time (Dore, 1976) is often accompanied by an increasing degree of differentiation in the level of qualifications obtained and therefore in the complexity of administrative records. Yet, all we really want to know is whether the person can do the job or not.

14.2.2 The problem of aggregation

When such a system is spelt out in detail, it will appear sensible to aggregate and compare according to some common denominator (whether in terms of resources such as labour or capital, or at an intermediate level in terms of particular levels of goods and services). The mistake which has been made only too often is to aggregate too far, too fast. For, although the physical quantities (whether of land, labour and capital, or of goods and services) *can* be converted into a common monetary or other unit and then aggregated, *this* conversion *assumes* a whole structure of production, distribution and exchange. It is therefore completely illegitimate to suppose that this aggregation has any meaning outside that particular structure. A more homely (North) example might help here. With fiscal harmonisation of the EEC due in 1992, the problem of harmonising government subsidies to physical and social infrastructure has arisen. In turn, this requires ways of assessing the quality of services that are provided. How do you trade off, for example, the exceptional convenience of the Paris Metro as compared to the London Underground against the (relative) lack of violence on the latter? The answer is that those kinds of issues have to be decided not by the parachuted-in social scientist, but as part of a democratic political process.

Obviously, it is sensible to bring together and compare findings from surveys in different areas (Edingbola et al, 1986) but it does not follow that the results should be aggregated to present an overall picture. For the particular mode of aggregation—including 'simple' addition—will benefit some groups and disadvantage others. Compromises are made in the process of decision-making, depending on the relative power of different groups. For a *post-hoc* analyst, these compromises imply a mode of aggregation and a set of weights; but they cannot be taken as the appropriate basis for future decision-making. The pressure to substitute a technical form of appraisal (e.g. cost-benefit analysis) for the essentially political process of decision-making must be resisted.

14.3 LAY REPORTING AND LOCAL-LEVEL MONITORING

Attempts to derive monitoring methods which are more appropriate on a local level are not new. In the mid 1950s the WHO explored ways of making use of data collected by non-medical personnel for studying crude cause of death (Uemura, 1988). But these attempts were overtaken by the emphasis on the technical aspects of computerisation. This led to a relative lack of attention to ensuring adequate quality in source data, to the practicalities and difficulties of collecting and preparing data for input, and to the capacity of health managers and decision makers to use the output.

In the 1970s UNRISD set up Development Monitoring Systems (DMS) at the local level (McGranahan et al, 1972). Scott (1988) draws on the experience in the Indian state of Kerala, to illustrate the possibilities and problems, where three of the initial 12 socio-economic observation areas are still functioning ten years later. Local level staff have been paid and trained to collect the data on a regular basis. This is not always easy: 'even one of the trained DMS interviewers read the height on the wrong side of the measuring rod for some time' (Scott, 1988, p.30).

However, although the data were intended for local use, local participation was virtually nil. Interpretation of statistical data always requires care: but the analysis of the causes of a moderate change in, say, infant mortality data or of a shift in the height-weight patterns (see Table 14.1) is complex. Even Scott is unable to explain what has happened despite substantial changes in IMRs and in indices of height-for-age and weight-for-age, partly because of the difficulty of interpreting movements on small rates, and partly because of the complexity of the inter-relations. At the policy level, people, used to relying on the state, did not see how the information could be used, as there is no provision for health in the *panchayat* budget. Nevertheless, a large mass of interesting data has been collected and should be analysed in detail together with the local community.

Table 14.1 Changes in infant mortality and in standardised weight for height

	Infant mortality Communities			*Percentages of children with 2 or more standard deviations below the median in community C*	
	A	*B*	*C*	*Height for age*	*Weight for height*
1981/82	26	47	24	42	29
1982/83	24	30	24	39	22
1983/84	17	20	42	33	16

Source: Scott, 1988.

Kirsch (1988) discusses the problem of assessing the effectiveness of the Expanded Programme of Immunisation (EPI). Routine global or national reporting of measles, poliomyelitis and tetanus suggests that EPI has had only limited impact on the incidence of the target diseases. Because country- and local-level reports suggested that there had been a considerable impact, the EPI also spawned a Local Area Monitoring Project (LAM) to supplement routine disease-reporting systems with sentinel site reporting.

In most cases, the sentinel sites were hospitals. The data presented by Kirsch (1988) suggest that EPI has had considerable impact. But whilst hospital data will tend to be of better quality and more reliable, there is the perennial problem of representativeness and of changes in the population served.

These problems are pervasive. In some cases, very simple rules appear to have been ignored. For example, Matomara (1989) reports on a survey conducted in Kenyan villages selected as part of a PHC programme. The data in Table 14.2 look convincing, until one begins to wonder about the inverse relationship between the number of villages surveyed and the numbers of children weighed!

Table 14.2 Nutritional status of under 5s as the programme area in 1982-85 using weight-for-age measurements (% of Harvard standard)

IMR		*Villages surveyed*	*Under 5s weighed*	*80% or more (%)*	*60% to 80% (%)*	*60% or less (%)*
161	1982a	3	1,049	57	33	10
101	1983a	9	2,469	62	29	9
121	1984b	9	512	61	37	2
85	1985b	13	483	41	58	1

a House-to-house survey – all under 5s found at home were weighed
b Under 5s gathered around the index household were weighed

Source: Matomara (1989).

Moreover, whilst many instruments for monitoring change on the local level have been devised, they are not always easy to interpret. The classic example is the measurement of arm circumference as part of growth monitoring. Even something very simple like monitoring the extent to which a community is acquiring latrines is not easy (Smith, 1988).

In AwHF, Stewart draws on evidence from a wide range of village studies and, in particular, on the birthweight data collected in Ghana by the Catholic Relief Services as a by-product of their feeding programmes in Ghanaian villages. It is obviously crucial in the absence of national data to collate this kind of data into as coherent a picture as possible. But the temptation to make a definitive pronouncement about trends, without very careful examination of possible variations in the quality of data and in reporting procedures over time, ought to be resisted. Moreover, it is to be hoped that these data were also presented to the villages concerned.

Indeed, the interest of the local community in the data must be recognised as paramount (see inset). There are three ways in which poor rural people can benefit from appraisal and research,

> the direct operational use of data; the changes in outsider's awareness, knowledge and understanding, leading subsequently to changes in their behaviour; and the enhanced awareness and capability of the rural poor themselves.
>
> (Chambers, 1983)

It has to be demonstrated that the community will benefit in at least one of these ways.

Surveillance of leprosy in Zaire

Another example from the field of leprosy surveillance illustrates the difficulty of 'involving the community'. Because of a high level of prevalence, a prospective incidence study was started in Yalisambo, Northern Zaire, in 1984. The study involved the annual examination of the total population, but of the 1,582 persons seen in 1984, only 833 were willing to participate in 1985 (55%). Mwanasangezi-bin-Moussa and Groenen (1987) interviewed 100 of the absentees. Their main criticism, cited by 92% as their reason for not showing up in 1985, was the lack of treatment. The survey team was well aware of the adage—no survey without service—and had provided several services, but these were not seen as appropriate by the population to the health problems in the area.

The development of a comprehensive lay reporting system will not always follow the same structure as a centrally devised system. The technical criteria of a 'good' surveillance system—such as sensitivity, specificity, representativeness, timeliness, simplicity, flexibility and acceptability—are obviously desirable. But the extent to which they can be met will be limited: increasing the sensitivity of a system to detect a greater proportion of a health event may improve representativeness and usefulness, but it also increases the cost and leads to more reporting of false positives (Thacker et al, 1988); second, it is crucially important to involve local people at all stages of planning and execution in order to obtain good quality data which may mitigate against the fulfilment of technical criteria. For whilst the perspectives of medical professionals and social scientists

> may help to structure and therefore 'see' empirical data which is not visible to the worker ... worker subjectivity, although containing false impressions, contains the seeds of empirical data and new conceptual starting points ... worker participation enhances the validity of collected data
>
> (Myers, 1985, cited in Thacker et al, 1988)

This is the problem for the next section.

14.4 COMMUNITY-BASED PARTICIPATORY APPROACHES

WHO reports community participation in the control of the spread of malaria through environmental control, larviciding and home spraying. In four other countries, communities have participated in trials to test the effectiveness and public acceptance of the use of mosquito coils and insecticide-impregnated bed nets. They also report the use of traps to control tsetse fly: several thousand traps are now in use in Angola, Congo, Cote d'Ivoire and Uganda. A report of a programme in five villages of the Congo shows how dramatic reductions in the tsetse fly were achieved (Gouteux et al, 1987). Village enthusiasm depends more on the level of tsetse fly than on the number of cases.

The word 'community' is used in a wide variety of ways. Midgley suggests that community has two main meanings in the development literature. The definition most used by those concerned with the *delivery* of (basic) services is the group of people living in a defined area (assumed to be sharing the same basic values and organisations). The more realistic definition refers to a group of people sharing the same basic interests or problems as the above example shows.

'Participation', similarly, has been used in a wide variety of ways, but there is the same basic contrast between the passive spectator ('weak' participation) and the issues of control and power ('strong' participation).

Rifkin et al (1988) point to three characteristics common to all definitions of strong participation. First, participation must be *active:* the purchase or receipt of services does not constitute participation. Second, participation involves *choice:* the right and responsibility to control, have power over, the decisions which affect their lives. Third, their choice must have the possibility of being *effective:* mechanisms must exist or can be created so that their choice can be implemented. ACE (an active effective choice) rather than PAP (passive acceptance of poverty).

None of this is easy:

> The social dimension of catalysis is ... elusive. Villagers readily participate in development projects but because administration is unable to respond rapidly and because of the organizational problems in the village that we have described, participation is often frustrating.
>
> (Feachem, 1980)

The weakness of village institutions contributes to shortages of publicly available resources. Villages in Africa do not usually have the power—or sanctions—to raise funds on a regular basis for maintenance. Whilst voluntary contributions in cash or labour may be easy enough to mobilise for a specific occasion, such as building of a new supply, to maintain it on a voluntary basis does not usually work.

On the basis of an analysis of over 100 case studies, Rifkin (1988) identifies six dimensions where the strength of participation can vary: needs assessment, leadership, organisation, resource mobilisation, management, and focus on the poor. Her argument is convincing but it should be emphasised that, whilst useful suggestions for monitoring participation—or any other aspect of welfare—can be brought from outside, the extent of participation can only satisfactorily be assessed by those who are meant to be participating! Thus Rifkin et al cite a study in Nepal using their framework of process indicators where, apparently, community involvement varied considerably between the villages. Whilst there is no reason to doubt the data, it appears that a uniform scale has been imposed by the researcher, rather than being agreed between (representatives of) the villagers.

Moreover, what counts as salient will vary over time: this is well illustrated by the Saradidi project (see Kaseje and Sempebura, 1989), where villages were asked what they thought were the priority problems at a seven-year interval. There is a shift in the perceived problems if one believes the two lists (see Table 14.3): the emphasis in 1979–80 is on death and material deprivation; the emphasis in 1986 is on management capability.

Table 14.3 Saradidi: priority problems

Priorities in 1979-80	*Priorities in 1986*
• Water	• Water
• Disease (e.g. malaria, measles, malnutrition, diarrhoea and vomiting)	• Low agricultural production
• Lack of health facilities	• Ineffective village leadership
• Too many and too frequent births	• Lack of viable income-generating activities
• High mortality rates, especially infants and children	• Low acceptance of family planning
• Lack of means of communication	• Measles attacking children before 9 months of age
• Poor agricultural production	• Illiteracy among adults
• Lack of knowledge	• Many school drop-outs due to school fees
• Poverty	• Lack of continuing education and technical facilities
• Lack of secondary schools	

Source: Kaseje and Sempebura (1989).

Lourie (1987) claims that cultural, political and social pressures—including the expectations that communities will make a material contribution—are following a demand for increased participation. The first question is whether communities can be fully involved in a monitoring process. Thus whilst simple instruments can be devised—see, for example, Smith's (1988) proposal for monitoring the acquisition of latrines—the issue is whether they are 'owned' by the community. Campbell (1988) describes the development of a household baseline survey and of water and sanitation profiles in Belize. He claims that villagers were involved at all stages, including survey design, counting the responses, and the use of the survey results for designing a local water supply and sanitation programme.

A systematic procedure for conducting such a survey is described in the context of educational planning in the Annex to this chapter.

The second crucial question is the extent to which communities have achieved any power. In another context, Piven suggests the following test of the effectiveness of a decentralisation programme:

> not merely by observing the shifts in inter-agency chains of command, or the formal procedures for 'citizen participation' or feedback, but by evaluating the actual political leverages in matters regarding the allocation of tangible resources, including the hiring and firing of personnel, which accrues to citizen groups, especially those citizen groups which have not previously been regarded as significant constituents of the agency. While such a 'test' of decentralisation may seem crude, in the turgid realms of bureaucratic policy, the simpler tests of power may be the most reliable.
>
> (Piven, 1977, p.289)

On the breadline, the issues are simpler. The poor peasant or slum dweller wants participation above all, in so far as it improves immediate consumption. More generally, given a real choice, the poor 'participant' is more likely to be interested in satisfying *consumer needs* than anything else, in the needs of the family today rather than those of the children tomorrow, and perhaps also in those of 'my' family rather than those of 'our' families.

This poses a dilemma for those promoting social participation from outside. First, given their emphasis upon emancipation, and upon creating bottom-up policies, programmes or projects with a participatory theme, they tend to concentrate on the educational and health care sector which are not always seen by the communities concerned as the most urgent priorities. Second, the political goals—the redistribution of power, structural change—are long term and do not usually offer short-term solutions to the immediate problems.

Just as there is no easy way to overcome the obstacles in the way of developing a lay monitoring system, there is no easy solution to the dilemma facing advocates of participatory approaches among poor communities.

ANNEX

Radicalising survey methodology

Freire argued:

> There is no such thing as a *neutral* educational process. Education either functions as an instrument which is used to facilitate the integration of the younger generation into the logic of the present system and bring about conformity to it, *or* it becomes the 'practice of freedom', the means by which men and women deal critically and creatively with reality and discover how to participate in the transformation of their world.
>
> (Freire, 1972, p.13)

On this basis, Freire developed his method of authentic-education for the oppressed whilst working with the peasants in north eastern Brazil. His method consisted first of discovering the basic vocabulary and living conditions of the group to be taught; then, through group dialogue, the fundamental interests of the students. They then realise that they need to know more about the world before they can act consciously to control their own lives.

The problem with Freire's method (or similar prescriptions for radical education) is that they only work *if people come to them,* whereas most people's experience of education (whether or not radical) is that the involvement and motivation by subjects of the learning process, which is crucial, cannot be assumed *ab initio*. In fact, one main reason why such methods work (as indeed they do) is because of the ideals and enthusiasm of the committed, highly skilled and motivated educators who employ them. Indeed, it is arguable that someone like Freire would be a successful educator—in terms of raising consciousness so that people can participate in the 'transformation of their world'—with almost any method.

The problem, therefore, is to develop a low-key method of awakening people's interest in the first place (the subsequent level and nature of their motivation cannot, of course, be determined in advance); a tool which will focus people's attention on the issue, without imposing counter-productive discussion on those who do not see any problem or who have no hope of effecting any change. Any approach to uninterested and unmotivated people must, *inter alia,* examine their educational experiences and the part these institutions have played in producing their immediate situation and particularly their understanding of, and reactions to, that situation. An early attempt was made by the author to use an interview/questionnaire approach as this requires a very low level of involvement on the part of the respondent and yet introduces ideas to him/her.

The difficulty is, that when people are asked their reaction to the education they have received or that they would desire for their offspring, the purpose and content of the slab of education being offered are often indeterminate. Even if made precise, there is little incentive for people to reply because they sense that the final decisions will be made elsewhere.

We can go some way towards compiling data on needs in a non-alienating and non-exploitative fashion by involving a selection of the population at each stage. In a pilot study in Brighton, England, in 1974, the following procedure generated considerable discussion about the purpose and content of educational programmes:

(a) an informal discussion with groups of individuals from the projected population, eliciting the categories in which people perceive the reality of their own lives and possible futures;
(b) a more directed semi-structured interview with the same group of individuals about the relevance of present and possible educational careers to their own lives; and
(c) a self-completion questionnaire for the population designed so as to compare the purpose and results of present formal educational systems and other forms of socialisation, with the way in which they live their own life and their hopes for improvement in its quality.

(taken from Carr-Hill, 1984)

The experience of the questionnaire suggested that it was possible for respondents to be clear and coherent about what are desirable outcomes of all kinds from all forms of education in terms of attitudes, roles and skills—and, moreover, that *everyone* is *capable* of distinguishing between different educational contexts and their effects on these outcomes for themselves.

15 Conclusion

The main objective of this study was to examine trends in social conditions in sub-Saharan Africa since the mid 1970s on the basis of a critical assessment of the available statistical data. A subsidiary purpose was to suggest ways in which existing monitoring systems might be improved.

The first draft of this book was written at a time when many saw Africa as in 'decline': apart from spectacular media coverage of famine 'caused' by drought and other 'natural' disasters, the well-publicised UNICEF study *Adjustment with a Human Face* (referred to as AwHF in the text) was only the latest in a long line of official reports from international agencies 'crying wolf'. Whilst the pronouncements of doom and gloom have been tempered in the last couple of years (see, for example, World Bank, 1989), the essential message remains the same: yet the evidential basis for these pronouncements is very weak.

The Institute of Development Studies set out their interpretation of the impact of structural adjustment policies on the basis of the wide range of studies of varying quality which were then available in 'Getting the Facts Straight' (IDS, 1985). They are right to emphasise the importance of assessing arguments and theories carefully in the light of the available evidence. But our knowledge about (trends in) the social conditions of the poor in Africa is, if anything, even more primitive: 'getting the facts straight' requires agreement both on the definition and measurement of development and progress, and on the quality of the data which are the basis for those facts.

First, the definition and measurement of development and progress. The rate of growth in GNP does not reflect the quality of the human condition either in the North or in the South. For the same kind of reason, there was little point in using net income per capita as a way of comparing social conditions across areas or between groups living in a wide variety of systems of production, distribution and exchange. On the breadline, people look for sustenance from a wide variety of sources (cf. Eicher and Baker, 1985), only some of them in cash. The human condition should be assessed directly in terms of health, learning, the opportunity for joyful participation in the community.

There have been some tentative moves in this direction with the Basic Needs Approach promoted by the ILO, which proposed that development policy should be oriented towards the provision of a certain number of specific goods and services (e.g. food, water, housing). But, in many cases, the intended policy implications of the approach have been significantly corrupted: instead of participatory control over the ends and means of community development, a variety of commercial packages have been produced often more oriented towards profit than towards the satisfaction of basic needs (Wisner, 1988). In general, more attention has been paid to the (financial) project inputs rather than to the impacts.

It is for this reason that *Adjustment with a Human Face* was welcome: precisely because it focussed on an assessment of the impact of macro-economic policies on the living standards of people. Their assessment is global, but restricted to the impact of macro-economic IMF adjustment policies; here the focus is on sub-Saharan Africa but the intention is to provide a general assessment of social trends since the mid 1970s.

15.1 THE QUALITY OF THE DATA

The assessments depend crucially upon the statistical series available. A major theme of this book has been that these are so unreliable that, whilst changes in some aggregate data series can be monitored, it is almost impossible to draw any conclusions about *per capita* social trends; and anthropological assessments are not always much more reliable. We can demonstrate widespread poverty at Independence and today; but a fundamental problem in assessing *per capita* trends is the accurate measurement of population growth. Published series of, e.g. food availability per capita or of, e.g. access to water and sanitation are based on 'guesstimated' populations. Many of the trends are assumed and constructed in Washington rather than based on empirical data collected and analysed in Africa.

The unreliability of the population data, of course, affects any assessment of *per capita* estimate. But other data series are also unreliable: the basis for assessments of food shortfalls depends, at best, upon *recorded* marketed production, and often upon inferences from import volumes; any sensible assessment of national trends is out of the question. Similarly, the assessment of actual access to a clean water supply remains a mystery. School enrolment data sometimes refer to initial, sometimes final enrolment, and can only be referred to a fixed age group with considerable difficulty; despite many attempts, the quality of schooling is still assessed in terms of inputs—such as teacher salaries or textbooks; and reliable literacy data series are non-existent. The major problems with assessing levels, let alone trends, in fertility and mortality are sufficient in themselves without trying to confront the problems of measuring morbidity; and so on.

This is not a new problem. Carr-Hill commented:

> One of the main faults with the Basic Needs approach is simply technical—the basic data which has, so far, been used is of very doubtful quality. This is not an anal concern with statistical precision—of being wrong by, say, 1 per cent or 2 per cent—but an observation that several of the data series that have been used in 'testing' such models have been chosen almost by default as the only available proxies for the real thing. At the same time, much of the data, whether or not it corresponds conceptually with the required variable, is grossly unreliable
>
> (Carr-Hill, 1978, p.127)

Not much has changed since then.

In consequence, much of the argument in Section 2 revolved around the quality of the data used for the assessments. Whilst many of the issues are specific to the particular statistical series considered, three general problems recurred.

The first general problem is ethnocentricity:

> The type of fertility research that attempts to provide social and economic explanation for fertility levels and trends has arisen almost entirely from Western quantitative sociology.
>
> The most serious distortion probably relates to the nature of the family as a social and economic unit ... in sub-Saharan Africa

> ... the nuclear family is the creation of the research worker, and further economic analysis based on such a unit is quite invalid.
>
> (Caldwell, 1977)

The second is that governments—not only in African countries—at various times, interfere with data collection and analysis, making the data very difficult to use analytically. Dasgupta and Seers (1975) suggest several ways:

(1) governments can ask statistical offices to manipulate or fabricate data. In Nigeria, both the 1963 and 1973 census were disputed (Udo, 1978, cited in Kpedekpo and Arya, 1981). It was in the interests of each state to inflate their own figures.
(2) statistical offices are 'requested' to suppress or suspend publication of inconvenient data. Obviously, political bias enters in several other ways.
(3) because of pressure from international or bilateral agencies, national statistical offices are asked to produce estimates that are neither needed by local policy-makers or analysts nor of defensible quality professionally. The World Health Organisation believes official responses to their enquiries are heavily spiced with political propaganda in some countries. For example, in Egypt the government has reported that the birth weights of children exceed 2,500 gms in 99.8% of all cases; even in Scandinavia the percentage of low birthweight babies does not fall below 4%.

Third, there are practical problems and difficulties in generating viable data. Data recorded have a strong institutional bias. But even for data emanating from official centres, practical data handling operations have a low priority. They may still be suspect. Problems of the lack of trained personnel and of communications are compounded by reluctance to respond and very slow processing of data. It is often difficult to assess even the coverage of the data, let alone their quality for purposes of comparison.

The poor quality of the data means not only that trend data are often unreliable but also that arguments about the causal factors which affect a trend on the basis of relationships observed in empirical data must be assessed very carefully.

15.2 WHAT DO WE 'KNOW'?

It would, of course, be silly to suggest that we know nothing about social conditions and trends in Africa. We know that public expenditure has stagnated and that the living standards of many of the most vocal have declined. But the focus of this book was not on state provision nor on the providers but on the experiences of the poor.

The brief summary below draws out some of the major themes of the earlier chapters, both about observed trends and about shifts in the pattern of contributory factors.

(1) *Food availability*

> Africa did experience a food crisis. The incidence of famine is proof of the most awful kind that there was a severe food crisis in several countries. But the unreliability of the data implies that researchers should re-examine with care prevailing notions of the extent and sources of the crisis at a country and regional level.
>
> (Borton and Clay, 1988, p.144)

For example, all writers agree that poor rains and drought were a significant factor in contributing to the crisis. However, there is disagreement over the relative importance of poor rains and inconsistency between accounts of their chronology. Partly this is because rainfall in Africa is highly variable in intensity both spatially and temporally so that localised drought can occur; mostly because data are almost non-existent.

Again, many authors blame continuing food crises upon unchecked population growth. In the long term and world wide, this is obviously true. Sustainable production depends upon maintaining the carrying capacity which is a pre-requisite to that production; in turn the earth's ecological carrying capacity depends upon limiting the demands made upon it by us all. But it is difficult to relate the African food crisis of the eighties to over population or unchecked population growth. For it is generally agreed (FAO, 1985a; ODI, 1985; USAID, 1986) that the countries worst hit with famine and widespread starvation by the food crisis of 1982–86 were Chad, Ethiopia, Mali, Mozambique and Sudan. None of these are or were thickly populated, even by African standards, whilst all of them but Mali were involved in a civil war at the time. Overall, Rimmer (1988) concludes 'the sign [direction] of the relationship between population growth in Africa and food supply per capita . . . is much less certain than the World Bank suggests'.

(2) *Woodfuel and water*

Accessibility to woodfuel is almost certainly deteriorating with women having to walk further to get small amounts of wood. Rapacious deforestation by international capitalism has not helped. But all that is casual observation rather than data based. There has been substantial investment in water and sanitation services in both urban and rural areas, but lack of maintenance has meant that much of the rural population have reverted to their traditional sources for water. Suggestions that women blindly conform to traditional practices in their choice of water sources are inappropriate. Whilst, because of lack of information, they might badly misjudge factors affecting health, they do give heavy weight to cleanliness and practicability, as well as to the interpersonal consequences of choosing a particular source (White, Bradley and White, 1972, p.262).

(3) *Health*

The levels of infant and child mortality have almost certainly decreased (= improved) over the last quarter of a century, although it is difficult to be precise. Recorded levels of malnutrition have always been high in Africa: they appear to have increased over this period. Assuming this is not an artefact of increased contact with marginal populations, this is probably due to the effects of commercialisation of peasant produce and of drought which have dislocated the patterns of food availability throughout much of Africa in the 1980s. It is, however, very difficult to assess exactly what is happening because of the lack of data:

> The UNICEF 'child survival and development campaign' with all its brilliant leadership, rests on a distressingly weak base of research and evaluation and UNICEF is putting distressingly little resources into improving that research base.
>
> (Bell, 1987)

Halstead et al (1985) and Mosley and Chen (1984) both draw attention to the need for careful studies of the potential of PHC and CSDR.

Information about levels of adult health and morbidity is even more sparse. The main apparent trend is the shift from infectious diseases to the pattern of chronic conditions observed in the North. Given the decline in state resources available for health care, the major debate has been over the effectiveness and practicability of cost recovery and of primary health care.

(4) *Education*

The rates of growth in educational provision and attainment registered in the 1960s and 1970s have slowed down in the 1980s. In a few cases, the rate of growth in enrolment in primary schools appears to be slower than the rate of growth of the corresponding population. Levels of literacy, which also appear to have increased substantially over this period, however, will probably continue to increase, albeit more slowly.

(5) *Inequalities*

The difficulty of assessing trends in the *per capita* satisfaction of basic needs is, of course, compounded when assessing trends in *inequality*. However, some of the signs are encouraging: for example, the appendices document—for a few countries—trends in educational provision and in health care facilities as between regions which suggest a movement towards equality. In respect of both education and health, there are also several countries where the status of women is improving, albeit agonisingly slowly.

The attention that has been focussed on drought and famine among rural populations has sometimes obscured the plight of the urban poor. Their prospects are poor because of the complexity of providing services for dense and overcrowded urban populations and data on relative incomes suggest a trend towards equality of emiseration. Finally,there is little sign of a reduction in environmental destruction or in militarisation, both of which affect the poor more than the rich.

Even these vague generalisations stretch the data to its limits. If we want to make more coherent statements about what is happening to the rural poor—or better, provide the opportunity for the rural poor to assess progress in their own communities—the development of reliable, and timely data collection procedures is crucial.

15.3 IMPROVING DATA COLLECTION

There is by now considerable agreement over what are some of the appropriate data elements of such a system, such as anthropometric data; birth weight, child and infant mortality rates; availability of food and water; and literacy and primary school attendance rates. Maine (1989) remarks on the relative neglect of maternal mortality in the 1970s and the 1980s, and the rush of interest at the end of the UN Decade for Women. Hence the necessity to agree on a coherent set of data. But these are difficult data to collect cheaply and reliably even under appropriate conditions; if coverage is only partial, it is very difficult to assess community trends. That difficulty is exacerbated by the annoying habit of using a composite indicator, such as the Physical Quality of Life Index (PQLI) to comment upon trends. Without knowing the weights people attach to different aspects of their living conditions, there is no justification for aggregation.

It is also difficult to collect reliable information on many of the influencing variables, assuming we can agree what those are. Statements about trends in environmental degradation, food production, water supply are all estimates. Whilst it is easier to be confident about coverage when monitoring expenditures, the links between expenditure and impact are often only tenuous. About the only thing one can say with certainty, is that war expenditures usually have a negative impact because the resources they involve could have been employed elsewhere.

In principle, the solution would be to ensure a well-functioning national data collection system; but since this will inevitably rely upon grass roots 'participation'—if only in providing the raw data!—such a system is unlikely to survive unless its purpose is clear and embraced by the majority of all the populations concerned. For example, in many African countries, cassava, a staple, does not appear in agricultural production statistics and consequently is not included in the calculation of food availability per capita. Equally, one is unlikely to find a count of the number of goats (the mobile food larder) or of donkeys (basic transport). Under these circumstances, the argument here is that, just as there is now a tendency to favour small scale projects, a preferable approach to monitoring is to build up local area monitoring systems based on data elements chosen by the community themselves. Whilst this will inevitably be a slow process, the information is more likely in this way to be routinely considered in the decision-making process and deliberations of the community. Just as it is self-evident—well almost—that people know best their own basic needs, they also know best how to assess whether or not they are being satisfied.

Cheater concludes her review of two books on the food crisis by commenting on the

> spate of publications on our non-fashionable food crisis [objecting that] . . . mere handful examine local realitities . . . Only 20 per cent of all the bibliographic references cited . . . were produced in Africa; and, of these, one third are official publications. Perhaps part of the contemporary African crisis is our apparent inability to construct our own priorities and realities ourselves, and to make them stick elsewhere
>
> (Cheater, 1988, p.111).

Finally a word of caution about making pronouncements about living conditions, even if a sophisticated national system of social statistics were to be developed. For it would not include data on many of the aspects of life that really matter: 'the average distance people have to carry water and food; the number without shoes; the extent of overcrowding; the prevalence of violence; how many are unable to multiply one number by another, or summarize their own country's history . . .' (Seers 1983, pp.5–6). Moreover, many of the more important social factors are inherently unquantifiable: how safe it is to criticise the government publicly, or the chance of an objective trial or how corruption affects policy decisions. On another level, the potential impact of, for example, the greenhouse effect, upon the current process of desertification must not be neglected. This cannot be considered here, but it implies that reducing the levels of energy consumption in the North may be as important as any aid package to the South.

The lack of these data do not negate the material presented in this book; for we can all agree that basic needs should be met and their attainment should be monitored. But it is important to realise that any assessment of the 'quality of life' beyond strict minima is not and can never be a technical procedure administered by bureaucrats within the constraints of our common humanity, it depends what people want out of life. But the construction of a system of social statistics which reflects what people value is only possible where people are valued. In this sense, participation is necessary not only to properly describe and measure the world but also to change it.

Appendix 1: Analysis of progress towards attaining basic needs

Sheehan and Hopkins (1979) examined the relationship between the basic needs indicators and other variables, including income level and income equality. They did not find income or distribution to be important for most indicators (pp. 82–4). Leipziger and Leuss (1980) considered the low-income and middle-income LDCs separately, and their correlational analysis suggested that (1) in low-income LDCs, income level is more important than distribution for improving basic needs performance, and (2) distribution seems more important in middle-income LDCs.

Regression results can be taken too seriously. Thus:

> more educated men and women are found to live healthier and longer lives. One recent multi-nation study demonstrated that a difference of one percentage point in the national literacy rate is associated with a two year gain in life expectancy, controlling for *per capita* income and food energy consumption.
>
> (World Bank, 1988, pp.24–5).

Given that national literacy rates in sub-Saharan Africa are around 40% and life expectancies are around 50, the implied suggestion is that life expectancies in those countries would overtake even those in Sweden if we could raise the national literacy rate to 53%!

Grosse and Perry (1982) use cross-sectional data on changes in life expectancy between 1960–65 and 1970–75 from the UN Estimates and Projections Sub-Division as a dependent variable in a multiple regression study of the determinants of life expectancy in developing countries. As Murray (1987) says, 'Unfortunately, when *change* in life expectancy is examined, little is left in the [dependent variable] except the UN's assumed rate of improvement.' Not surprisingly, Grosse and Perry noted that 'life expectancy at birth has risen about ten years in the past twenty in *most* of the less developed countries ...' (p.276; cited in Murray, 1987, p.780).

As Shourie (1974, p.28) remarked several years earlier:

> About 15% of the estimates of Sri Lanka's GDP were then derived from assumed trends, e.g. that value added at current prices grew at the same rate as the population. Hence 'the time series enthusiast may well find himself regressing a variable on another variable from which the former was estimated in the first place: what appears to be an economic coefficient is no more than a measure of the consistency in statistical procedures'.

Ram (1985) uses 1983 data from the World Bank on calorie intake, protein intake, life expectancy, infant mortality rate, medical personnel supply, elementary school enrolment rate and adult literacy rate. Only the data on medical personnel and elementary school enrolment can be derived from records, and whilst the latter has well-known deficiencies, it has the virtue of attempting to record a characteristic of people rather than of provision.

Ram then divided his sample into low-income LDCs (with a conventional GDP *per capita* of US$400 or less in 1970) and others. His sample includes 10 African countries: Botswana, Gabon, Cote d'Ivoire, Liberia, Malawi, Sierra Leone, Sudan, Tanzania, Uganda and Zambia. After correlating the basic needs indicators with income level and a measure of income inequality (income share of the poorest 40% households) he concludes that 'income level seems important in almost all cases: but the importance of income inequality is observed only on a limited scale' (p.589).

In a later article, Ram (1988) tests the hypothesis that the relationship between the level of economic development and income inequality is U-shaped: the presumption being that, as with financially measured economic growth, societies move from relatively equal distribution to relatively unequal distribution and then back again. Using cross-sectional data from both developed and developing countries (N=32), Ram found some support for the hypothesis; but among the 24 developing countries he found no relationship. Of these 24 countries, eight were in sub-Saharan Africa and the basic data are given in Table A1.1. None of the rank correlations between the three indices of inequality and the two income *per capita* measures in this table are significant.

Table A1.1 Distribution data for Ram's analysis

	Share of income of			*GDP per capita*	
	Bottom 20%	*Bottom 40%*	*Gini Coefficient*	*International*	*Conventional*
Egypt	5.8	16.5	0.40	841	336
Kenya	2.7	9.0	0.59	448	260
Sierra Leone	5.6	15.2	0.44	504	227
Sudan	4.0	13.0	0.44	731	219
Tanzania	5.8	16.0	0.42	374	131
Zambia	3.4	10.8	0.56	732	438

Source: Ram (1988), p.1376.

The problem, of course, is that data on income distribution are even more unreliable, if that were possible, than income *per capita:* do Egypt and Tanzania really have almost identical income distributions?

Murray (1987) also takes two economists to task for over-interpreting spurious data. First, Sen (1981b), who uses expectation of life at birth data from the World Bank in 1960 and 1977 to calculate percentage decline in longevity shortfall—defined as 80 years minus observed life expectancy. He then identifies 'best performances' in improving longevity (and/or literacy). Murray comments:

> the list of performers includes North Korea and Mongolia, whose estimates are based on neighbouring countries and includes Congo, Vietnam and Tanzania, all of whose estimates are highly questionable. ... his choice of top performers, who largely have good mortality measurements, is inevitably based on a comparison with the non-empirical measurements of the rest of the developing countries.
>
> (Murray, 1987, p.781)

Second, Murray criticises Stewart's (1985) analysis of the relationship between life expectancy and GNP *per capita*. The exceptional performers she identifies based on the analysis of World Bank data for 1981 include countries whose mortality estimates are questionable. Murray comments:

> This type of cross-sectional analysis of a largely non-empirical data set produces results that can legitimately be doubted.
>
> (Murray, 1987, p.781)

Finally, Scholing and Timmerman (1988) provide us with a remarkable display of statistical virtuosity, in developing a path model of the factors determining economic growth. They claim statistical validity for latent factors such as climate, ethnic homogeneity, intensity of governmental control, infrastructure and availability of raw materials. Their faith in the reliability of their data sources, unmentioned, is touching. Before unleashing computer power, econometricians using macro data must first assess the variance due to unreliability: in most cases it will swamp any effect they might be looking for.

Appendix 2: Inequalities in health and in access to health care

There are several kinds of inequalities in health and health care. This appendix presents some indicative material on inequalities in birthweight, in child malnutrition and mortality, and on access to 'modern' health care facilities.

A2.1 BIRTHWEIGHT AND POVERTY

There have now been several studies of the relation between socio-economic status and low birthweight (Mbise and Boersma, 1979; Olusi, Ademowore and Ajani, 1979; Oduntun, Odunlami and Ayeni, 1977; Lewis, 1974; Rehan and Tafida, 1980; Olowe, 1981; Ladipo and Adelusi, 1977; Osuhor and Yakasai, 1981).

Not all studies give a clear result. Seyoum, Kidane, Gebru and Sevenhuysen (1986) studied all households with children under 5 from two communities in Ethiopia, one growing mainly khat and the other mainly staple food crops. They expected to find an association between income and nutritional status but found no effect due to income after allowing for variations in age and sex of child, and family size.

Oni and Ariganjoye (1986) collected data on all births in November/December 1983 at Ilorin Hospital in Nigeria. They interviewed the mothers of 49 LBW babies and 156 'controls' (babies of normal birthweight born during the same 24 hour period). Although they reported no association, 20% of those with no education gave birth to an LBW baby compared to 16% of those with any education at all.

Typical data from Benin are given in Table A2.1. The high overall incidence of low birthweight (22%) is either extremely worrying or due to selection factors again. The authors also argue that the observed relationship between occupation and birthweight is not due to maternal malnutrition but to differential appreciation of the importance of malaria prophylaxis.

Table A2.1 Birthweight by occupational group

	Total	*Mean birthweight (kg)*	*% LBW*
Civil Servants	364	2.82	18
Traders	87	2.83	15
Peasants	1,106	2.74	23
Other	45	2.74	31
	1,602	2.76	22

Source: Sargent, McKinney and Wetherington (1986), Tables 1b, p.93 and 2, p.94.

They base this claim on the relationship of low birthweight to distance from the clinic and the absence of any seasonal variation on the rate of low birthweight. However, their description of the region suggests a relatively rich agricultural area and we know that maternal malnutrition has to be severe to have a significant effect upon birthweight (Stein and Susser, 1975). But the fundamental problem, illustrated by the distance–lowbirthweight relationship, is the selection bias in all these clinic- or hospital-based studies.

A2.2 INFANT MORTALITY

Sindiga (1985) presents infant mortality rates in Kenya before and after 1967, but says ‘there probably are no accurate statistics on trends in infant and child mortality in the rural areas’ (p.81). Yet there were substantial gains in the 1970s.

Large variations can be observed within a province. For example, De Boer and McNeil (1989) show variations between different altitude zones in the Meru district of Kenya.

Table A2.2 Kenya: infant mortality rates by current province of residence during the 1960s and 1970s

Province	*Pre-1967*	*1967-1976*	*1978*
Nairobi	100	75	82
Central	88	56	72
Coast	156	129	na
Eastern	100	77	89
Nyanza	162	128	na
Rift Valley	103	64	80
Western	116	109	114

Note: na = not available
Sources: columns 1 and 2, Republic of Kenya (1981); column 3, Kenya Fertility Survey cited in Mwangi and Mwabu (1986).

Table A2.3 Mortality before ages 1, 2 and 5 years according to altitude zone and compared with available national and district figures for Meru district (rates per thousand)

Mortality before age	*Altitude zone*			*Kenya 1979*	*Meru district 1979*
	High/middle	*Low*	*Total*		
1	37	73	56	72	–
2	41	87	59	–	75
5	46	102	68	156	104

Source: De Boer and McNeil (1989).

Determining which are the important factors is not easy. Oni (1988) reports on a household survey in Ilorin, Nigeria at the end of 1983. Out of a sample of 932 households in three residential strata, 913 married women were interviewed. He analyses for the effect of a wide range of socio-economic variables (woman's education, husband's education, type of union, religion, woman's occupation, parity, contraceptive use, area of residence, presence of indoor tap water, presence of refrigerator) on child mortality. Although all the inter-correlations are statistically significant (see Table A2.4), in a multivariate analysis nearly all the variables enter significantly except woman's education, type of union, religion and woman's occupation.

Table A2.4 Correlations between mortality ratio and socio-economic variables

	Woman's education	*Husband's education*	*Area of residence*	*Source of water*	*Use of refrigerator*
Mortality ratio	–0.28	–0.29	–0.31	–0.25	–0.29
Woman's education	1	0.65	0.64	0.54	0.60
Husband's education		1	0.55	0.50	0.58
Area of residence			1	0.58	0.62
Source of water				1	0.54
Use of refrigerator					1

Source: G.A. Oni, 1988, Table 6.

A2.3 MALNUTRITION

Data from both Kenya and Tanzania show substantial geographical disparities or variations in malnutrition by province. However, in both countries, whilst there is a relation between the geographical variation in malnutrition and socio-economic indicators, it is not exact. More detailed data from Zimbabwe demonstrate inequalities between occupational groups.

Table A2.5 Kenya: nutritional indicators and selected factors by province

Province	*N*	*% Stunted*	*% Wasted*	*Mortality 0-5/000*	*% Mothers with no education*	*% no piped water*	*Person/per arable land*
Coast	419	36	5.0	206	77	79	87
Nyanza	788	29	3.6	220	52	98	211
Western	787	26	2.0	187	46	96	247
Eastern	1,195	23	2.7	128	46	88	33
Central	907	20	2.8	85	30	77	254
Rift Valley	1,227	20	3.0	132	55	89	101
National	5323	24	3.0	156	49	88	138

Source: Republic of Kenya, *Third Child Nutrition Survey*

(1) *Kenya*

The data for Kenya in Table A2.5 show how variations in the percent stunted and percent wasted corresponds quite closely with variations in child mortality and with the percent of mothers with no education, but not with variations in the percent with no piped water or with the numbers of persons per arable land.

One should caution against over-interpretation, as data on the percent stunted and wasted for Kenya only 5 years earlier do not put the provinces in the same order (Table A2.6). Mwangi and Mwabu (1986) also suggest that there may be more complete reporting in Nairobi than elsewhere. Moreover, movements over time in the percent wasted do not correspond to movements in the percent stunted.

Table A2.6 Kenya: percent of children stunted or wasted by provinces

	Stunted (Height for Age less than 90%)			*Wasted (Height for Height less than 90%)*		
Province	*1977*	*1978/9*	*1982*	*1977*	*1978/9*	*1982*
Coast	19	37	36	7.5	10.8	5.0
Eastern	38	24	23	5.0	4.2	2.7
Central	31	22	20	3.0	2.4	2.8
Rift Valley	29	25	20	4.5	7.0	3.0
Nyanza	26	32	29	2.5	5.7	3.6
Western	21	27	26	5.0	1.8	2.0
National	21	26	24	4.5	4.8	3.0

Source: for 1977 and 1978–79 Mwangi and Mwabu (1986); for 1982, Sindiga (1985).

Mott and Mott (1980) say:

> Kenya's modest gain in socio-economic development appears to have been somewhat exaggerated. Empirical studies in fact reveal growing poverty and endemic malnutrition and under-nutrition in many parts of the country.

They agree that there was no aggregate food shortage in Kenya during the period 1965–81 with an average daily *per capita* availability of over 2,380 calories and over 62.5g of protein (compared to FAO/WHO recommended averages of 2,362 calories and 46g of protein). They suggest that 'children have adapted very well [to] chronic food shortage ... by reducing their stature.' However, there are no clear trends in Table A2.6.

(2) *Tanzania*

Jakobsen (1987, p.240) reports on a study of child malnutrition in the Southern Highlands of Tanzania (see Table A2.7) and finds that

> more malnourished children are found in the areas with high cash incomes than in areas with a subsistence oriented economy. Why don't the rich families have better fed children than the poor? ... [there is] ... the issue of control over the distribution of resources for various consumption items within the family. Increasing monetarisation has taken the form of accumulation of resources in the hands of the husbands.

Table A2.7 Tanzania, Southern Highlands

	Estimated family income in Tsh	*Proportion underweight*
South	1,300	30
North	1,500	39
Central	4,700	41
West	4,700	44
East	3,200	57
Rungwe/Kyela	na	41

Source: Jakobsen (1987), Chap. 9.

(3) *Zimbabwe*

Loewenson (1986) surveyed health indicators and factors affecting health status in four areas of Mashonoland in order to compare the health status of different occupational groups. Based on a review of Zimbabwe's economic history, he predicts that:

> the broader political and economic inequalities between classes would be reflected in inequalities between labour groups in 1980, with workers on commercial farms in the worst position, followed by mine labour and urban workers.
>
> (Loewenson, 1986, p.49)

The results (Table A2.8)) broadly confirm his predictions: a repeat survey in 1983 showed the same gradient although there had been an overall decrease in levels of both stunting and wasting in all areas.

Table A2.8 Health status in four occupational groups

	Commercial	*Communal*	*Mining*	*Urban*
Wasting (weight for height ≤ 80% NCHS standard)				
0–6 months	12	9	2	0
6 months – 2 years	28	19	8	12
2–5 years	7	8	5	16
Stunting (height for age ≤ 90% NCHS standard)				
0–6 months	33	51	23	0
6 months – 2 years	38	27	20	9
2–5 years	24	25	10	6
Access to health and educational services				
Hospital utilisation	23	na	32	42
BCG immunization	18	96	56	90
School attendance	19	36	34	59

Source: Loewenson (1986)

His description of access to and quality of housing, water supplies, sanitation and fuel supplies confirms the poor situation of the commercial farming areas. Moreover, similar patterns were shown in the access to health and educational services.

A2.4 GEOGRAPHICAL ACCESS TO HEALTH CARE

This has been examined in two ways: the distribution of facilities by province and the percentage of population within a certain distance. The Nigerian government present data showing that whilst dispensaries are relatively equitably distributed, other facilities are not (Table A2.9).

The lack of equity is due to the favoured position of the urban population: this is illustrated by the fall-off in use among villages further away (Table A2.10).

Table A2.9 Coefficients of distribution of health facilities in Nigeria

	Gini[a]	*Correlation Coeff.*[b]
Hospitals	33	0.06
Hospital beds/doctors	21	0.32
Health centres	32	0.04
Maternity centres	30	0.15
Dispensaries	18	0.49

a Gini coefficient compares proportion of health care facilities in each State with proportion of population.
b Correlation coefficient looks at correlation between population and number of health care facilities.
Source: Okafor (1987).

Table A2.10 Nigeria, Kano State

Utilisation rate (visits per 100 people per year)	*Number of villages at distance*			
	0 – 4km	*4 – 6km*	*6 + km*	*Total*
None	3	4	7	14
Under 10	4	4	13	21
10 and under 20	7	8	5	20
20 and under 30	7	8	2	17
30 and up	15	1	1	17
Total	36	25	28	89

Note: $x^2 = 33.8$, with 8 df. $p<0.05$
Source: Understanding Health Care Behaviour
Data from 1,194 individual interviews with patients at 2 facilities, 1976–77.

While accessibility improved between 1979 and 1982 through the establishment of more dispensaries and maternity and child welfare centres (MCW), Ayeni et al (1987) argue that the relative efficiency of locations has remained low. Alternative locations would have increased accessibility (cols. 3 & 6) and utilisation of MCW and dispensaries by an estimated 12% and 16% respectively (Table A2.11).

Table A2.11 Accessibility of health facilities to people, Ogun State, Nigeria, 1979, 1982

	MCW			*Dispensaries*		
	1979	*1982 Actual*	*1982 Optimum*	*1979*	*1982 Actual*	*1982 Optimum*
Number of facilities	32	53	53	43	63	63
Percent population without facilities	60	56	54	57	54	52
Average distance of people from places without facilities	6.4	4.9	4.0	5.5	4.7	3.7

Source: Ayeni et al (1987), Tables 2, 3 and 7.

Table A2.12 presents similar data for Tanzania. There is a clear inverse correlation between the level of access in 1972 and the extent of improvement over the next ten years, reflecting a concern for equity at least between the administrative regions.

Table A2.12 Percentage of population within 10 km of any health facility

	1972	*Rank*	*1978*	*Increase*	*Rank*
Arusha	79	6	84	5	13=
Dodma	78	7=	92	14	9=
Iringa	67	14=	87	22	4
Kagera	85	4	90	5	13=
Kigoma	89	3	91	2	15=
Kilimanjaro	97	1	98	1	17
Mara	59	17	98	39	1
Mbeva	78	7=	83	7	12
Morogoro	83	5	92	9	11
Mtwara	76	9	91	15	8
Mwanja	73	11	98	25	3
Pwani	67	14=	93	26	2
Puvuma	69	12	88	19	5
Shinvanga	68	13	86	18	6
Singida	75	10	85	10	10
Tabora	61	16	77	16	7
Tanaga	93	1	95	2	15
Mean	76		90	17	

Note: Rank correlation between percentage in 1972 and increase 1972–1982 = –0.92.

Although Zambia has a similar commitment to equitable distribution of health care resources, in the period 1980–82 the *per capita* health expenditure in rural health centre areas was K0.6 as compared to K12.3 in Lusaka (Table A2.13). Whilst the ratio of personnel to population has steadily improved, large differences between provinces remain (Table A2.14). Overall, both the Copperbelt and Lusaka provinces are privileged relative to elsewhere, and this inequality worsened over the early 1980s.

Table A2.13 *Per capita* health expenditure in rural health centre areas; Zambia

	Population (1980)	*Expenditure*			
		1981	*1982*	*1983*	*1984*
Headquarters, training, research	na	23	29	28	20
Copperbelt	22	18	16	16	20
UTH and Lusaka Province	12	19	20	19	22
All other provinces	66	40	35	37	38

Source: GPZ Financial Reports quoted in Freund (1986).

Table A2.14 Population per category of health personnel; Zambia

	Doctors					
	1978	*1981*	*% Decrease*	*Nurses 1978*	*Medicine 1981*	*% Decrease*
Central	11.716	8.702	25.7	6.862	1.375	80.0
Copperbelt	5.259	4.311	18.0	1.959	0.695	64.5
Eastern	26.573	21.611	18.7	12.472	1.963	84.3
Luapta	33.127	14.505	56.2	9.696	2.052	78.8
Lusaka	2.514	2.998	–19.2	2.079	0.847	59.3
Northern	31.010	17.730	42.8	10.022	2.376	76.3
North Western	13.660	12.357	9.5	4.413	1.065	75.9
Southern	17.492	12.191	30.3	9.246	1.049	88.7
Western	22.526	15.993	29.0	9.097	2.350	74.2
Zambia	8.447	7.139	15.5	4.302	1.142	73.5

Source: Akhtar, R. and Izhar, N. (1986).

Appendix 3: Equity and inequalities in education

A3.1 UNIVERSAL PRIMARY EDUCATION: A RIGHT TO KNOWLEDGE

Why UPE? There are five possible rationales.

(1) *Education as a human right.* The UN International Declaration in Human Rights claimed 'Everyone has a right to education. Education shall be free, at least in the elementary and fundamental stages. Elementary education shall be compulsory ...' (UNESCO, 1949, p.279). Exactly why this should be so, why especially for children, and why it should be '*compulsory*' are rarely discussed. Children drop out, or refuse to attend, for what appear to them or their elders to be good or unavoidable reasons. Bray (1986) cites examples from Ghana and Nigeria, where communities have reacted strongly to the imposition of school. Shouldn't children have the right *not* to attend school?

(2) *Education as an investment.* Here the assertion is that primary education produces a stream of benefits for the individual or for the society, which (after appropriate discounting) are greater than the current costs of education. Little (1984) supports a relation between education and agricultural productivity but concludes that the evidence of productivity in the urban sector 'is too scattered to provide generalisations' (Little, 1984, p.102).

(3) *UPE promotes equity.* Usually thought of in terms of gender, region, rural/urban, or social group. Even if formal equity of access is attained, the *quality* of primary schooling provided may vary between genders, regions, rural/urban and social groups.

(4) *UPE for national cohesion.* It helps to develop a 'sense of national belonging or identity: it may be the only means of achieving national unity' (Smith, 1979, p.7). In fact, school systems reflect, to a large extent, the societies in which they operate, so it is perhaps unrealistic to expect too much of school. On the other hand, the argument that school systems teach a national language obviously has some merit.

(5) *UPE for reduction of fertility and improvements in health.* The surveys conducted as part of the World Fertility Survey suggest that a little bit of education may increase fertility, because it increases the ability to have live births; but that after three or four years of schooling, increases are positively correlated with reductions in fertility. The evidence about better health status usually relates to adult literacy.

It seems clear that the social reasons for advocating or promoting UPE are stronger than the economic ones; the issue of compulsion should be carefully considered before making a total commitment. If UPE is adopted, then issues of quality and the necessary infrastructural support to a UPE policy should not be neglected.

A3.2 INEQUALITIES IN EDUCATION

There have been two main types of study of inequality in primary school education concerned with regions and socio-economic groups.

In many countries, formal regional disparities in primary school attendance have been reduced substantially, although there are still considerable disparities at secondary and tertiary levels. Several case studies are presented and discussed in Carron and Chau (1981) and the reader is referred to that as the best source. More recent data, for example, those for Zambia presented by Kaluba and Karlsson (1987), confirm this trend towards formal equality, although urban–rural disparities in the quality of educational services (as measured by, for example, number of text books) persist. The focus here is, instead, on evidence about inequalities between socio-economic groups.

Heyneman and Loxley (1983) ask 'whether countries with high *per capita* income distribute primary school resources more equally'. They have analysed data for 29 countries, although we are only concerned here with the two in Africa. They constructed an index of school quality based on the significant indicators emerging from country-specific regressions of 'achievement' (measured as transfer to the next level—posing obvious problems of interpretation where there is only a small transition rate from one level to the next) upon whatever data they could lay their hands on. As they say in a table of international comparisons, the means are not comparable as the indices of school quality were constructed separately for each country.

They then ranked individual primary school students in each country from high to low on the basis of their access to school quality (as defined above). Heyneman and Loxley (1983) conclude that 'the distribution of school quality appears more equal, on average, than the distribution of personal income'.

> It seems that countries are able to distribute school quality more equally than income
>
> (Heyneman and Loxley, p.115)

Table A3.1 Distribution of personal income and school quality within high-, medium-, and low-income countries

	Percentage shared by bottom 40%		*Percentage shared by top 20%*	
	Income	*School quality*	*Income*	*School quality*
Low-income countries	14	29	53	27
Middle-income countries	14	30	48	28
High-income countries	17	29	44	28
Average	15	29	48	28

Note: Low income = below US$300; Middle income = US$300–750; High income = above US$750; N = 29 for school quality distribution; N = 66 for income distribution.

Data for Kenya over the 1970s show, in fact, a relatively rapid movement towards equality at the primary level (Table A3.2). Martin (1984) argues that this occurred because 'the popular social classes ...

have taken up the slack in increased educational provision' (p.97). Meanwhile the Kenyan bourgeoisie have secured a segregated sector of high cost, high quality schooling (p.110).

Table A3.2 Percentage distribution of households and students in Kenya, 1969 and 1977

	1969			*1977*		
	Households	*Students*	*Diff.*	*Households*	*Students*	*Diff.*
Farmers only	42	31	–11	24	18	–6
Semi- and unskilled workers	25	15	–10	42	43	+1
Self employed	18	31	+13	13	14	+1
White collar worker	12	15	+3	16	18	+2
Prof. civil servant	3	8	+5	5	7	+2

Source: Adapted from Martin, 1984, Table 3, p.105.

A3.3 INEQUALITIES IN ADULT EDUCATION

In principle, one would be interested in variation in participation according to social group. But the only breakdowns available on official data, apart from male/female, are according to age and administrative region. Age breakdowns are difficult to interpret. First, the age distributions within the populations of the different countries vary considerably, so that the same proportion of *enrolment* in a particular age group corresponds to a different proportion of the population. Second, the age structure of participation in the *regular* education system differs; which, correspondingly, affects the likelihood of individuals of that age enrolling in *adult* education. The appropriate comparison is of each proportion of each age group, according to whether or not they have attended regular education; but such data are rarely available for the age groups required. Given all these caveats, it is still surprising to see that, for the two countries where data were available (Botswana and Swaziland), 72% and 83% of those enrolled were under 30: it is not obvious that the term 'adult education' is appropriate.

The analysis of regional disparities leads to similar problems. If there are differences in enrolment among regions in a country, these may or may not reflect differences in the needs—or these days 'wants'—of the populations of different regions. Without detailed information of that kind, it is difficult to evaluate the extent of any 'disparity': for example, one would expect major differences in enrolment in literacy programmes if there are major differences in literacy rates. A related problem is lack of data on fields of study on a regional basis. A given degree of disparity would be evaluated very differently depending on what kind of adult education is involved.

There are also more technical problems. The coverage of the data varies. The size and number of regions varies very widely between countries. *In extremis,* a country divided into two regions might show no disparity in enrolment, even though within each region there are major disparities which, had the country been divided into more regions, would have become apparent. That is why it would have been misleading to have tried to summarise disparities with one figure (e.g. a Gini coefficient) for each country (shown in Table A3.3).

Table A3.3 Disparities in adult education in different regions within single countries

	Number of regions	*Index of adult education*	
		lowest rating region	*highest rating region*
Egypt	14	31	491*
Liberia	4	90	108
Sierra Leone	4	10	255
Tanzania	20	47	155**

* Primary education only.
** Literacy programmmes only.

Data are available for four countries. In Egypt and Tanzania, where we have data on enrolment at the first level only, high enrolment scores seem to correspond to the more remote areas; in Sierra Leone, high enrolment rates correspond to the more developed regions.

If there is any conclusion to be drawn, it is that while the more basic adult education tends to be directed at the least industrialised regions, more advanced education is concentrated in the towns.

Bibliography

Abel-Smith, B. (1986a), 'The world economic crisis.Part 1: repercussions on health', *Health Policy and Planning,* vol.1, no.3, pp.202–13.

Abel-Smith, B. (1986b), 'The world economic crisis.Part 2: health manpower out of balance', *Health Policy and Planning,* vol.1, no.4, pp.309–16.

Adediji, A. (1989), Executive Secretary of the UN Economic Commission for Africa, Addis Ababa (reported in the Washington Post, April 15th).

Adelman, I. and Morris, C.T. (1973), *Economic Growth and Social Equity in Developing Countries,* Stanford, Calif: Stanford University Press.

AED, Academy for Educational Development (1985), *Lessons from five countries: Honduras, the Gambia, Swaziland, Ecuador, Peru: Report on the communication for child survival project.* Washington DC.Academy for Educational Development.

Agarwal, B. (1986), *Cold Hearths and Barren Slopes: The Woodfuel Crisis in the Third World,* London, Zed.

Akhtar, R. (1987)(ed.), *Health and Disease in Tropical Africa,* Switzerland, Harwood.

Akhtar, R. and Izhar, N. (1986), 'The Spatial Distribution of Health Resources Within Countries and Communities: Examples from India and Zambia', *Social Science and Medicine,* vol.22, no.11, pp.1115–29.

Aldous, J. (1962), 'Urbanization, the Extended Family, and Kinship Ties in West Africa', *Social Forces,* vol.41.

Allison, C. (1983), 'Constraints to UPE: More than just a question of supply?' *International Journal of Educational Development,* vol.3, no.3, pp.263–76.

Allison, C. and Green, R. (1985), *Sub-Saharan Africa: Getting the Facts Straight,* Institute of Development Studies Bulletin, vol.16, no.3.

Amanam, A. Udo (1980), 'The Use of Socio-economic and Accessibility Information for Improving MCH/FP Services. The Nigerian Case', *J. Tropical Paediatrics,* vol.26, pp.203–8.

Amin, S. (1987), 'Preface' to Gakou (1987), *op.cit.*

Amnesty Internatonal (various years), *Annual Reports,* London, Amnesty International Publications.

Anker, R. and Knowles, J. (1980), 'An Empirical Analysis of mortality differentials in Kenya at the macro and micro level', *Economic Development and Cultural Change,* vol.29, pp.165–85.

Ankerl, Guy (1986), *Urbanisation Overspeed in Tropical Africa, 1970–2000,* IWU Press.

Anon (1979), *The OECD Social Indicator Programme: for Individual Well-Being or for Social Control?* London, BSSRS, Radical Statistics No.4.

Anyinam, C. (1987), 'Availability, Accessibility, Acceptability and Adaptability: Four Attributes of African Ethno-Medicine', *Social Science and Medicine,* vol.25, no.7, pp.803–11.

Ashe, J. (1979), *Assessing Rural Needs: a Manual for Practitioners,* Mt.Rainier, Maryland VITA (Volunteers in Technical Assistance).

Asrat, D. (1983), *Report on the strengthening of statistical activities in Botswana,* Lusaka, UNICEF.

Ayeni, B., Rushton, G. and McNulty, M.L. (1987), 'Improving the Geographical Accessibility of Health Care in Rural Areas: A Nigerian Case Study', *Social Science and Medicine,* vol.25, no.10, pp.1083–94.

Basta, S.S. (1977), 'Nutrition and health in low income urban areas of the third world', *Ecology of Food and Nutrition,* vol.6, pp.113–14.

Baster, N. (1981), *'The Measurement of Women's Participation in Development: the Use of Census Data',* Brighton, Institute of Development Studies, University of Sussex (Discussion Paper No.109).

Baster, N. (1985), 'Social Indicator Research: some issues and debates', pp.23–46, in Hilhorst, J.G.M. and Klatter, M. (1985), *Social Development in the Third World: Level of Living Indicators and Social Planning,* London, Croom Helm.

Bedri, B. (1988), 'Housework and the productivity of housewives', *The Afhad Journal,* vol.5, no.7, pp.24–9.

Bell, D. E. (1987), 'Innovations in reproductive health and child survival', Remarks to the Biennial Conference of the Association for Women in Development, Washington DC, 16 April 1987.

Benefice, E., Chevassus-Agnes, S. (1985), 'Variations anthropometriques saisonnieres des adultes appartenant a deux populations differentes de l'Afrique de l'Ouest', *Rev Epid et Sante Publique,* vol.33, pp.150–60.

Bennett, F.J. (1989), 'The dilemma of essential drugs in primary health care', *Social Science and Medicine,* vol.28, no.10, pp.1085–90.

Benyoussef, A., Culter, J.C., Baylet, R. et al (1973), 'Sante, migration et urbanization: une etude collective au Senegal', *Bulletin OMS,* vol.49, pp.517–37.

Berg, E. (1975), *The Recent Economic Evaluation of the Sahel,* Ann Arber, Centre for Research on Economic Development, University of Michigan.

Berry, B. (1973), *The Human Consequences of Urbanization,* London, Macmillan.

Berry, S. (1983), 'Agrarian crisis in Africa? A review and an interpretation', in P.Lawrence (ed.), *World Recession and the Food Crisis in Africa (1986),* London, James Curry, ROAPE.

Bibeau, G. (1985), 'From China to Africa: The Same Impossible Synthesis Between Traditional and Western Medicines', *Social Science and Medicine,* vol.21, no.8, pp.937–43.

Birdsall, N. and McGreevey, W.P. (1983), 'Women, poverty and development', in Buvinic, M., Lycetts, M.A. and McGreevey, W.P. (eds.), *Women and poverty in the third world,* Baltimore, Maryland, Johns Hopkins University Press.

Blacker, J.G.C. (1987), 'Health Impacts of Family Planning', *Health Policy and Planning,* vol.2, no.3, pp.193–203, Oxford University Press.

Blades, D.W. (1980), 'What do we know about levels and growth of output in developing countries? A critical analysis with special reference to Africa', in R.C.O.Matthews (ed.), *Economic Growth and Resources,* vol.2, London, Macmillan for the International Economic Association.

Blaxter, M. (1981), *The Health of the Children,* SSRC/DHSS Studies in Deprivation and Disadvantage 3, London, Heineman

Bleek, W. (1987), 'Lying Informants: A Fieldwork Experience from Ghana', *Population and Development Review,* vol.13, no.2, June, pp.314–22.

Boerma, T. (1987), 'The magnitude of the maternal mortality problem in sub-Saharan Africa', *Social Science and Medicine,* vol.24, no.6, pp.551–8.

Boersma, E.R. and Mbise, R.L., (1979), 'Intrauterine growth of live born Tanzanian infants', *Tropical Geographical Medicine,* vol.31, no.7.

Bondestam, L. (1973), *Some Notes on African Statistics: Collection, Reliability and Interpretation,* Research Report No.18, Uppsala, Scandinavian Institute of African Studies.

Borton, J. and Clay, E. (1988), 'The African Food Crises of 1982–1986: A Provisional Review', pp.140–67, in Rimmer (ed.) (1988), *op.cit.*

Bowman, M.J. (1984), 'An Integrated Framework for Analysis of the Spread of Schooling in Less Developed Countries', *Comparative Education Review,* vol.28, no.4, pp.563–83, November.

Bradley, J. (1972), in White, G.F., Bradley, D.J., and White, A.U. (1972), *op.cit.*

Bradley, J. and White, G.F. (1972), in White, G.F., Bradley, D.J., and White, A.U.(1972), *op.cit.*

Bray, M. (1986), 'If UPE is the Answer, what is the Question? A Comment on Weaknesses in the Rationale for Universal Primary Education in Less Developed Countries', *International Journal of Educational Development,* vol.6, no.3, pp.147–58.

Brekke, T. (1985), 'The hut belongs to the husband', *New Internationalist, Woman to woman: a World Report,* no.149.

Brink, E.W., Aly, H., Dakrovry, A.M.et al (1983), 'The Egyptian National Nutrition Survey 1978', *Bulletin OMS,* vol.61, pp.853–60.

Bryceson, D.F. (1989), 'Nutrition and the Commoditization of Food in Sub-Saharan Africa', *Social Science and Medicine,* vol.28, no.5, pp.425–40.

Cairncross, S. (1988), 'Domestic Water Supply in Rural Africa', pp.46–63, in Rimmer, D. (ed.), *op.cit.*

Cairncross, S. and Cliff, J. (1987), 'Water use and health in Mueda, Mozambique', *Trans Royal Society, Tropical Medicine and Hygiene,* vol.81, pp.51–4.

Cairncross, S. and Feachem, R.G. (1977), 'Operations and maintenance of rural water supplies', *EEC-ACP Courier,* vol.43.

Caldwell, J.C. (1977), 'The economic rationality of high fertility: an investigation illustrated with Nigerian survey data', *Population Studies,* vol.31, no.1, pp.5–27.

Caldwell, J.C. (1982), *Theory of Fertility Decline,* London, Academic Press.

Callaway, B.J. (1984), 'Ambiguous consequences of socialisation and seclusion of Hausa women', *Journal of Modern African Studies,* vol.22, no.3, pp.429–50.

Campbell, C.A. (1984), 'Nestlé and Breast vs Bottle Feeding: Mainstream and Marxist Perspectives', *International Journal of Health Services,* vol.14, no.4, pp.547–67.

Campbell, D. (1988), 'Data collection for the design of water and sanitation projects in Belize', *Waterlines,* vol.6, no.3, January, pp.26–8.

Carlson, B.A. (1985), 'The Potential of National Household Survey Programmes for Monitoring and Evaluating Primary Health Care in Developing Countries', *World Health Statistics Quarterly,* vol.38, pp.38–63.

Carr-Hill, R.A. (1976), *Population and Educational Services,* Educational Policy and Planning, UNESCO, Paris.

Carr-Hill, R.A. (1978), 'Social Indicators and the Basic Needs Approach: Who Benefits From Which Numbers?', in Coles, S. and Lucas, H. (eds), *Models, Planning and Basic Needs,* Oxford.

Carr-Hill, R.A. (1984a), 'The Political Choice of Social Indicators', *Quality and Quantity,* vol.18, pp.173–91.

Carr-Hill, R.A. (1984b), 'Radicalising Survey Methodology', *Quality and Quantity,* vol.18, pp.275–92.

Carr-Hill, R.A. (1987), 'When Is A Data Set Complete: A Squirrel With a Vacuum Cleaner', *Social Science and Medicine,* vol.25, no.6, pp.753–64.

Carr-Hill, R.A. and Lintott, J. (1985), *Comparative Statistics on Adult Education from 84 Countries,* Paris, UNESCO Office of Statistics.

Carron, G. and Chau, T.G. (1981), *Reducing Regional Disparities: The Role of Educational Planning,* Paris, IIEP.

Carron, G., Mwiria, K. and Righa, G. (1989), *Functioning and Effects of the Kenyan Literacy Programme,* Paris, IIEP, Research Report No.73.

Cash, R., Kuesch, G.T. and Lamstein, J. (1987), *Child Health and Survival—The UNICEF GOBI Program,* London, Croom Helm.

Cates, W., Smith, J.C., Rochot, R.W. and Grimes, D.A., (1982), 'Mortality from abortion and childbirth: are the statistics biased?' *Journal of the American Medical Association,* vol.248, pp.192–6.

Central Bureau of Statistics, Kenya (1977), 'The rural Kenya nutrition survey, 1977', *Social Perspectives,* vol.2 no.4.

Central Bureau of Statistics, Kenya (1979), *Report of the child nutrition survey 1978/79,* Ministry of Economic Planning and Development, Nairobi, Kenya, Nairobi, CBS.

Central Bureau of Statistics, Kenya (1983), *Third rural child nutrition survey 1982,* Kenya, Nairobi, CBS.

Central Statistical Office, Ethiopia (1983), *Rural Health and Nutrition Survey,* (1982–1983), Ethiopia, Addis Ababa, CSO.

Central Statistical Office, Ethiopia (1983), *The rural integrated household survey programme: methodological report,* Central Statistical Office, Ethiopia, Addis Ababa, CSO.

Central Statistics Office, Botswana (1983), *Evaluation of the Primary Health Care in Botswana,* Gaberone, CSO.

Centre for Development Research (1989), *Mobilization and Women's Integration in Tanzania: Case Study from the Village of Peramiho 'A', Ruvuma Region,* Dar-es-Salaam, Centre for Development Research.

Chambers, R. (1974), *Managing Rural Development: Ideas and Experience from East Africa,* Scandinavian Institute of African Studies, Uppsala.

Chambers, R. (1982), 'Health, Agriculture and Rural Poverty: Why Seasons Matter', *Journal of Development Studies,* vol.18, no.2, pp.217–38.

Chambers, R. (1983), *Rural Development: Putting the Last First,* London, Longman.

Chapman, S., Ball, K., Gray, N., Nostbakken, D. and Omar, S. (1986), 'Smoking control in Africa: problems and prospects', *Health Policy and Planning,* vol.1, no.3, pp.222–31.

Cheater, A. (1988), 'Review of Food in Sub-Saharan Africa and World Recession and Food Crisis in Africa', *Journal of Developmental Studies.*

Chenery, H. et al (1977), *Redistribution with Growth,* London, Oxford University Press.

Chenery, H. and Syrquin, M., (1975), *Patterns of Development, 1950–1970,* London, Oxford University Press.

Chojnacka, H. and Adegbola, O. (1984), 'The determinants of Infant and Child Morbidity in Lagos, Nigeria', *Social Science and Medicine,* vol.19, no.8, pp.799–810.

Choolun, R. (1989), 'The Mauritius Health Service: The Population's Changing Needs and Demands', *International Journal of Health Planning and Management,* vol.4, no.1, pp.63–72.

Christensen, C.et al (eds.)(1981), *Food Problems and Prospects in Sub-Saharan Africa: The Decade of the 1980s,* US Department of Agriculture, Foreign Agricultural Report No.166.

Coale, A. and Demeny, P. (1966), *Regional Model Life Tables and Stable Populations,* Princeton University Press, Princeton, N.J.

Collinson, M. (1981), 'A Low Cost Approach to Understanding Small Farmers', *Agricultural Administration,* vol.8, no.6, November, pp.433–50.

Comber, I.C. and Keeves, J.P. (1973), *Science Education in Nineteen Countries,* New York, Wiley.

Conti, A. (1979), 'Capitalist Organisation of Production through Non-Capitalist Relations: Women's Role in a Pilot Resettlement in Upper Volta', *Review of African Political Economy,* vols 15/16, pp.75–92.

Coombs, P.H. and Ahmed, M. (1974), *Attacking Rural Poverty: How Education Can Help,* Baltimore, Johns Hopkins University Press.

Coombs, P.H., Prosser, R.C. and Ahmed, M. (1973), *New Paths to Learning for Rural Children and Youth,* New York, Int.Council for Educational Development.

Corbett, J. (1988), 'Famine and Household Coping Strategies', *World Development,* vol.16, no.9, pp.1099–112.

Cornia, G.A., Jolly, R. and Stewart, F. (1987), *Adjustment with a Human Face: Protecting the Vulnerable and Promoting Growth,* Oxford, Clarendon Press.

Cornia, G.A., Jolly, R. and Stewart, F. (1988), *Adjustment with a Human Face: Ten Country Case Studies,* Oxford, Clarendon Press.

Coughenour, C.M., Frankenberger, T. and Skertvedt, E. (1985) 'Women farmers in rural settlements in North Kordofan, Sudan', *The Ahfad Journal,* vol.2, no.2, pp.9–21.

Coulibaly, N. (1981), 'Place et approches des problemes de la tuberculose en Abidjan', *Medicin Afrique Noire,* vol.28, pp.447–9.

Cumper, G. (1987), 'The Resource Requirements for Basic Health Care in Developing Countries, with Special Reference to Africa', *Journal of Tropical Paediatrics,* vol.33, supplement 1, pp.18–25, Oxford University Press.

Dasgupta, B. and Seers, D. (1975)(eds), *Statistical Policy in Less Developed Countries,* Brighton, Institute of Development Studies, University of Sussex (IDS, No.114).

Davis, I. (1984), 'The squatters who live next door to disaster', *The Guardian Third World Review,* 7 December 1984.

Davis, K. (1965), 'The urbanization of human populations', *Scientific American,* vol.213, (3).

Day, D.G. (1988), 'Problems with Hydrological Monitoring: Case of the Australian Representative Basins Program', *Water International,* vol.13, pp.230–4.

De Bethune, X., Alfani, S. and Lahaye, J.P. (1989), 'The influence of an abrupt price increase on health service utilization: evidence from Zaire', *Health Policy and Planning,* vol.4, no.1, pp.76–81.

De Boer, C.N. and McNeil, M. (1989), 'Hospital outreach community-based health care; the case of Chogona, Kenya', *Social Science and Medicine,* vol.28, no.10, pp.1007–18.

Deck, F.L.O. (1986), 'Community Water Supply and Sanitation in Developing Countries 1970–1990: An Evaluation of the Levels and

Trends of Services', *World Health Statistics Quarterly,* vol.39, pp.2–31.

De Kadt, E. (1989), 'Making health policy management intersectoral: issues of information analysis and use in less developed countries', *Social Science and Medicine,* vol.29, no.4, pp.503–14.

Dettwyler, K.A. (1987), 'Breastfeeding and Weaning in Mali: Cultural Context and Hard Data', *Social Science and Medicine,* vol.24, no.8, pp.633–44.

DEVRES (1980), *The Socio-Economic Context of Fuelwood Use in Small Rural Communities,* AID Evaluation Special Study No.1, USAID, August.

DeWolfe Miller (1986), 'Boiling drinking water: a critical look', *Waterlines,* vol.5, no.1, July, pp.2–5.

Dey, J. (1981), 'Gambian Women: Unequal Partners in Rice Development Projects?' *Journal of Development Studies,* vol.17, no.3, April, pp.109–22.

Digerness, T.H. (1977), 'Wood for Fuel—The Energy Situation in Bara, the Sudan', mimeo, Department of Geography, University of Bergen, Norway, July (cited in Agarwal (1986), *op.cit.*).

Donohue, J.J. (1982), 'Facts and Figures on urbanisation in the developing world', *Assignment Children,* vols 57–8, pp.21–41.

Dore, R. (1976), *The Diploma Disease: Education, Qualification and Development,* London, George Allen and Unwin.

Dougna, K.D. (1987), 'Crise Economique et Crise de l'Education en Afrique', Paris, IIEP mimeo (IIEP/KD/87.06).

Dowler, E.A., Payne, P.R., Young, O.S., Thomson, A.M. and Wheeler, E.F. (1982), 'Nutritional Status Indicators: Interpretation and policy making role', *Food Policy,* May 1982, pp.99–111.

Dunlop, D.W. (1983), 'Health Care Financing: Recent Experiences in Africa', *Social Science and Medicine,* vol.17, no.24, pp.2017–25.

Earthscan (1983), 'Earthscan Press Briefing Document No.37', mimeo, London, International Institute for Environment and Development.

Economic Commission for Africa (annual), *Demographic Handbook for Africa,* UNECA.

Edingbola, L.K., Walts, S.J., Kale, O.O., Smith, G.S. and Hopkins, D.R. (1986), 'A Method of Rapid Assessment of the Distribution and Endemicity of Dracunculiasis in Nigeria', *Social Science and Medicine,* vol.23, no.6, pp.555–8.

Egero, B. (1973), 'Errors in the census of the population of Tanzania' and 'Non-sampling errors', in Egero, B. and Henin, R.A. (eds.)(1973), *The Population of Tanzania: An Analysis of the 1967*

Population Census, Census vol.6, Dar es Salaam, Bureau of Statistics.

Eicher, C.K. and Baker, D.C. (1982), *Research in Agricultural Development in Sub-Saharan Africa: A Critical Survey,* East Lansing, My.Dept.of Agric.Econ., MSU International Development Paper No.1.

Ei Nagar, S.E.H. (1988), 'Changing patterns of participation of women in petty-trading activities in Khartoum', *The Ahfad Journal,* vol.5, no.7, pp.14–23.

Elkan, W. (1988a), 'Energy in Rural Africa: an Economist's Approach', pp.64–76, in Rimmer, D. (ed.), *op.cit.*

Elkan, W. (1988b), 'Alternatives to Fuelwood in African Towns', *World Development,* vol.16, no.4, pp.527–33.

Ellis, R.P. (1987), 'The revenue generating potential of user fees in Kenyan government health facilities', *Social Science and Medicine,* vol.25, no.9, pp.995–1002.

Enabor, E.E. (1976), 'Wood consumption requirements in Nigeria: a reassessment', *Nigerian Journal of Economic and Social Studies,* vol.18, no.1, pp.121–45.

Ernst, E. (1977), 'Fuel Consumption Among Rural Families in Upper Volta, West Africa', mimeo, Ouayadougou, Peace Corps, July 5 (cited in Argawal (1986), *op.cit.*).

Eveleth, P.B. and Tanner, J.M. (1976), *Worldwide Variations in Human Growth,* New York, Cambridge University Press.

Faniran, A. (1986), 'The perception of water quality among rural communities in South-Western Nigeria: Lessons for Planners', *Water International,* vol.11, pp.169–74.

FAO, Food and Agricultural Organisations (1985), 'Food and Agriculture Situation in African Countries Affected by Calamities in 1983–85', Report No.7, FAO/WFP Task Force, Rome.

Fassin, D. (1987), 'Illicit sale of pharmaceuticals in Africa: sellers and clients in the suburbs of Dakar', *Tropical Geographical Medicine,* vol.40, no.2, pp.166–70.

Fassin, D. and Fassin, E. (1988), 'Traditional medicine and the stakes of legitimation in Senegal', *Social Science and Medicine,* vol.27, no.4, pp.353–7.

Feachem, R.G. (1980), 'Community Participation in Appropriate Water Supply and Sanitation Technologies: The Mythology for the Decade', *Proceedings of the Royal Society,* B209, pp.15–29, London, The Royal Society.

Feachem, R., Burns, E., Cairncross, S., Cronin, A., Cross, P., Curtis, D., Kahn, M., Lamb, D. and Southall, H. (1978), *Water, Health and Development: an Interdisciplinary Evaluation,* Tri-Med. Books.

Federal Office of Statistics, Nigeria (1982), *National Integrated Survey of Households: health and nutrition module,* Nigeria, Lagos, FDS.

Federal Office of Statistics, Nigeria (1983), *The Health of Nigerians,* Nigeria, Lagos, FDS.

Federal Office of Statistics, Nigeria (1983), *National Integrated Survey of Households: reports of the general household survey,* Nigeria, Lagos.

Federal Office of Statistics, Nigeria (1985), *National Integrated Survey of Households, 1983–84,* Lagos, Federal Office of Statistics.

Ferguson, A. (1986), 'Women's Health in a Marginal Area of Kenya', *Social Science and Medicine,* vol.23, no.1, pp.17–29.

Fetter, B. (1985), 'Decoding and Interpreting African Census Data: Vital Evidence from an Unsavoury Witness', in *Proceedings of American African Studies Association,* pp.83–105.

Fieldhouse, D.K. (1986), *Black Africa, 1945–80, Economic Decolonization and Arrested Development,* London, Allen and Unwin.

Fleuret, P.C. and Fleuret, A. (1978), 'Fuelwood Use in a Peasant Community: A Tanzanian Case Study', *The Journal of Developing Areas,* 12 April.

Floor, W.M. (1977), 'The Energy Sector of the Sahelian Countries', mimeo, Policy Planning Section, Ministry of Foreign Affairs, The Netherlands (cited in Agarwal 1986, *op.cit.*).

Floud, R. (1984), *Measuring the Transformation of European Economies: Income, Health and Welfare,* Discussion Paper No.33, Centre for Economic Policy Research, London.

Fluitman, F. (1983), *Socio-Economic Impact of Rural Electrification in Developing Countries: A Review of the Evidence,* International Labour Offices, Geneva Working Paper, November 1983.

Fortney, J.A. Susanti, I., Gadalla, S., Saleh, S., Rogers, S.M. and Potts, M. (1986), 'Reproductive mortality in two developing countries', *American Journal of Public Health,* vol.76, pp.134–8.

Freire, P. (1972), *Pedagogy of the Oppressed,* Penguin, Harmondsworth.

French, D. (1985), 'Economics of bioenergy in developing countries' in Egneus, H.et al (eds), *Bioenergy 84,* vol.5, London, Elsevier, pp.161–70.

Fresco, L. (1987), 'Cassava shifting cultivation: a systems approach to agricultural technical development in Africa', *Royal Tropical Institute,* Amsterdam.

Freund, P.J. (1986), 'Health care in a declining economy: the case of Zambia', *Social Science and Medicine,* vol.23, no.9, pp.875–88.

Fuller, B. (1986), 'Is Primary School Quality Eroding in the Third World?' *Comparative Education Review,* vol.30, no.4, pp.491–508.

Gakou, M.L. (1987), *The Crisis in African Agriculture,* UNU, Studies in African Political Economy.

Gelfand, M., Mavi, S. and Loewenson, R. (1981), 'The urban N'anga in practice', *Central African Journal of Medicine,* vol.27, no.5, pp.93–5.

Gilbert, A. and Gugler, J. (1981), *Cities, Poverty and Development, Urbanization in the Third World,* Oxford, Oxford University Press.

Goldsmith, E. (1985), 'Is Development the solution or the problem', *Ecologist,* no.15, p.211.

Goldstein, J.S. (1985), 'Basic Human Needs: The Plateau Curve', *World Development,* vol.13, no.5, pp.595–609.

Gomez, F.et al (1955), 'Malnutrition in infancy and childhood with special reference to Kwashiorkor', in *Advances in Paediatrics,* vol.VII, Chicago, Ill., Yearbook Publishers.

Good, C.M. (1980), 'A comparison of rural and urban ethnomedicine among the Kamba of Kenya', in Ulin, P. and Seagall, M.H. (eds), *Traditional Health Care Delivery in Contemporary Africa,* New York, Syracuse Univ.Press.

Gordon, G. (1979), 'The Hungry Season in the Savanna of West Africa', presented to conference on *Rapid Rural Appraisal* held at the Institute of Development Studies, University of Sussex, 4–7 December.

Gorstein, J. and Akre, J. (1988), 'The Use of Anthropometry to Assess Nutritional Status', *World Health Statistics Quarterly,* vol.41, pp.48–57.

Gouteux, J.P., Bansimba, P., Bissadidi, N. and Noireau, F. (1987), 'La prise en charge de la lutte contra les tsetse par les communautes rurales: premiers essais dans cinq villages congolais', *Ann. Soc. Belge Med. Trop.,* vol.67, pp.37–49.

Goyea, H.S. (1988), 'The Low Income Preschools in Benin City: some health aspects of the children', *Tropical Geographical Medicine,* vol.40, no.4, pp.369–72.

Graham, W. and Airey, P. (1987), 'Measuring maternal mortality: sense and sensitivity', *Health Policy and Planning,* vol.2, no.4, pp.323–33, Oxford University Press, 1987.

Granotier (1977), cited in Ankerl, G. (1986), *op.cit.*

Grant, J.P. (1973), 'Development: The end of trickle down?' *Foreign Policy,* vol.12.

Gray, C.S. (1986), 'State-Sponsored Primary Health Care in Africa: The Recurrent Cost of Performing Miracles', *Social Science and Medicine,* vol.22, no.3, pp.361–8.

Green, C. and Kirkpatrick, C. (1982), 'A Cross Section Analysis of Food Insecurity in Developing Countries.Its Magnitude and Sources', *Journal of Development Studies,* vol.18, pp.185–204.

Greenstreet, M. (1981), 'Females in the Agricultural Labour Force and Non-Formal Education for Rural Development in Ghana'.Institute for International Studies, The Hague, August 1981 (Occasional Papers No.90).

Greiner, T., Almroth, S. and Latham, M. (1979), *The Economic Value of Breast Feeding,* Cornell International Monograph, Series No.6.

Grosse, R. and Perry, B. (1982), 'Correlates of life expectancy in less developed countries', *Health Policy and Education,* vol.2, pp.275–304.

Gunnar, J. (1968), *Provisional Estimates of Fertility, Mortality and Population Growth for Tanzania,* Dar es Salaam: Central Bureau of Statistics, Min.of Economic Affairs and Development Planning.

Guyer, J.I. (1984), 'Women's work and production systems: a review of two reports on the agricultural crisis', *Review of African Political Economy,* no.27/28.

Haaga, J. (1986), 'Cost-effectiveness and cost-benefit analyses of immunization programmes in developing countries', in Jelliffe, D.B. and Jelliffe, E.F.P. (eds.), *Advances in International Maternal and Child Health,* Oxford, Clarendon Press, pp.195–220.

Haaga, J., Kenrick, C., Test, K. and Mason, J. (1985), 'An Estimate of the Prevalence of Child Malnutrition in Developing Countries', *World Health Statistics Quarterly,* vol.38, pp.331–47.

Habicht, B. and Chamie, J., *Estimates and Projections of Infant Mortality Rates,* New York, Population Association of America/United Nations Population Division, 1982.

Habicht, J.P., Martorell, R. and Yarborough, C. et al (1974), 'Height and weight standards for pre-school children: are there really ethnic differences in growth potential?' *Lancet,* vol.1, pp.611–15.

Hale, S. (1985), 'Private and public labour: the Sudanese woman worker in the 1980s—a pilot study', *The Afhad Journal,* vol.2, no.2, December, pp.36–40.

Hall et al (1982) cited in Elkan (1988a), *op.cit.*

Halstead, S.B., Walsh, J.A. and Warren K.S. (eds) (1985), *Good health at low cost: Proceedings of a conference held at Bellagio, Italy, 29 April–2 May 1985,* New York; Rockefeller Foundation.

Haper, N. (1981), Women, Subsistence and the Informal Sector: Towards a Framework of Analysis.Discussion Paper 163.August, Brighton, Institute of Development Studies, University of Sussex.

Harpham, T. (1986), 'Review article: Health and the Urban Poor', *Health Policy and Planning*, vol.1, no.1, pp.5–18.

Harrison, I.E. (1979), 'Traditional Healers: a neglected source of health manpower', in Z.A.Ademuwagun et al (eds), *African Therapeutic Systems*, Waltham, Mass., Cross Roads Press.

Heligman, L.et al (1978), *Measurement of Infant Mortality in Less Developed Countries*, Washington DC, US Bureau of the Census.

Henderson, R.H., Keja, J., Hayden, G., Galazka, A., Clements, J. and Chan, C. (1988), 'Vacciner les enfants du monde: progres et perspectives', *Bulletin de l'Organisation mondiale de la Sante*, vol.66, no.6, pp.699–707.

Hey, R.W. and Rukuni, M. (1988), 'SADCC Food Security and Strategies', *World Development*, vol.16, no.9, pp.1013–24.

Heyneman, S.P. (1983), 'Education during a period of austerity: Uganda, 1971–1981', *Comparative Education Review*, vol.27, no.3, October, pp.403–16.

Heyneman, S.P. and Loxley, W.A. (1983), 'The Impact of Primary School Quality on Academic Achievement across Twenty-Nine High- and Low-Income Countries', *American Journal of Sociology*, vol.88 (6) June, pp.1162–94.

Heyneman, S.P. and Loxley, W.A. (1983), 'The Distribution of Primary School Quality within High- and Low-Income Countries', *Comparative Education Review*, vol.27, no.1, pp.108–18.

Hicks, N. and Streeton, P. (1979), 'Indicators of development: the search for a basic needs yardstick', *World Development*, vol.7, no.6, pp.567–80.

Hildebrand, P.E. (1981), 'Combining Disciplines in Rapid Appraisal: the Sondeo Approach', *Agricultural Administration*, vol.8, no.6, November, pp.423–32.

Hill, A.G. and Graham, W.J., (1987), *Sources of Health and Mortality Information in Mali, Senegal, The Gambia and Sierra Leone*, Technical Report, Ottawa, Canada, IDRC.

Hirschorn, N. (1987), 'Oral Rehydration Therapy: The Programme and the Promise', in Cash, Kuesch and Lamstein (eds), *op.cit.*, pp.21–46.

Hogh, B. and Petersen, E. (1984), 'The Basic Health Care System in Botswana: A Study of the Distribution and Cost in the Period 1973–1979', *Social Science and Medicine*, vol.19, no.8, pp.783–92.

Horton, S., Kerr, T. and Diakosavvas, D. (1988), 'The Social Cost of Higher Food Prices: Some Cross-Country Evidence', *World Development,* vol.7, no.16, pp.847–56.

Hunter, J.M. (1967), 'Seasonal hunger in a part of the West African savanna: a survey of body weights in Nangodi', *Trans. Inst. Br. Geog.,* publication no.41, pp.167–85.

Hussain, M.A. (1985), 'Seasonal variation and nutrition in developing countries', *Food and Nutrition,* vol.11, no.2, pp.23–7.

Illsley, R. and Mitchell, R.G. (1984), *Low Birthweight: A Medical.Psychological and Sociological Study*, Chichester, John Wiley.

Imo State Evaluation Team (1989), 'Evaluating water and sanitation projects: lessons from Imo State, Nigeria', *Health Policy and Planning,* vol.4, no.1, pp.40–49.

Imperato, P.J. (1974), 'Traditional medical practitioners among the Bambara of Mali and their role in the modern health care delivery system', *Rural Africana,* vol.26, pp.41–54.

ILO, International Labour Office (1976), *Employment Growth and Basic Needs: A One World Problem,* ILO, Geneva.

ILO, International Labour Office (1984), *Rural Development and Women in Africa,* ILO/WEP Study, Geneva.

Jacobson, B. (1986), 'Third World Women—the invisible tobacco users', *Health Policy and Planning,* vol.1, no.4, pp.357–9.

Jakobsen, O. (1987), 'Economic and Geographical Factors Influencing Child Malnutrition in the Southern Highlands, Tanzania', in Akhtar, *op.cit.,* pp.203–44.

Jamal, V. (1982), *Rural-urban gap and income distribution in Africa: the case of Kenya, Lesotho, Nigeria, Sierra Leone, Somalia, Tanzania.* Six separate case studies, Addis Ababa, ILO/JASPA.

Jamal, V. (1988), 'Getting the crisis right', *International Labour Review,* vol.127, no.6, pp.655–78.

Jamal, V. and Weeks, J. (1988), 'The vanishing rural-urban gap in sub-Saharan Africa', *International Labour Review,* vol.127, no.3, pp.271–92.

Jameson, K.P. (1983), 'A Critical Examination of 'The Patterns of Development'', *The Journal of Development Studies,* vol.18, no.4, pp.431–6.

Jazeiri, N.T. (1976), *Approaches to the Development of Health Indicators,* Paris, OECD, Special Studies No.2.

Johansson, S. (1976), *The Theory of Social Reporting,* Swedish Institute of Social Research, Stockholm.

Johnston, A., Kaluba, H, Karlsson, M. and Nyström, K. (1987) *Education and Economic Crisis,* Stockholm, SIDA (Education Division Documents no.38)

Johnston, A. and Nyström, K. (1987), *Education Support to Mozambique: A Question of Survival,* in A. Johnston, H. Kaluba, M. Karlsson and K. Nyström (1987) *op.cit.*

Jolly, R. and Cornia, G.A. (1984), *The Impact of World Recession on Children,* Oxford.

Kahn, A.R. (1976), 'Basic Needs: an illustrative exercise in identification and quantification with reference to Bangladesh', mimeo, Geneva, ILO.

Kalache, A. (1986), 'Ageing in developing countries: are we meeting the challenge?' *Health Policy and Planning,* vol.1, no.2, pp.171–5.

Kaluba, H. and Karlsson, M. (1987), 'Education Support to Zambia: Keeping up Coverage and Standards', in Johnston, A., Kaluba, M., Karlsson, M. and Nyström, K., *op. cit.*

Kaseje, D.C.O. and Sempebura, E.K.N. (1989), 'An integrated rural health project in Saradidi, Kenya', *Social Science and Medicine,* vol.28, no.10, pp.1063–72.

Keller, W. and Fillmore, C. (1983), 'Prevalence of protein energy malnutrition', *World Health Statistics Quarterly,* vol.36, pp.129–66.

Kennedy, E. and Cogill, B. (1988), 'The Commercialization of Agriculture and Household-level Food Security: The Case of Southwestern Kenya', *World Development,* vol.16, no.9, pp.1075–81.

Kerejan, H. and Konan, N. (1981), 'Approche des problemes alimentaires et nutritionels d'une megalopolis africaine', *Medicin Afrique Noire,* vol.28, pp.479–82.

Khadam, M.A.A. (1988), 'Factors influencing per capita water consumption in urban areas of developing countries and their implications for management, with special reference to the Khartoum Metropolitan Area', *Water International 13 (1988),* pp.226–9.

Kielmann, A.A. (1978), 'Mortality at Young Ages as an Indicator for Evaluation of Health Programmes in Developing Countries', *Ann. Soc. Belge Med. Trop.,* 1987, vol.67, suppl.1, pp.83–96.

King, J. and Ashworth, A. (1987), 'Historical review of the changing pattern of infant feeding in developing countries: the case of Malaysia, the Caribbean, Nigeria and Zaire', *Social Science and Medicine,* vol.25, no.12, pp.1307–20.

King, M., 'The Present State of Health in Africa' (1987), *Journal of Tropical Paediatrics,* vol.33, supplement 1, pp.6–12, Oxford University Press.

Kiray, M. (1970), 'Squatter housing—fast depeasantisation and slow workerisation in underdeveloped countries', Paper presented at *World Congress of Sociology,* Varna, Bulgaria.

Kirsch, T.D. (1988), 'Local Area Monitoring', *World Health Statistics Quarterly,* vol.41, pp.19–25.

Ki-Zerbo, J. (1981), 'Women and the Energy Crisis in the Sahel', *Unasylva,* vol.33, no.11 (cited in Agarwal (1986), *op.cit.*).

Knight, J.B. (1972), 'Rural-urban income comparisons and migration in Ghana', *Bulletin* (Oxford Institute of Economics and Statistics), May.

Knight, J.B. and Sabot, R.H. (1982), 'From migrants to proletarians: employment experience, mobility and wages in Tanzania', *Bulletin* (Oxford Institute of Economics and Statistics), August.

Koley, C. (1973), 'Agricultural data' in Egero and Henin (eds), 1973, *op.cit.*

Kossoudji, S. and Mueller, E. (1983), 'The economic and demographic status of female-headed households in rural Botswana', *Econ. Devl. Cult. Change,* July, pp.831–59.

Kpedekpo, G.M.K. (1967), 'The nature and extent of errors in the 1960 Ghana population census', *West African Journal of Science,* vol.12, pp.149–63.

Kpedekpo, G.M.K. (1970), *Studies on Vital Registration Data from Compulsory Registration Areas of Ghana, Vol 2: An Analysis of Seasonality of Births and Deaths,* Legon, Accra, Institute of Statistical, Social and Economic Research, University of Ghana.

Kpedekpo, G.M.K. and Arya, P.L. (1981), *Social and Economic Statistics for Africa,* London, George Allen and Unwin.

Kravis, I. (1981), *Real GDP per capita for more than one hundred countries,* Baltimore, Johns Hopkins University Press.

Kravis, I., Heston, A. and Sommers, R. (1982), *World Product and Income: International Comparisons of Real Product,* Baltimore, Johns Hopkins University Press.

Kumar, S.K. (1988), 'Effect of Seasonal Food Shortages on Agricultural Production in Zambia', *World Development,* vol.16, no.9, pp.1051–63.

Kuznets, S. (1972), 'Problems in comparing recent growth rates for developed and less developed countries', *Economic Development and Cultural Change,* vol.2, 2, pp.185–209.

Kweka, A.N. (1989), 'Women in Literacy Programmes and Underdevelopment: the Case of Tanzania', paper presented at 1989

Symposium of the Nordic Association for the Study of Education in Developing Countries on 'Women and Literacy—Yesterday, Today and Tomorrow', Hasselby-Slott, Sweden, June 8–10.

La Belle, T.J. (1982), 'Formal, non-formal and informal education: a holistic perspective on lifelong learning', *International Review of Education,* vol.28, no.2.

Ladipo, O.A. and Adelusi, B. (1977), 'Birthweights of Nigerian children at Ibadan', *East African Medical Journal,* vol.54, p.31.

Lawrence, P. (ed.)(1986), *World Recession and Food Crisis in Africa,* London, James Currey for ROAPE.

Lawrence, P. (1988), 'The Political Economy of the 'Green Revolution' in Africa', *Review of African Political Economy,* no.42, pp.59–75.

Lechtig, A. et al (1977), 'Low birth weight babies: world wide incidence, economic cost and program needs', pp.17–30 in Rooth, G. and Engstrom, L. (eds), *Perinatal care in developing countries,* Sweden, Uppsala, Perinatal Research Laboratory and WHO.

Lee, K.H. (1988), 'Universal Primary Education: An African Dilemma', *World Development,* vol.16, no.12, pp.1481–91.

Leipziger, D.M. and Leuss, M.A. (1980), 'Social indicators, growth and distribution', *World Development,* vol.8, no.4, pp.299–302.

Leslie, J. (1988), 'Women's Work and Child Nutrition in the Third World', *World Development,* vol.16, no.11, pp.1341–62.

Leslie, J. (1989), 'Women's time: a factor in the use of child survival technologies?' *Health Policy and Planning,* vol.4, no.1, pp.1–16.

Levi, J.F.S. (1973), 'Migration from the land and urban unemployment in Sierra Leone', *Bulletin* (Oxford Institute of Economics and Statistics), November.

Lewin, K.M. (1987), *Education in Austerity: options for planners,* Paris, IIEP (Fundamentals of educational planning No.36).

Lewis, B. (1984), 'The Impact of Development Policies on Women', in M.J.Hay and S.Stichter (eds), *African Women South of the Sahara,* Longman.

Lewis, J.R. (1974), 'Birthweights of infants in the Cameroon grasslands', *Bulletin World Health Organisation,* vol.50, p.575.

Lewis, O. (1965), *La Vida: a Puerto Rican family in the culture of poverty; San Juan and New York,* London, Secker and Warburg.

Lipton, M. (1977), *Why Poor People Stay Poor: a Study of Urban Bias in World Development,* London, Temple Smith.

Lipton, M. (1980), 'Migration from Rural Areas of Poor Countries: The Impact on Rural Productivity and Income Distribution', *World Development,* vol.8, no.1, pp.1–24.

Lisk, F. and Stevens, Y. (1987), 'Government Policy and Rural Women's Work in Sierra Leone', in C.Oppong (ed.), *Sex Roles, Population and Development in West Africa,* ILO.

Little, A. (1984), 'Education, earnings and productivity—the eternal triangle', in J.Oxenham (ed.), *Education Versus Qualifications,* London, George Allen and Unwin.

Loewenson, R. (1986), 'Farm Labour in Zimbabwe: a comparative study in health status', *Health Policy and Planning,* vol.1, no.1, pp.48–57.

Looney, R. (1988), 'Military Expenditure and Socio-Economic Development: a Survey of Recent Political Research', *Journal of Modern African Studies,* vol.26, no.2, pp.319–25.

Lourie, S. (1987), *Are Consequences of Adjustment Policies on Education Measurable?,* International Institute for Educational Planning (UNESCO), Paris.

Lucas, H. (1981), 'Review of *Data Collection in Developing Countries* by D.J.Casley and D.A.Lury', Oxford: Oxford University Press, in *Journal of Development Studies,* vol.17, pp.384–5.

MacCormack, C.P. (1988), 'Health and the Social Power of Women', *Social Science and Medicine,* vol.26, no.7, pp.677–83.

Macoloo, G.C. (1988), 'Housing the Urban Poor: A Case Study of Kisumu Town, Kenya', *Third World Planning Review,* vol.10, no.2, pp.159–74.

Madsen, B. (1984), *Women's Mobilisation and Integration in Development: A Village Case Study from Tanzania,* Centre for Development Research Copenhagen, CDR Research Report No.3.

Maine, D., (1989), 'Attention and Inattention to Maternal Mortality in International Agencies', in Maine, D. et al (eds), *Women and Crisis in Southern Africa,* pp.84–89.

Maine, D., Rosenfield, A., Wallace, M., Kimbalt, A.M., Kiyast, B.E., Papiernik, E. and White, S. (1987), *Prevention of maternal mortality in developing countries: programme options and practical considerations,* Background paper prepared for the International 'Safe Motherhood' Conference, Nairobi, 10–13 February 1987.

Manton, K.G. (1988), 'The Global Impact of non-communicable diseases: estimates and projections', *World Health Statistics Quarterly,* vol.41, pp.255–66.

Maro, P.S., 'Reducing Inequalities in the Distribution of Health Facilities in Tanzania', in Akhtar, *op.cit,* pp.415–26.

Martin, C.J. (1984), 'Education and Inequality: The Case of Maragoli, Kenya', *Int.J.Educational Development,* vol.4, no.2, pp.97–112.

Martorell, R. and Habicht, J-P. (1986), 'Growth in early childhood in developing countries', in Tanner, J. (ed.), *Human Growth: a comprehensive treatise,* New York, Plenum Press (2nd ed.).

Matomara, M.K.S. (1989), 'A people-centred approach to primary health care implementation in Mvumi, Tanzania', *Social Science and Medicine,* vol.28, no.10, pp.1031–8.

Mbise, R.L. and Boersma, E.R. (1979), 'Factors associated with low birthweight in the population of Dar es Salaam, Tanzania', *Tropical Geographical Medicine,* vol.31, p.21–32.

Mburu, F.M. and Steinkuller, P.G. (1983), 'Ocular needs in Africa: Increasing priorities and shrinking resources', *Social Science and Medicine,* vol.17, no.22, pp.1687–91.

McGranahan, D.V., Richard-Proust, C., Sovani, N.V. and Subramanian, M., (1972),*Contents and Measurement of Socio-Economic Development,* New York, Praeger for UNRISD.

McKeown, T.S. (1976), *The Role of Medicine: Dream, Mirage or Nemesis?* London, Nuffield Hospital Trust.

Mehaniah, J. and Kimpianga M. (1981), 'La Structure Multidimensionnelle de Guerison a Kinshasa, Capitale du Zaire', *Social Science and Medicine,* vol.158, no.3, pp.341–9.

Midgley, J. with A.Hall, M.Hardman and D.Narine, (1986)(ed.), *Community: Participation, Social Development and the State,* London, Methuen.

Miles, I. (1985), *Social Indicators for Human Development,* London, Pinter, for United Nations University.

Mingat, A. and Tan, J.P. (1985), 'Subsidization of Higher Education Versus Expansion and Primary Enrollments: What Can a Shift of Resources Achieve in Sub-Saharan Africa?' *International Journal of Educational Development,* vol.5, no.4, pp.259–68.

Morley, D. (1987) 'Medical Needs of African Children—Can they be met by the Year 2000', *J. Tropical Paediatrics,* vol.33, Supplement 1, pp.9–12.

Morris, M.D. (1979), *Measuring the Conditions of the World's Poor:. The Physical Quality of Life Index,* New York.

Mosley, W.H. and Chen, L.C. (1984), 'An Analytical Framework for the Study of Child Survival in Developing Countries', *Population and Development Review,* vol.10, supplement, pp.25–45.

Mosley, W.H. and Chen, L.C. (1984), *Child Survival: strategies for research,* Cambridge, Cambridge University Press.

Mott, F.L. and Mott, S.M. (1980), 'Kenya's record population growth: a dilemma of development', *Population Bulletin,* vol.35, no.1, p.2.

Mueller, E. (1977), 'The economic value of children in peasant agriculture', in R.G.Ridker (ed.), *Population and Development,* Baltimore, Johns Hopkins University Press.

Murdock, G.P. (1967), *Ethnographic Atlas,* University of Pittsburgh, Pittsburgh, Penn.

Murray, C.J.L. (1987), 'A Critical Review of International Mortality Data', *Social Science and Medicine,* vol.25, no.7, pp.773–81.

Mustafa, M. El Murtada (1985), 'Women, work and development: a view from Sudan', *The Afhad Journal,* vol.2, no.1, pp.39–45.

Mwabu, G.M. (1986), 'Health care decisions at the household level: results of a rural health survey in Kenya', *Social Science and Medicine,* vol.22, no.3, pp.315–19.

Mwanasangezi-bin-Moussa and Groenen G. (1987), 'Reasons for non-response during an ongoing leprosy survey in Northern Zaire', *Annales Soc. Belge Med. Trop.,* pp.271–5.

Mwangi, W.M. and Mwabu, G.M. (1986), 'Economics of Health and Nutrition in Kenya', *Social Science and Medicine,* vol.22, no.7, pp.775–80.

Nabarro, D. and Graham-Jones, S. (1987), 'Appropriate information systems for primary health care', paper presented to Conferences on *Health Interventions and Mortality Change in Developing Countries,* University of Sheffield, 9–11 September, 1987.

Nelson, J. and Mandl, P.E. (1978), 'Peri-urban malnutrition: a neglected problem', *Assignment Children,* vol.43, pp.25–46.

Nelson, N. (1981), 'Introduction' to Special Issue on African Women in the Development Process, vol.17, no.3, April, pp.1–9.

Nestel, P. (1986), 'A Society in Transition: Developmental and Seasonal Influences on the Nutrition of Maasai Women and Children', *Food and Nutrition Bulletin,* vol.8, no.1, pp.2–18.

NEIDA, Network for Educational Innovations and Development in Africa, *Education and Productive Work in Africa,* UNESCO/BREDA/NEIDA, Dakar, n.d. (c.1979).

Newman, Jeanne S. (1984), *Women of the World: Sub-Saharan Africa,* US Bureau of the Census, US Office of Women in Development, August 1984.

Nissinen, A., Bothig, S. Granroth, H. and Lopez, A.D. (1988), 'Hypertension in developing countries', *World Health Statistics Quarterly,* vol.41, pp.141–54.

Nordberg, E. (1986), *Invisible Needs (Past household surveys in Third World countries. A review of methods.* Stockholm, Karolinska Institutet, International Health Care Research.

Nordhaus, W.D. and Tobin, J. (1973), 'Is growth obsolete?', in Moss, M. (ed.), *The Measurement of Economic and Social Performance,* New York, National Bureau of Economic Research.

Odebiyi, A.I. and Togonu-Bickersteth, F. (1988), 'Deafness in the Yoruba medical system', *Social Science and Medicine,* vol.24, no.8, pp.645–9.

Ojedide, A.D. et al (1977), 'Traditional healers and mental illness in the city of Ibadan', *African Journal of Psychiatry,* vol.3, pp.99–106.

ODI, Overseas Development Institute (1985), 'Africa's Food Crisis', *Briefing Paper,* London.

Oduntan, S.Olu, Odunlami, V.B. and Ayeni, O. (1977), 'The birthweights of Nigerian babies', *Environmental Child Health,* vol.23, pp.141–4.

OECD, Organisation for Economic Cooperation and Development (1970), *List of Social Concerns,* Paris, OECD.

Okafor, S.I. (1987), 'Inequalities in the distribution of Health care facilities in Nigeria', in Akhtar (1987)(ed.), *op.cit,* pp.383–402.

Olowe, Samuel A. (1981), 'Standards of intrauterine growth for an African population at sea level', *Journal of Paediatrics,* vol.99, p.489.

Olukoya, A.A. (1986), 'Traditional Child Spacing Practices of Women: Experiences from a Primary Care Project in Lagos, Nigeria', *Social Science and Medicine,* vol.23, no.3, pp.333–6.

Olusanya, O., Ogbemi, S., Unuigbe, J. and Oronsaye, A. (1986), 'The pattern of rape in Benin City, Nigeria', *Tropical Geographical Medicine,* pp.215–20.

Olusi, S.O., Ademowore, A.S. and Ajani, G.Bola (1979), 'Biochemical assessment of the nutritional state of growth of different socio-economic classes at the Wesley Guild Hospital, Ilesha, Nigeria', *Journal of Tropical Medicine and Hygiene,* vol.82, p.8.

Oni, G.A. (1988), 'Child mortality in a Nigerian city: its levels and socio-economic differentials', *Social Science and Medicine,* vol.27, no.6, pp.607–14.

Oni, G.A. and Ariganjoye, O. (1986), 'A Study of some of the predisposing factors to low birthweight in a Nigerian community', *East African Medical Journal,* vol.63, no.2 (February), pp.121–30.

Oppong, C. (1987)(ed.), *Sex Roles, Population and Development,* London, James Currey.

Osuhor, P.C. and Yakasai, B.A. (1981), 'Low birthweight in Kano City, northern Nigeria', *Public Health Lond.95,* p.36.

Oyebola, D.D.O. (1980), 'The method of training of the traditional healers and midwives among the Yoruba of Nigeria', *Social Science and Medicine*, vol.14A, no.1, pp.31–38.

Packard, R.M. (1986), 'Agricultural Development, Migrant Labour and the Resurgence of Malaria in Swaziland', *Social Science and Medicine*, vol.22, no.8, pp.861–7.

Palmer, I. (1985), *Women: Roles and Gender Differences in Development: the Impact of Male Outmigration on Women in Farming*, New York, Population Council.

PANOS Institute (1989), *Aids and the Third World* (revised edition), London, Panos Institute, Dorner No.3.

Papanek, G.F. (1978), 'Economic Growth, Income Distribution and the Political Process in Less Developed Countries', in Z.Grilliches, W.Krelle, H-J.Krupp and O.Kya, *Income Distribution and Economic Inequality*, New York, Halstead, pp.259–73.

Peattie, L. (1975), 'Tertiarisation and urban poverty in Latin America', *Latin American Urban Research*, vol.5, pp.109–23.

Pickering, H. (1985), 'Social and Environmental Factors Associated with Diarrhoea and Growth in Young Children: Child Health in Urban Africa', *Social Science and Medicine*, vol.21, no.2, pp.121–7.

Piven, F.F. (1977), 'The Political Uses of 'Planning' and Decentralisation in the United States', in *Inter Sectoral Educational Planning*, Paris, OECD, pp.268–89.

Piwoz, E.G. and Viteri, F.E. (1985), 'Studying Health and Nutrition Behaviour by Examining Household Decision-Making, Intra-Household Resource Distribution, and the Role of Women in these Processes', *Food and Nutrition Bulletin*, vol.7, no.4, pp.1–31.

Population Council (1986), *Socio-Economic Indicators of Women's Status in Developing Countries 1970–80*, New York, The Population Council.

Psacharopoulos, G. (1984), 'The contribution of education to economic growth: international comparisons', in J.W.Kendrick (ed.), *International Comparisons of Productivity and Causes of the Slowdown*, American Enterprise Institute/Ballinger, Cambridge.

Raikes, P. (1986), 'Flowing with milk and honey: agriculture and food production in Africa and the EEC', in Peter Lawrence (ed.), *World Recession and the Food Crisis in Africa*, (1986), London, James Curry, ROAPE, pp.160–76.

Rakodi, 'Urban Agriculture: Research Questions and Zambian Evidence', *Journal of Modern African Studies*, vol.26, no.3.

Ram, R. (1985), 'The Role of Real Income Level and Income Distribution in Fulfillment of Basic Needs', *World Development,* vol.13, no.5, pp.589–94.

Ram, R. (1988), 'Economic Development and Income Inequality: Further Evidence on the U-Curve Hypothesis', *World Development,* vol.16, no.11, pp.1371–6.

Reardon, T., Matlon, P. and Delgado, C. (1988), 'Coping with household-level food insecurity in drought affected areas of Burkina Faso', *World Development,* vol.16, no.9, pp.1065–974.

Rehan, N. and Tafida, D.S. (1980), 'Multiple births in Hausa women', *British Journal of Obstetrics and Gynaecology,* vol.87, p.997.

Republic of Kenya (1981), 'Infant Mortality in Kenya: past and present differentials', *Social Perspectives,* vol.6, no.1, p.2.

Republic of Kenya (1983), *Third Rural Child Nutrition Survey 1982,* Central Bureau of Statistics, Ministry of Finance and Planning, Nairobi.

Riessman, L. (1964), *The Urban Process,* New York, Macmillan.

Rifkin, S.B., Muller, F. and Bichmann, W. (1988), 'Primary Health Care: On Measuring Participation', *Social Science and Medicine,* vol.26, no.9, pp.931–40.

Rimmer, D. (1988), 'Introduction', pp.1–15 in D.Rimmer, *op.cit.*

Rimmer, D. (ed.)(1988), *Rural Transformation in Tropical Africa,* London, Pinter.

Robertson, C.C. (1984), 'Formal or Nonformal Education? Entrepreneurial Women in Ghana', *Comparative Education Review,* vol.28, no.4, pp.639–58.

Rosenfield, A. and Maine, D. (1985), ' Maternal Mortality in Developing Countries: a note on the choice of denominator' (a letter), *International Journal of Epidemiology,* vol.13, no.4, pp.246–7.

Rosetta, L. (1988), 'Seasonal changes and the physical development of young Serere children in Senegal', *Annals of Human Biology,* vol.15, no.3, pp.179–89.

Rossi-Espagnet, A. (1984), *Primary Health Care in Urban Areas: Reaching the Urban Poor in Developing Countries,* A State of the Art Report by UNICEF and WHO, Report No.2499M, Geneva, WHO.

Royston, E. (1982), 'The Prevalence of Nutritional Anaemia in Women in Developing Countries: A Critical Review of Available Information', *World Health Statistics Quarterly,* vol.35, pp.52–91.

Royston, E. and Lopez, A.D. (1987), 'On the Assessment of Maternal Mortality', *World Health Statistics Quarterly,* vol.40, pp.214–24.

Rutstein, S.O. (1983), *Infant and Child Mortality Levels, Trends and Demographic Differentials, Revised Edition,* World Fertility Survey Comparative Studies, No.43.

Safilios-Rothschild, C. (1986), *Socioeconomic Indicators of Women's Status in Developing Countries, 1970–1980,* The Population Council, May.

Salamone, F. (1977), 'The methodological significance of the living informant', *Anthropological Quarterly,* vol.50, no.3, pp.117–24.

Salau, A.T. (1979), 'The Urban Process in Africa', *African Urban Studies,* vol.4 (Spring 1979), pp.27–34.

Sanders, D. and Carver, R. (1985), *The Struggle for Health: Medicine and the Politics of Underdevelopment,* London, Macmillan.

Sargent, C., McKinney, C. and Wetherington, R.K. (1986), 'Socioeconomic status and the incidence of low birthweight among the Bariba of Benin', *East African Medical Journal,* vol.62, no.2, pp.91–8.

Saunders, R.J. and Warford, J.J. (1976), *Village Water Supply: Economics and Policy in the Developing World,* Baltimore, John Hopkins University Press.

Scandizzo, (1984), 'Aggregate supply response: empirical evidence on key issues' In Horton, Kerr and Diakosavvas, *op. cit.*

Schatz, S.P. (1986), 'African Food Imports and Food Production: an Erroneous Interpretation', *Journal of Modern African Studies,* vol.24, no.1, pp.177–8.

Schiefelbein, E. and Simmons, J., *The determinants of school achievement: a review of research for developing countries,* Ottawa, IDRC, 1981.

Scholing, E. and Timmerman, V. (1988), 'Why LDC Growth Rates Differ: Measuring 'Unmeasurable' Influences', *World Development,* vol.16, no.11, pp.1271–94.

Schuftan, C. (1981), 'Nutrition Intervention Programmes for Rural Areas: African Experiences', *Journal of Tropical Paediatrics,* vol.27, pp.177–81.

Schumacher, E. (1973), *Small is Beautiful: Economics as if People Mattered,* London, Blond and Briggs.

Schwartz, A. (1983), 'Tradition et Changements dans la Societe Cruere (Cote d'Ivoire)', Paris, Office de la Recherche Scientifique et Technique Outre-Mer (ORSTROM).

Scott, W. (1988), 'Community-based health reporting', *World Health Statistics Quarterly,* vol.41, pp.26–31.

Scott, W. with Argalis, H. and McGranahan, D.V. (1973), *The Measurement of Real Progress at the Local Level,* Geneva, UNRISD.

Scott-Emuakpor, M.M. and Okafor, U.A. (1986), 'Comparative Study of Morbidity and Mortality of Breast-Fed and Bottle-Fed Nigerian Infants', *East African Medical Journal,* vol.63, no.7, pp.452–7.

Scrimshaw, N.S. (1987), 'Summarising the UNICEF Conference on Child Health and Survival: A Personal Opinion', in Cash, Kuesch and Lamstein (eds), *op.cit.,* pp.244–250.

Seers, D. (1979), 'The meaning of development, with a postscript', in Lehmann, D. (ed) (1979), *Development Theory: Four Critical Studies,* Bournemouth, Cass.

Seers, D. (1975), 'The Political Economy of National Accounting' in A.Cairncross and M.Puri (eds), *Employment, Income Distribution and Development Strategy,* London, Macmillan.

Seers, D. (1983), *The Political Economy of Nationalism,* Oxford University Press.

Segall, M. and Vienonen, M., 'Haikko declaration on actions for primary health care', *Health Policy and Planning,* vol.2, no.3, pp.258–65.

Sen, A.K. (1981a), *Poverty and Famine,* Oxford, Clarendon Press.

Sen, A.K. (1981b), 'Public action and the quality of life in developing countries', *Oxford Bull. Econ. Statist.,* vol.43, pp.287–319.

Senaratne, S.P.F. (1978), 'Economic Development and the Sociological Consultant', paper for the Social Sciences Research Council Workshop, University of Sussex, Brighton, 1–2 July.

Senghor, D. and Diop, M. (1988), *L'utilisation des Medicins Traditionnels a Dakar,* Dakar, ENDA.

Seyoum, E., Kidane, Y., Gebru M. and Sevenhuysen, G. (1986), 'Preliminary Study of Income and Nutritional Status Indicators in Two Ethiopian Communities', *Food and Nutrition Bulletin,* vol.8, no.3, pp.37–41.

Sheehan, G. and Hopkins, M. (1979), *Basic Needs Performance: An Analysis of Some International Data,* ILO, Geneva.

Shepard, D.S., Sanoh, L. and Coffi, E. (1986), 'Cost-effectiveness of the expanded programme of immunization in the Ivory Coast', *Social Science and Medicine,* vol.22, pp.369–77.

Shourie, A. (1974), 'Sri-Lanka's National Accounts', *Marga,* vol.2, no.3 (Colombo).

Sindiga, I. (1985), 'The Persistence of High Fertility in Kenya', *Social Science and Medicine,* vol.20, no.1, pp.71–84.

Singer, H.W. (1977), 'Reflections on Sociological Aspects of Economic Growth Band on the Work of Bert Hoselitz', *Economic Development and Cultural Change,* vol.25, Supplement.

Sircar, B.K. and Dagnow, M.B. (1988), 'Beliefs and Practices Related to Diarrhoeal Diseases among Mothers in Gondar Region, Ethiopia', *Tropical and Geographical Medicine*, pp.259–63.

Sivard, R.L. (1983), *World Military and Social Expenditure*, Washington DC.

Sivard, R.L. (1985), *Women: a World Survey*, Washington DC, World Priorities.

Smith, C. (1988), 'The latrine acquisition curve: a tool for sanitation evaluation', *Waterlines*, vol.7, no.1, July 1988, pp.22–4.

Smith, R.L. (1979), 'Summary of Discussions' in Commonwealth Secretariat, *Universal Primary Education in Asia and the Pacific: Report of a Commonwealth Regional Seminar, Bangladesh*, London, Commonwealth Secretariat.

Stein, C.M., Gora, N.P. and Macheka, B.M. (1988), 'Self-medication with Chloroquine for Malaria Prophylaxis in Urban and Rural Zimbabweans', *Tropical and Geographical Medicine*, pp.264–68.

Stein, Z. and Susser, M. (1975), 'The Dutch Famine 1944–45 and the reproductive process', *Paediatric Research*, vol.9, no.70.

Sterky, G. and Millander, L. (eds)(1978), *Birth-Weight Distribution—An Indicator of Social Development*, Stockholm, SAREC Report No.R:2.

Stevenson, D., 'Inequalities in the distribution of health care facilities in Sierra Leone', in Akhtar, *op.cit*, pp.403–14.

Stewart, F. (1985), *Planning To Meet Basic Needs*, London, Macmillan.

Stewart, F. (1987) in G.A. Cornia, R. Jolly and F. Stewart, *op. cit.*

Stock, R. (1986), ''Disease and Development' or 'The Underdevelopment of Health': A Critical Review of Geographical Perspectives on African Health Problems', *Social Science and Medicine*, vol.23, no.7, pp.689–700.

Streeten, P. (1977), 'Basic Needs: an issues paper', Washington IBRD, mimeo.

Streeten, P.P. (1979), 'Basic Needs: Premises and Promises', *Journal of Policy Modeling*, vol.1, pp.136–46.

Stromquist, N. (1988), 'Recent Developments in Women: Education Closer to a Better Social Order', mimeo Stanford International Institute of Comparative Education.

Sule, B.F. and Oni, O.A. (1988), 'A New Approach for locating public standpipes in a water supply distribution network', *Water International*, vol.13 (1988), pp.85–91.

Swantz, M.L. (1985), *Women in Development: A Creative Role Denied? The Case of Tanzania*, Hurst and Co.

Tanner, J.M. (1982) 'The Potential of Auxological Data for Maintaining Economic and Social Well-Being', *Social Science History,* vol.6, no.4.

Tarrant, J.R. (1980), *Food Policy,* Chichester, John Wiley.

Teokul, W., Payne, P. and Dugdale, A. (1988), 'Seasonal variations in nutritional status in rural areas of developing countries: a review of the literature', *Food and Nutrition Bulletin,* vol.8, no.4, pp.7–10.

Thacker, S.B., Gibson Parrish, R., Trowbridge, F.L. and Surveillance Coordinating Group (1988), 'A Method for Evaluating Systems of Epidemiological Surveillance', *World Health Statistics Quarterly,* vol.41, pp.11–18.

Tietze, C., (1977), Maternal mortality—excluding abortion mortality, *World Health Statistics Report,* vol.30, pp.312–39.

Tjon a Ten, W.A., Kusin, J.A. and De With, C. (1985), 'Birthweight distribution in the Mantsonyane Area: Lesotho', *Tropical and Geographical Medicine,* pp.131–6.

Todaro, M.P. (1969), 'A model of urban unemployment and migration for less developed countries', *American Economic Review,* March.

Togolese Federation of Women in the Legal Profession (1986), 'Women's participation in development: the case of Togo', Chapter 1, pp.21–52, in UNESCO, *Women's Concerns and Planning a Methodological Approach for their integration into local, regional and national planning,* Socio-Economic Studies, vol.13.

Tsui, A.O., DeClerque, J. and Mangani, N. (1988), 'Maternal and socio-demographic correlates of child morbidity in Bas Zaire: the effects of maternal reporting', *Social Science and Medicine,* vol.26, no.7, pp.701–74.

Tuppen, C.J.S. and Deutrom, P.E.B. (1982), 'Comparisons of Educational Standards of Achievement when Opportunities for Education are Unequal', *Comparative Education Review,* vol.26, pp.69–77.

US Bureau of the Census (1983), *World Population 1983—Recent Demographic Estimates for Countries and Regions of the World,* 1983, Government Printing Office, Washington DC.

Uemura, K. (1988), 'World health situation and trend assessment from 1948 to 1988', *Bulletin of the World Health Organisation,* vol.66, no.6, pp.679–87.

Ulin, P.R. (1975), 'Traditional healers of Botswana in a changing society', in I.Harrison and D.W.Dunlop, *Traditional Healers: Use and Non-Use in Health Care Delivery,* Michigan, Michigan State University, The African Studies Center.

UN Annual Conference 116/5/Add 3, December 1984. Report of the Secretary General, Part 2.Development in Sectoral Areas, Health and Nutrition (replies to Part II of UN Questionnaire).

UN, United Nations (1974), *World Housing Survey,* UN Dept.of Economic and Social Affairs, Geneva (E/C.6/129, Sept.5).

UN, United Nations (1983), *Indirect Techniques for Demographic Estimation,* New York, United Nations, Department of International, Economic and Social Affairs (Population Studies, No.81).

UN, United Nations (1984a), *Data Bases for Mortality Measurement,* New York, United Nations Department of International Economic and Social Affairs, (Population Studies, No.84).

UN, United Nations (1984b), *Levels and Trends in Mortality since 1950.*

UN, United Nations (1985a), *World Population Prospects: Estimates and Projections as Assessed in 1982,* United Nations, New York.

UN, United Nations (1985b), *World Population Prospects, Trends and Policies: Monitoring Report,* United Nations, New York.

UN, United Nations (annual), *Demographic Yearbook,* New York, UN Statistical Office, Department of Economic and Social Affairs.

UN, United Nations Commission on Housing (1971), *The Improvement of Slums and Squatter Settlements,* New York.

UN, United Nations Commission on Housing (1984), *Improvement of Slums and Squatter Settlements: infrastructure and services,* New York.

UN Economic and Social Council, Economic Commission for Africa (1984), *The Role of Women in the Situation of the Food Crisis in Africa (implementation of the Lagos Plan of Action),* September.

UN Economic and Social Council, Economic Commission for Africa (1984), *Review and Appraisal of the Achievements of United Nations Decade for Women,* 1976–1985, August.

UNESCO, United Nations Educational Scientific and Cultural Organisation (1949), *Human Rights: Comments and Interpretations,* Allan Wingate, London.

UNESCO, United Nations Educational, Scientific and Cultural Organisation (1979), *Final Report of the Regional Seminar on the Applicability of Socio-Economic Indicators for Analysis and Planning in Africa,* Paris, UNESCO, Division of Socio-economic Analyses (55–79/WS/5).

UNESCO, United Nations Educational Scientific and Cultural Organisation (1988), *Compendium of Statistics on Illiteracy,* Statistical Reports and Studies no.30, Paris, UNESCO.

Unger, J.P. and Killingsworth, J.R. (1986), 'Selective Primary Health Care: A Critical Review of Methods and Results', *Social Science and Medicine,* vol.22, pp.1001–12.

UNICEF, United Nations International Children's Fund (1984), *Urban basic services: reaching children and women of the urban poor,* Occasional Paper Series No.3, New York, UNICEF.

UNICEF, United Nations International Children's Fund (1987), *Children on the Front Line,* New York, UNICEF.

UNICEF, United Nations International Children's Fund (1989), *The State of the World's Children,* New York, UNICEF.

UNICEF/Government of Somalia (1986), *Review of PHC 1986, North West Region,* Mogadisco Somalia Democratic Republic.

UNRISD, United Nations Research Institute for Social Development (1977), *Measurement of Real Progress at the Local Level: An Overview,* Geneva (UNRISD/77/C.25).

US Department of Commerce (1967), 'Basic Data on the Ethiopian Economy', *Overseas Business Reports,* Feb.1967, cited in Bondestam (1973), *op.cit.*

US Department of Commerce, Bureau of the Census (1985), *Women of the World: A Chartbook for Developing Regions,* Women in Development Bureaux, March.

USAID, US Agency for International Development (1986), *The US Response to the African Famine, 1984–86,* Washington DC.

Uyanga, J. (1980), 'Rural-urban differences in child care and breastfeeding behaviour in southeastern Nigeria', *Social Science and Medicine,* vol.14, pp.23–9.

Van Damme, J.M.G. (1985), 'The essential role of drinking water sanitation in primary health care', in *Tropical and Geographical Medicine,* pp.S21–S32.

Van der Geest, S. (1987), 'Self-Care and the Informal Sale of Drugs in South Cameroon', *Social Science and Medicine,* vol.25, no.3, pp.293–305.

Van Norren, B., Boerma, J.T. and Sempebura, E.K.N. (1989), 'Simplifying the evaluation of primary health care programmes', *Social Science and Medicine,* vol.28, no.10, pp.1091–7.

Vaughan, M. (1989), 'Measuring Crisis in Maternal and Child Health: an Historical Perspective', in D. Maine et al (eds), *Women and Crisis in Southern Africa,* pp.125–41.

Vella, V. and Adkinson, S. (1987), *Review of Community Based Health Care in Uganda,* Kampala/UNICEF.

von Braun, J. (1988), 'Effects of Technological Change in Agriculture on Food Consumption and Nutrition: Rise in a West African Setting', *World Development,* vol.16, no.9, pp.1083–98.

Vu, M. (1985), *World Population Projections 1985, Short- and Long-Term Estimates by Age and Sex With Related Demographic Statistics,* World Bank, Washington DC.

Waddington, C. and Enimayou, K. (1989), 'Impact of user changes in the Ashanti-Akim District of Ghana', *Int. J. of Health Planning and Management,* vol.6, pp.17–47.

Wagner, D.A., Spratt, J.E. and Klein, G.D. (1990), 'The Myth of Literacy Relapse', *International Journal of Educational Development.*

Waldron, I. (1987), 'Patterns and Causes of Excess Female Mortality Among Children in Developing Countries', *World Health Statistics Quarterly,* vol.40, pp.194–213.

Walsh, J.A. (1987), 'Immunization: A Question of Priorities', in Cash, Kuesch and Lamstein, *op. cit.,* pp.63–74.

Walsh, J.A. and Warren, K.S. (1979), 'Selective primary health care: an interim strategy for disease control in developing countries', *New England J. of Medicine,* vol.301, pp.967–74.

Waterlines (1988), 'Technical Briefing No.17, Health, Water and Sanitation, 1', *Waterlines,* vol.7, no.1, July 1988, pp.15–8.

White, G.F. and White, A.U. (1986), 'Potable Water for all: the Egyptian Experience with Rural Water Supply', *Water International,* vol.11, pp.54–63.

White, G.F., Bradley, D.J. and White, A.U. (1972), *Drawers of Water: Domestic Water Use in East Africa,* Chicago University Press.

WHO Division of Family Health (1980), 'The Incidence of Low Birthweight: A Critical Review of Available Information', *World Health Statistics Quarterly,* vol.33, no.3, pp.197–224.

WHO Offset Publication No.90, *Women, Health and Development,* Geneva 1985.

Wilson, M. (1984), 'Retentivity and Educational Standards of Achievement', *Comparative Education Review,* vol.28, no.3, pp.485–90.

Winikoff, B. and Laukaran, V.M. (1989), 'Breastfeeding and bottlefeeding controversies in the developing world: evidence from a study in four countries', *Social Science and Medicine,* vol.29, no.7, pp.859–68.

Winikoff, B. and Sullivan, M. (1987), 'Assessing the role of family planning in reducing maternal mortality', *Studies in Family Planning,* vol.18, pp.128–43.

Wirth, L. (1938), 'Urbanism as a Way of Life', *American Journal of Sociology,* vol.44.

Wisner, B. (1976), 'Health and the geography of wholeness', pp.81–100, in Knight, C.G. and Newman, J.L. (eds), *Contemporary*

Africa: Geography and Change, Englewood Cliffs NJ, Prentice-Hall.
Wisner, B. (1980), 'Nutritional consequences of the articulation of capitalist and non-capitalist modes of production in eastern Kenya', *Rural Africana,* nos.8–9, Fall-Winter 1980–81.
Wisner, B. (1988a), *Power and Need in Africa: Basic Human Needs and Development Policies,* London, Earthscan.
Wisner, B. (1988b), 'Gobi versus PHC? Some Dangers of Selective Primary Health Care', *Social Science and Medicine,* vol.26, no.9, pp.963–9.
World Bank (1973), cited in Gakou (1987), *op.cit.*
World Bank (1980), *Women in the urban labor markets of Africa: the case of Tanzania,* World Bank Staff Working Paper No.380, April 1980.
World Bank (1988), *Education in Sub-Saharan Africa, Policies for Adjustment, Revitalization and Expansion,* January 1988.
World Bank (annual), *World Development Reports.*
World Bank and UNDP (1989), *Africa's Adjustment and Growth in the 1980s,* Washington, World Bank.
WFS, World Fertility Survey (1985), *Kenya Report,* International Statistical Institute, The Hague.
WFS, World Fertility Survey (1983), *Comparative Studies,* no.4, September 1983, International Statistical Institute, The Hague.
WFS, World Fertility Surveys (1988), *Comparative Studies,* no.8, International Statistical Institute, The Hague.
WHO, World Health Organisation (1968), *Nutritional Anaemias,* Technical Report Series no.405, Geneva, WHO.
WHO, World Health Organisation (1986), 'Maternal mortality rates: a tabulation of available information', Geneva, WHO/FHE/86:3.
WHO, World Health Organisation (1986), 'Maternal mortality: helping women off the road to death', *WHO Chron.,* vol.40, no.5, pp.175–83.
World Health Statistics Annual, various years, Geneva, World Health Organisation.
Wunsch, G. (1983), 'Maternal and Child Health in the Developing Countries: Problems of Data Collection' in *World Health Statist.Quart.,* vol.36, pp.62–71.

Name Index

Subject Index